HSS. 18.12.89 46.80
J2

THE MIDAS TOUCH

By the same author

Drum, a Venture into the New Africa
The Treason Cage
Commonsense about Africa
South Africa: Two Views of Separate Development
Anatomy of Britain
Anatomy of Britain Today
Macmillan: a Study in Ambiguity
The New Europeans
The New Anatomy of Britain
The Sovereign State
The Seven Sisters
The Arms Bazaar
The Money Lenders
The Changing Anatomy of Britain
Empires of the Sky
Black and Gold

ANTHONY SAMPSON

THE MIDAS TOUCH

MONEY, PEOPLE AND POWER FROM WEST TO EAST

BBC BOOKS

Hodder & Stoughton

LONDON · SYDNEY · AUCKLAND · TORONTO

British Library Cataloguing in Publication Data
Sampson, Anthony, *1926–*
The Midas touch.
1. Money. Sociological perspectives
I. Title
306′.3

ISBN 0-340-48793-3
ISBN 0-563-20853-8 BBC

Copyright © Anthony Sampson 1989

First published in Great Britain 1989

All rights reserved. No part of this publication may be reproduced or transmitted in any form or by any means, electronic or mechanical, including photocopying, recording, or any information storage and retrieval system, without either prior permission in writing from the publisher or a licence permitting restricted copying. In the United Kingdom such licences are issued by the Copyright Licensing Agency, 33–34 Alfred Place, London WC1E 7DP.

Published by Hodder & Stoughton,
a division of Hodder and Stoughton Ltd,
Mill Road, Dunton Green, Sevenoaks, Kent TN13 2YA
Editorial Office: 47 Bedford Square, London WC1B 3DP
and BBC Books,
a division of BBC Enterprises Ltd, Woodlands, Wood Lane,
London W12 0TT

Photoset in Linotron Galliard by
Rowland Phototypesetting Ltd,
Bury St Edmunds, Suffolk
Printed in Great Britain by
Mackays of Chatham plc, Chatham, Kent

CONTENTS

ILLUSTRATIONS

between pages 84 and 85

Acknowledgements
[1]Mansell Collection [2]Mick Csaky [3]Basil Pao
[4]Greg Evans Photo Library [5]Camera Press
[6]Morgan Library [7]A.R.S.

INTRODUCTION

No man but a blockhead ever wrote except for money.

DR SAMUEL JOHNSON

This is a book about money and people; about the explosion of mobile and global money in our time, and how it has affected people's attitudes and lives round the world. It is about motives, not economics; why people want money, how they use it, how it changes them, and how money 'makes the world go round'.

The book focuses on the changes during the boom of the eighties – a decade of individual money-making and shifts in the balance of values unprecedented since the nineteenth century. And it tries to show how people in different parts of the world were influenced by some of the experiences of the eighties, including the rapid globalisation of markets, the crash of '87, and the shift of financial power to the East. But it also tries to set those events in some historical perspective, particularly in comparison to the earlier upheavals of the first industrial revolution.

In some respects this book follows my earlier books which have dealt with the workings of multinational corporations and business: including *The Seven Sisters* about the oil companies, *The Money Lenders* about banks, and *The Arms Bazaar* about arms sales. As in those books, I try to describe some of the global forces that are changing ordinary people's daily lives and horizons, through the viewpoints of key participants. But this book looks much less at organisations, and more at the money-motivations that lie behind them.

I am very conscious of the dangers of trying to describe these far-reaching global changes while we are all still in the midst of them. No doubt it will take many years – as it did in the nineteenth century – before the full social and political implications of the financial upheavals of the eighties become clear. But as a reporter rather than a historian I believe it is worth trying to convey the feel of them, and to look at the connections between very separate societies.

I do not attempt to present a comprehensive global picture which includes all countries. I have selected countries or regions which appear to be of special importance in the changing money-map, and which epitomise particular aspects and problems of money. Specifically I look at the United States for the resurgence of individual fortunes, detached from industry and communities; at Japan to observe the process of building up a financial surplus, and what people want to do with it; at two kinds of Chinese, on the mainland and abroad, to show how people in exile rapidly become money-motivated as they never were at home; at Latin America, and particularly at Argentina, for an extreme case of a debtor-country which appears unable to escape from its debtorholic psychology; and at Africa as the continent that has been left behind by the transformations elsewhere, and particularly at Ghana as the most dramatic case-history of both past failures and current hopes of recovery and realism. I have left out the Soviet Union and Eastern Europe, not to play down their importance to the rest of the world, but because their relationship with the global economy remains fragile, with a future that is hard to assess.

I have approached the daunting problems of money in a personal way, offering myself as an informal guide and questioner through the jungle. No doubt my own assumptions and prejudices emerge, as a sceptical individualist detached from any organisation. As a writer I have had my own confusing experiences with money which suddenly appears and disappears, and which can provide discipline and inspiration as well as burdens. I cannot avoid the perspective of my own country which has seen world financial power come and go, and which has seen many past swings between obsessive concerns with money-values and extreme rejections of them. But I have tried to expose myself to a range of different attitudes in different countries and to reflect them fairly and vividly.

In this book I have had the advantage of also writing and presenting a television series, which has provided the opportunity for more extensive interviews and research than is normally available to a topical book-writer. These interviews have allowed me to present a succession of major players in the money-world, giving in their own words a continuing commentary and argument through the book, often at variance with my own views. And I therefore owe a special debt to many busy people – ranging from Sir James Goldsmith in Paris to Carlos Menem in Argentina, from Paul Volcker in New York to Fang Li-zhi in Beijing, from Akio Morita in Tokyo to Sir Kit McMahon in London – who have given their time to record their own views, often with striking candour.

I also owe a great deal to members of the television team who have provided much patient and generous support. I am specially grateful to Mick Csaky, the producer of the TV series and director of five of the six episodes, who originally had the idea of broaching the difficult subject of money on television, and who pushed through the arrangements and conducted many interviews. His energetic and good-humoured encouragement – all the more after I had a heart-attack in the middle of filming – provided a revelation of how far a masterly colleague can underpin an individual accustomed to working alone. I am also in debt to Patrick Forbes, the researcher for the TV series, who provided his own vigorous ideas and interpretations and organised interviews and research with great efficiency. Rosalind Bentley, the archive researcher, and Gina Hobson, the unit manager, provided their own valuable expertise. The cameramen Peter Greenhalgh and Michael Miles were both impressive artists and very welcome companions. Mel Morpeth, the film editor, contributed tremendous dedication and some very helpful ideas and suggestions. Joanie Blaikie, the associate producer, and Fiona Freed, the production assistant, were wonderfully competent and tolerant of a lone outsider. Mick Gold, who directed the episode dealing with money and art, provided useful research and ideas which are reflected in chapter 12. Christopher Ralling, the consultant to the series, contributed his experienced eye both to television episodes and to ideas reflected in this book; while at Antelope Films Peter Montagnon added his own intellectual approach. At the BBC Peter Armstrong, the Head of Television South and East, added his own critical eye and very positive suggestions, which I specially appreciated in writing the last chapter.

In Japan I must record a double indebtedness to TV Asahi for the development of this book. It was their invitation to me to give lectures in Tokyo in January 1988 which first thoroughly stimulated my interest in the contrasts and comparisons between East and West. I gained many insights from my host Masuhiko Hirobuchi who guided me and my wife through an enlightening and most entertaining visit. The President of TV Asahi, Kikuo Tashiro, took a warm personal interest in my visit and in the idea of a television series, which was supported by Yasubumi Hiyoshi, the director of the International Division, and which led to TV Asahi becoming co-producers with the BBC. When I returned to Tokyo for filming many people at TV Asahi gave both ideas and technical support, including Yoshi Tsubaki who provided close liaison with our team and Mariko Nakamura, our resourceful assistant and interpreter. Other friends in Tokyo contributed insights and perspectives, including Shigeki

Hijino and Tasuku Asano of *Newsweek* Japan, Yuriko Koike of Inter-communication Forum, Masataka Itoh of the *Asahi Journal*, and Hiroshi Hayakawa of Hayakawa Publishing.

In many other cities I have too many personal debts to list, but I specially appreciated the help of friends who made my task much more agreeable. In New York old friends including George Soros, John Heimann, Arthur Schlesinger and Clay Felker were always enlightening. In Hong Kong I owed much to the photographer Basil Pao who accompanied me to Shanghai. In China I was much helped by Dorinda Elliott of *Newsweek* in Beijing and Han Zihui of the Shanghai Journalists' Association. In my home city, London, I had very useful insights on financial questions from Jeremy Hardie, Percy Mistry and Christopher Beauman; while on patterns of consumption I was much helped by my friends Tom Jago of United Distillers, and Jeremy Bullmore and Judie Lannon of J. Walter Thompson.

As in previous books, I have enjoyed consistent support from Hodder and Stoughton, my publishers in London for the last quarter-century; specially from Michael Attenborough, Eric Major and my editors Jane Osborn and Morag Lyall. For the index, I am full of admiration for Douglas Matthews who compiled it with extraordinary speed and thoroughness. I am again grateful to my London agents Michael Sissons and Pat Kavanagh of Peters Fraser and Dunlop, and to Anthony Gornall of the Intercontinental Literary Agency for his highly competent arrangements. In New York I was again supported by my agent Sterling Lord, and in Tokyo I received special encouragement from Tom Mori.

In preparing the book itself I am deeply grateful to Carla Shimeld for seeing it all through the word-processor with amazing skill, organising my wayward files and repeatedly producing order out of chaos. In proof-reading I have had help from my daughter Katie Sampson. And more than ever I am grateful to my wife Sally, both for her advice and encouragement with the book, and for seeing me through a tense period of my life.

The Midas Touch: a Csaky/Antelope Film production, written and presented by Anthony Sampson for BBC Television South & East, in association with TV Asahi of Japan and Channel 7 of Australia.

Anthony Sampson, London, August 1989

THE MIDAS TOUCH

CHAPTER ONE

THE WORLD'S RELIGION

Money alone sets all the world in motion.

PUBLILIUS SYRUS: MAXIMS, 1st century BC

If an ancestor were brought back to life in the late twentieth century he would surely assume that the world was under the sway of a powerful new religion. He would see the glittering buildings reaching up to the sky, dwarfing the old churches or shrines alongside them. He would see the same architectural styles, as alike as Gothic cathedrals, proclaiming the same beliefs. Inside the cathedrals he would come into high atria, with the same hushed, self-contained atmosphere, always with the same temperature and humidity, the same kind of foliage, like flowers on altars. And in the surrounding cloisters he would see hundreds of acolytes sitting silently in front of flickering screens, watching mystical patterns of digits taking shape, and pressing keys as if reciting ritual responses or telling beads.

He would see these new cathedrals across half the world, whether in New York, Tokyo, London, Hong Kong or Singapore – all apparently dislocated from time and space, their glass and steel interchangeable across the continents. They look much more like each other than like the surrounding low-lying buildings, as did the temples which stared over the far-flung colonies of ancient Greece. And everywhere the same screens display the same magic numbers, subjugating a hundred different cultures and traditions to the same universal homage to its language, proclaiming with total faith the first commandment: that money makes the world go round.

Our ancestor would certainly be right to assume that money had taken over many attributes of a religion. Like a religion it binds together different parts of the world, providing the means by which people and nations judge each other. Like a religion it demands great faith, a huge priesthood with rituals and incantations which few ordinary people understand. Like missionaries, the bankers and brokers travel the still unconverted parts of the world, bringing the deserts and jungles into the same system of values, seeking to convert still more tribes to their own faith in credit, interest rates and the sacred bottom line. Today it is the bank managers rather than priests who are the guardians of people's secrets and confessionals, who see the world (as they say) 'with their trousers down'. The old language of religion is transmuted into the language of money: redemption means the future repayment of government stock; creed means credit; miracle means high economic growth; forgiveness means the forgiveness of debt, and is transformed from a virtue to a vice. And this new religion has the kind of credibility which Christianity, Buddhism or Islam never had: for it is based on pure reason. All its effects can be measured, all its movements explained, as part of the elaborate mechanism which makes the world work.

While bishops or cardinals turn to fund-raising, the bankers and economists take over the role of preachers, depicting money as the central instrument of morality and goodness. 'Money is more than an economic artefact,' says the long-haired American prophet of monetarism Professor Robert Mundell, in his own creed, endorsed by Sir Jeremy Morse the chairman (or is he the abbot?) of Lloyds Bank in Britain: 'it is an idea, a central feature of civilisation, the health of which depends, in a liberal society, on the predictability of its value, its stability, not only today but in the distant future.'* The discipline has become much stricter since the brief victory of inflation, the ultimate heresy against the faith in the seventies, which inspired the triumphant crusade against infidels; while the eighties saw the collapse of another heresy, Marxism, all over the world.

Now politicians provide their own reinterpretation of the old-fashioned religions to bring them in line with the new faith in money, celebrating not the Creation, but wealth creation. As Mrs Thatcher told the Church of Scotland in 1988: 'The tenth commandment – thou shalt not covet – recognises that making money and owning things could become selfish activities. But it is not the creation of wealth that is wrong, but love of money for its own sake. The spiritual dimension comes in deciding what one does with the wealth.' Only a few Church leaders cared to argue with her priorities which put the spiritual dimension so firmly in its place. 'You cannot really talk about wealth creation unless you also consider the opportunity for wealth distribution,' said the Catholic Archbishop of Liverpool, Derek Worlock.†

*See Sir Jeremy Morse: 'The Great Inflation and its Aftermath', *Lloyds Bank Review*, London, October 1987, p.1.
†Interview in Liverpool, October 28, 1988.

The power and mystery of the new religion was massively increased in the eighties by the rapid development of global markets and the movements of capital, which detached money much more completely from ordinary goods or trade, and created far bigger scope for those who understood it. For those who could see what was happening it was an awesome development. This is how it looks to John Reed, the chairman of Citicorp – the biggest American bank:

> We see about 400 billion dollars every day of foreign exchange transactions going through the system. It's a little bit like the physicist who created the atomic bomb . . . It didn't take them long to recognise that this was a force that obviously had changed the nature of the world in both a positive and a negative way. You couldn't uninvent. We're not going to uninvent the capital markets of the world. Those of us who are practitioners and see the large sums of money and the velocity of change, what it means in terms of moving money around, recognise that some of these forces are large compared to day-to-day economic activities; and in that sense overwhelming, awesome. On the other hand you recognise that there's some good; you can translate the saving of that Japanese household into economic well-being for somebody in south Italy or Spain. The practitioners clearly see the size of the system, the imperfections, the risks, the possibility for a destructive event of some sort economically speaking; but also that we as a society have to harness and make use of the ability to transmit change and to bring economic well-being to all of us.*

But the remoteness and ramifications produced a still less human relationship. As Felix Rohatyn of Lazard's Bank in New York puts it:

> People buy and sell blips on an electronic screen. They deal with people they never see, they talk to people on the phone in rooms that have no windows. They sit and look at screens. It's almost like modern warfare, where people sit in bunkers and look at screens and push buttons and things happen. That environment really takes away a lot of the old controls on behaviour or how you run your business, because there's no quality control, there's no manufacturing efficiency, there's no servicing the customer. There's just a lot of buying and selling. That's difficult because it's also so dehumanised.†

*Interview in London, May 9, 1989.
†Interview in New York, November 17, 1988.

There is nothing new about the association of money with religion. Money in its origins was closely linked to worship: early coins emerged from temples, and the word Moneta – 'she who warns' – was the title of the goddess Juno, whose temple was used by the Romans as a workshop to make coins. The earliest currencies were otherwise useless objects, like shells, dog's teeth or stones, which were invested with special magic or respect, and became a substitute for simple barter. The invention of money as a means of exchange was an essentially practical device which (said Adam Smith) distinguished men from animals: 'Nobody ever saw a dog make a fair and deliberate exchange of one bone for another with another dog.' And this brilliant invention became the basis of all subsequent commerce. As Geoffrey Crowther (later editor of *The Economist*) described it:

> Money is one of the most fundamental of all Man's inventions. Every branch of knowledge has its fundamental discovery. In mechanics it is the wheel, in science fire, in politics the vote. Similarly, in economics, in the whole commercial side of Man's social existence, money is the essential invention on which all the rest is based.*

But as money developed from a 'medium of exchange' to a 'store of value' it acquired its own magic and awe as an instrument of worldly power. Gold, which was sometimes worshipped, sometimes used for ornament, became also the ultimate store of value and symbol of wealth. The desire to turn other substances into gold through alchemy became an obsession lasting into the eighteenth century, preoccupying not only misers but also scientists including Sir Isaac Newton.

As the power of money grew, most religious teachings, including the Old and New Testaments, warned about the corruptions of riches. Jesus threw the moneylenders out of the temple; the rich man was like the camel passing through the needle; St Paul said that the love of money (though not money itself) was the root of all evil. The interpretation of usury or interest became a battleground for theologians. Interest was essential for any system of loans or realistic finance, but most religious leaders found it hard to justify the idea of money breeding without work, using God's time. And Christian bankers including the Medici felt impelled to re-pay money to the 'ultimate creditor' to atone for the sin of usury. But the Christian Churches accumulated their own hypocrisies

*Geoffrey Crowther: *An Outline of Money*, Thomas Nelson, London, 1945, pp.16–17.

as they acquired property and wealth and bishops became landowners. Jews who developed a more rational attitude to money were reviled as usurers while Christians used them to finance splendour and wars.

The power of gold, to corrupt, control and dominate men's lives, became the recurring theme for myths and poets and playwrights, who saw the worship of the glittering metal as a kind of anti-religion. As Volpone proclaimed it in Ben Jonson's play:

> Good morning to the day; and next, my gold:
> Open the shrine, that I may see my saint.
> Hail the world's soul, and mine . . .
> That lying here, amongst my other hoards,
> Show'st like a flame by night; or like the day
> Struck out of chaos, when all darkness fled
> Unto the centre.*

Shakespeare described all the corrupting powers of money when Timon of Athens discovers gold when digging in the earth – a passage much admired by Karl Marx, who commented that Shakespeare 'excellently depicts the real nature of money'.†

> This yellow slave
> Will knit and break religions, bless th'accurst,
> Make the hoare leprosy adored, place thieves
> And give them title, knee and approbation
> With senators on the bench.

This picture of mobile, secretive money kept recurring: a sinister force which could disrupt a stable and honest society. As bank-notes, bills of exchange and international loans took over more of the role of gold, money appeared still more insidious as the means of invisible corruption. As Alexander Pope depicted it in 1733, after the South Sea Bubble:

> Blest paper-credit! Last and best supply!
> That lends Corruption lighter wings to fly!
> Gold imp'd by thee, can compass hardest things,
> Can pocket states, can fetch or carry kings;

*Ben Jonson: *Volpone*, 1605, Act I, Scene 2.

†William Shakespeare: *Timon of Athens*, Act 4, Scene 3. Karl Marx: *Capital*, vol 1 (Pelican edition 1976), p.230. For an analysis of Marx's attitude see also Laurence Lerner's essay on 'Literature and Money' in *Essays & Studies*, collected for the English Association, John Murray, London, 1975, pp.106–22.

A single leaf shall waft an army o'er,
Or ship off senates to a distant shore . . .*

Both poets and prophets (including Marx) tended to ignore the more prosaic and indispensable character of money, as the only means by which daily transactions and trade were made possible, as part of the machinery of civilisation: what Dickens called: 'those little screws of existence – pounds, shillings and pence'.† But Dickens, like so many of his Victorian contemporaries, was bewildered by the paper money which was spreading its power:

> That mysterious paper currency which circulates in London when the wind blows gyrated here and there and everywhere. Whence can it come, whither can it go? It hangs on every bush, flutters in every tree, is caught flying by the electric wires.‡

By the nineteenth century the sheer momentum of industrialisation and commerce was sweeping away religious obstacles. 'Money is the God of our Time,' said the poet Heine (who was a friend of the Rothschilds) 'and Rothschild is his prophet.' Technology, unlike goodness or happiness, could be accurately measured, which gave it a growing advantage over the claims of religion. As David Landes, the historian of European industrialisation, describes it:

> This world, which has never before been ready to accept universally any of the universal faiths offered for its salvation, is apparently prepared to embrace the religion of science and technology without reservation.§

The idea of credit – which means trust – required an unquestioning faith in money. Karl Marx in *Das Kapital* analysed how money, like other commodities, had become a fetish, and how credit required its own beliefs: 'Public credit becomes the credo of capital. And with the rise of national debt-making, lack of faith in the national debt takes the place of the sin against the Holy Ghost, for which there is no forgiveness.'‖

Money was becoming so all-enveloping in industrial society that like a religion it gave its own meaning and purpose to life. As the German philosopher Georg Simmel described it in 1907:

*Alexander Pope: 'Epistle to Lord Bathurst', 1733, 11.68–73.
†Letter to Henry Austin, January 1835.
‡Charles Dickens, *Dombey and Son*, 1846–8, chapter 12.
§David Landes: *The Unbound Prometheus*, Cambridge University Press, 1969.
‖Marx, op cit, p.919.

> Money is everywhere conceived as purpose, and countless things that are really ends in themselves are thereby degraded to mere means. But since money itself is an omnipresent means, the various elements of our existence are thus placed in an all-embracing teleological nexus in which no element is either first or last . . .*

But industrialisation and capitalism required much more than a devotion to money: they needed an elaborate social organisation and discipline, which many countries lacked. Protestants in Northern Europe and North America began to see themselves with a special vocation and aptitude for capitalism. In his famous study in 1904, *The Protestant Ethic and the Spirit of Capitalism*, Max Weber argued that Calvinism, by making its followers more worried about their individual salvation, encouraged asceticism, diligence and thrift, which were the virtues required by the capitalist system. Weber's theory led to endless academic debates about the relationship between religion and money. The British historian R. H. Tawney developed it in his *Religion and the Rise of Capitalism* in 1926. The Italian Catholic economist Fanfani (who later became President of Italy) argued in his own study in 1935 that capitalism existed long before Protestantism, and was much more influenced by the general liberation of the individual under the Renaissance.† The post-war economic achievements of Catholic countries like Italy and Spain helped to undermine the earlier Protestant confidence and theorising; and later historians have thrown doubt on the extent of the self-denial of the Calvinists anyway.‡

Today the skills of money-making seem less directly connected with any religion, and more with the surrounding social and psychological conditions. The Jews had traditionally been associated with a special ruthlessness over money, going back to their role as usurers in the early Middle Ages. But as people of other religions became more mobile and more preoccupied with money, the Jews were depicted more as the forerunners of a much-needed rationality. 'One of the greatest contributions the Jews made to human progress,' as Paul Johnson puts it in his *History of the Jews*, 'was to force European culture to come to terms with money and its power.'§ The role of

*Georg Simmel: *The Philosophy of Money* (English translation), Routledge, Kegan Paul, London, 1978, p.431.

†Amintore Fanfani: *Catholicism, Protestantism and Capitalism* (English translation), Sheed and Ward, London, 1935.

‡See for instance Simon Schama: *The Embarrassment of Riches*, Collins, London, 1987, pp. 322–3.

§Paul Johnson: *A History of the Jews*, Weidenfeld and Nicolson, London, 1987, p.247.

religion has been frequently confused with the role of exile and persecution, which detached religious minorities from their territory and strengthened their common bonds. Jews, Quakers or Huguenots were each bound together with their own codes and networks which gave them a special effectiveness in finance. Once settled among a majority of their own people, their commercial dynamic becomes less evident. 'Look how unsuccessful commercially Israel has been,' says Sir James Goldsmith, 'and how successful the Jewish communities are outside Israel.'*

It remained clear that the puritan virtues in their broadest sense of self-denial and discipline clearly played a critical role in the organisation of industry and economic growth. As David Landes wrote, they 'were more than a new version of the appetite for wealth. They constituted in effect an imposition of the criterion of efficiency on every activity, whether or not directly connected with getting and spending.'† But over the last three decades the Western nations have lost any sense of monopoly of these efficient virtues, as they watched Asian countries overtaking them in economic organisation.

It was in the Far East that puritan virtues showed themselves with the most devastating efficiency (see chapter 6). The old religions of Buddhism, Shintoism, even Marxism, which had long been seen as obstacles to economic growth, now all seemed secondary to the god which had performed such visible miracles. In Japan, Taiwan or Korea the religion of money seems now more powerful than anywhere, as rows of worshippers gaze up at the graphs and statistics which have transformed their existence in a lifetime.

Time and Money

The religion of money exacts its harshest tribute in its demands on time. The banker begins his day with a pre-breakfast meeting before the power breakfast. The lawyer times his telephone discussion with a stop-watch to charge his client by the minute. The foreign exchange dealer watches his digital clocks in three time-zones at once. The arbitrageur telephones from cars, restaurants or planes. They all accept the commandment that their time must be governed by money. The old cathedral clocks which summoned monks to prayer and measured the time which belonged to God have long ago been superseded by the digital microseconds which measure the time which belongs to money.

*Interview in Paris, October 12, 1988.
†Landes: op cit, p.24.

'Remember that time is money,' said Benjamin Franklin, in his *Advice to a Young Tradesman* in 1748: and the bleak refrain re-echoed through industrial America and Britain. 'Take away *time is money*, and what is left of England?' wrote Victor Hugo in *Les Misérables* in 1862. Max Weber took Franklin's dictum as his starting-point in analysing the spirit of capitalism, and it was no accident that the watch industry had been based since the sixteenth century on Geneva, where Calvin's teaching abjured jewellery but endorsed watch-making.*

The tyranny of time became far more dominant with the spread of railways in the 1840s and 1850s, enforced by more reliable clocks: a 'Time Table' was first used for the Liverpool and Manchester Railway in 1838, and timetables were soon applied to schools and factories. The huge station clock became the stern reminder of unchangeable minutes: the great clock-faces of the former Gare d'Orsay in Paris still stare across the Seine as monuments to the railway age. The strains of minute-by-minute punctuality at the railway station provided a sharp contrast with the slow seasonal rural rhythms of sunrise and sunset. The pace of the train itself could bewilder Victorians as much as jet-lag confuses air-travellers today, as we see in *Dombey and Son*. 'Been travelling a long time, Sir, perhaps?' asks the waiter of Mr Carker after a hectic journey through France when he could not remember whether it was Wednesday or Thursday.

> 'Yes.'
> 'By rail, Sir?'
> 'Yes.'
> 'Very confusing, Sir. Not much in the habit of travelling by rail myself, Sir, but gentlemen frequently say so.'†

The telegraph provided instant communication across the continents which gave huge benefit to financiers who could make use of it. When Anthony Trollope wrote *The Way We Live Now* in 1873 – six years after the first submarine telegraph – he described how his financial villain Melmotte 'had the telegraph at his command and had been able to make as close inquiries as though San Francisco and Salt Lake City had been suburbs of London'.‡ The new speed of communications soon compelled nations to co-ordinate their time-keeping: the US in 1883 first instituted time-zones for its different

*David Landes: *Revolution in Time*, Belknap Press of Harvard University Press, Cambridge, Mass, 1983, p.238.
†Dickens: op cit, chapter 55.
‡Anthony Trollope: *The Way We Live Now*, London, 1875.

regions and the next year all nations (except of course the French) agreed to accept Greenwich Mean Time as the measure to which all other times were related.

Mass-production required a still stricter discipline of punctuality. American industrialists began equating time and money more literally after the 1880s, when F. W. Taylor applied principles of scientific management beginning with the steel industry in the years of depression, through 'time and motion' and incentive payments. But it was not until the assembly-line of Henry Ford, and the spread of machines for 'clocking in' in the twenties that 'Taylorism' was more widely applied, and output and man-hours were closely related to human performance.

By the 1960s space travel was putting a far greater premium on the measurement of time by seconds rather than minutes. Olympic races called for split-second timing, and the microseconds whirring round on TV screens across the world gave a new frenzy and unity to the passage of time. The spread of cheap digital watches increased the sense of exact timing among ordinary people. Even railway stations now have digital clocks showing the seconds, to encourage the punctuality of their trains.

The spread of global finance in the eighties, when billions crossed the exchanges every hour, created a far more tense relationship between time and money: a billion dollars at 10 per cent interest rate was earning three dollars a second. The need for speed produced a new species of young dealer across the world whose style belonged to a race-track rather than a bank, and who could exhaust himself by the age of thirty. The dealing across time-zones added to the strain: a dealer in London might have to reach his office by dawn to catch Tokyo before it closed.

Parcels of time became smaller and smaller. Businessmen and bankers began rationing their appointments in quarter-hour or even five-minute slots, finding extra bits of time in cars or planes. Diaries cut up the day into smaller slices, and the proliferation of the electronic organiser and the Filofax – which surprisingly spread from Britain to Japan – provided a new spur to time-consciousness. Busy-ness, with no spare time for reflection, became the mark of the important man. 'Our business is helping those who are short of time, not money,' says an advertisement for Lloyds Bank International in 1989.* The time-miser has taken over from the money-miser as the symbol of meanness, and even retired executives like to boast: 'never been

**Newsweek*, May 29, 1989.

busier in my life'. Michael Young in his book *The Metronomic Society* complains how:

> In my home city, London, I have only to telephone an executive, a senior civil servant, or still worse, a professor – they are all busynessmen and women now – to be told that this next week or month is quite impossible, there is an important meeting in Glasgow or Brighton or Washington that has to be prepared for or gone to – as if one needs to be humiliated cut by cut by a tally of all the other calls on his or her time which are so much more important than mine.*

Contemporary intellectuals are inevitably ambivalent about time. 'Those of us who live under tight time discipline deplore it and flee it when we can,' wrote David Landes in 1983. 'We seek vacations in places where we can put our watches away and let nature wake us up and put us to sleep. For others, though, submission to time is the price of modernisation, productivity, potential affluence. Who are we to deprecate what we live by and, living, have gotten rich by?'† Michael Young still looks forward to machines liberating men from the pressures of time. 'Machines could enslave themselves to their own master machine, the clock, so that we should no longer be required to treat ourselves as though we were machines.'‡ This option should already be technically possible; but the clock is still tightening its psychological hold on humans, as the minutes tick by.

The Japanese developed far more demanding time-disciplines. Their work-teams have progressed far beyond clocking in or time-and-motion study as they exert their own self-discipline, while computers, robots and information technology set a rigid pace for their human partners. Productivity, first mentioned at the beginning of the century, acquired a greater power when it defined the man-hours required to build a car or computer; and Western nations anxiously watched their productivity figures decline compared to the Asians. A new tyranny of time emerged when Toyota invented a new computerised system which came to be known as just-in-time (JIT) – as opposed to just-in-case. The system did away with the need for inventories by linking the buyers and agents directly to the suppliers and assembly-line, synchronising components to reach the factory as required. The combinations of just-in-time with robots and computer-integrated manufacturing (CIM) soon speeded up the

*Michael Young: *The Metronomic Society*, Thames and Hudson, London, 1988, p.220.
†Landes: *Revolution in Time*, op cit.
‡Young, op cit, p.261.

productivity of Japanese plants, with robots setting the pace: the Yamasaki Machinery Works claims to make machine-tools in unmanned plants working a twenty-four-hour day.*

The rigours of punctuality and precision made new difficulties for Third World countries accustomed to more leisurely concepts of time and 'mañana'. The vagueness and delays of African time or Arab time were not merely the legacy of a pre-industrial time-scale: they were part of a culture which put personal relationships before timetables. It was an insult to cut short a friendly discussion to make room for another appointment. The importance of an official could be judged by his capacity to keep people waiting: Arab princes would expect foreign salesmen to wait day after day in their ante-rooms. Societies where time was limitless, with elaborate courtesies and rituals to help pass the day, could never easily adjust to the strange notion that time is money. In many African countries the airport and the railway station are the sole, and often fitful, guardians of punctuality. Automated factories can make impossible demands on easy-going workers who are required to join a regime in which every part depends on another, every minute. And many Third World people still baulk at paying the tribute of time to the new religion.

The world religion of money, with its statistics and digital clocks, can offer far more measurable miracles – including liberation from poverty and hardship – than were ever provided by the old religion. But it demands ever-stricter payments of time. 'What will you do with the time you have saved?' asks the African of the hectic businessman as he races through the Third World. But the businessman cannot answer the question. For the religion of money abhors any relaxation or contemplation whose benefits cannot be measured by clocks.

The long arm of money makes its demands on time still further into the future. Keynes described how money provides the link between past, present and future: now time is defined as a currency itself. It is the art of the banker – like a trout-angler, as the Belgian banker Louis Camu described it – to be able to operate simultaneously in the two elements of liquidity and time. The process of investment, dividends and interest repayments commits everyone to stake out the future with an orderly allocation of time. As the market becomes more global, investments longer-term and shareholders more widespread, the commitment becomes more complex and binding. International debts are rescheduled to enforce repayments thirty or forty

*See *Transnational Corporations in World Development*, UN Centre on Transnational Corporations, New York, 1988, pp.45–8.

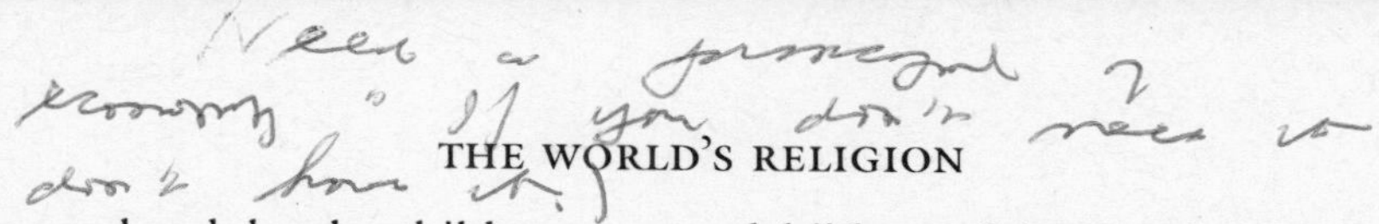

years ahead, by the children or grandchildren of the people who first contracted them.

Yet by the end of the eighties there were some signs of cracks in the faith in the world religion. Several of its high priests were worrying that global money, as it extended its influence, was showing some dangerous signs. In the first place, it was becoming much more disconnected from any actual production. As Felix Rohatyn puts it:

> Financial deregulation and technology and world markets, and the fact that money just carooms around the world at infinite speeds, has made it possible for people to speculate on a huge scale with very little money of their own committed to it. Since the returns on those kinds of speculation were always bigger than if you really had to go to work and build a factory or develop a new product, the so-called financial industry became the biggest growth industry in the world.*

Or in the words of Paul Volcker, who was chairman of the Fed during most of the eighties:

> It seems to be easier to make money in some sense, with paper chasing paper, than in investing in real goods and services. If you're doing some research and the pay-off is coming in fifteen years or twenty years at today's interest rates, it's hard to envisage a big enough pay-out to justify the investment that you make today.†

Secondly, the relationship between money and time has become very perverse. The bigger and more mobile the sums of money that float round the world, the shorter the time-scale in which they can be used, while the most serious problems of the world and its environment can only be solved by bold commitments for decades ahead. In the words of John Reed of Citicorp:

> The global markets and large pools of capital have had the effect of shortening our time horizons . . . we define out of existence certain types of problems that have a longer time-cycle. I've always felt that interest rates reflect the value of time. If your basic interest rate cost of capital in Japan is 4 per cent then that gives you twenty-five years to get something done. If the value of money in England is 10 per cent you only have ten years. Now there are lots of problems that you can't get done in ten years, but which you could very well address in twenty-five . . . In the underdeveloped

*Interview, November 17, 1988.
†Interview in New York, November 19, 1988.

> part of the world which does not have access to the global sophisticated economy today, the cost of money is very high, with interest rates of maybe 30 per cent or 40 per cent. That really says that they can't deal with problems that have much more than a three-year time-frame. Dealing with the Amazon rain-forest – a forty-year problem – is a luxury that simply doesn't exist under that kind of pricing system . . . We are going to have to find a way of changing that reality in some way . . .*

The dedication to this all-powerful religion of money is in striking contrast to the lack of interest in the long-term future, with which so many older religions have been concerned. While the world's people pursue money still more hectically they are inclined to forget the real wealth of the planet they inhabit, its land, oceans, atmosphere and population.

*Interview, May 9, 1989.

CHAPTER TWO

THE NEW FACE OF MIDAS

King Midas asked the god Dionysus that everything he touched should be turned to gold. But when he found that even his food turned to gold, he pleaded to lose his gift.

King Midas returned to his Western kingdom in the 1980s in apparent triumph. The rich, particularly in America, were now proclaimed and classified as never before. The millionaire had long ago been made commonplace by inflation and booms: by 1988 there were over a million millionaires in America, and more than 20,000 households worth 10 million dollars or more. Some fastidious social arbiters, like Lewis Lapham or Michael Thomas, insist that assets of 20 million are now the minimum for being described as rich.* Only a quarter-billionaire is likely to attract much interest in the media, which are now much more precise in their reckoning of wealth. Every year *Forbes* magazine publishes its list of the 400 richest people in America: in 1988 it reckoned that the new 400 had an average fortune of over half a billion dollars ($551m).† As its owner-editor Malcolm Forbes put it to me: 'There have never been so many so quick with so much.'‡

The speed of some new fortunes had been breathtaking: among the 400, thirty-three men all under forty had earned most of their fortunes over twelve years, in real-estate, entertainment and above all finance – several with the help of the 'grand sorcerer' of Wall Street, Michael Milken (see chapter 4), who turned out to have earned over half a billion dollars in a single year, 1987. Eight of the 400 fortunes belonged to men in their thirties, and most of the new rich came from outside traditional backgrounds: only 242 of the 400 were graduates of any kind, and only twenty-four came from Yale, fifteen from Harvard. Two hundred and twenty-four of them had made

*'How Rich is Rich?', *M* magazine, New York, August 1988.
†*Forbes* magazine, November 24, 1988.
‡Interview in New York, October 18, 1988.

their fortune 'without any significant inheritances', and twenty-four were immigrants; only 154 had inherited most of the money they controlled. Of the very rich families of a century earlier only David Rockefeller, the grandson of the first oil tycoon John D. Rockefeller, remained among the 400.

The explosion of new American wealth has been frequently compared to the explosion a century earlier, when money poured into New York from railroads, oil and new industries to create the first multimillionaires. But the new face of Midas looks different in two critical respects. In the first place private wealth is now celebrated more straightforwardly, with little guilt and much publicity. The new rich advertise their opinions and life-stories with an openness and individualism very unlike their predecessors. John D. Rockefeller had insisted – however hypocritically – that 'God gave me the money.'* Andrew Carnegie said that 'surplus wealth is a sacred trust.'† But the new rich have no such reservations, and there is far less effective critique of their roles – whether from socialism or Marxism, Christianity or traditional puritanical restraints.

In the second place, the new rich are much more detached from productive industry. Only seventy-five of the 400 fortunes in 1988 came mainly from manufacturing – seventeen fewer than two years before. There were a few staggering new fortunes from computers, including the billionaire William Gates of Microsoft, still only thirty-two; and the former billionaire Steve Jobs, the co-founder of Apple computers who had now set up his own company, Next. But most of the quick fortunes had been far removed from industry. Sixty-five of the 400 came mainly from financial operations (compared to fifty-nine two years earlier). Real-estate provided eighty-seven, twenty-seven of them from New York. The media provided seventy-three: almost as many as manufacturing.‡ The media barons were beginning to take the place of the railroad barons of the previous century: both in making quick fortunes, and in acquiring political power and influence. As railroads and the telegraph controlled communications and information in the 1880s, so television, newspapers and satellites controlled them in the 1980s, increasingly interlocked with other financial dealings. But apart from computers, the communications industry was more closely involved with consumption than production, and far less central to the industrial economy than the old railroads.

*Allan Nevins: *John D. Rockefeller*, Scribner's, New York, 1940, vol 2, p.713.
†Andrew Carnegie: 'Wealth', *North American Review*, June 1889.
‡*Forbes* magazine, October 24, 1988, and October 26, 1987.

The new face of Midas is aptly represented by Donald Trump, the real-estate financier in New York, who is publicised and admired, not as a captain of industry, nor as a master-banker, but as a showman-dealer. The son of a prosperous Swedish-American builder in Brooklyn, Trump claimed by the age of forty-one to be a billionaire. His name is now blazoned across the rich heart of Manhattan, with a triangle of prominent skyscrapers gazing at each other – Trump Tower, Trump Parc and the Plaza Hotel – which in turn are linked to his two big casinos in Atlantic City, headed by Trump's Castle. The centre of his kingdom is Trump Tower, the luxury apartment-block with its resplendent atrium including a waterfall and brand-name boutiques, with his own offices above. Trump's own face is equally famous, with the style of a playboy – defiant half-open mouth and shock of hair – accompanied by his wife Ivana, a former Czech athlete and model who displays daring fashions.

Trump cultivates conspicuous extravagance. He bought a 118-roomed mansion in Palm Beach which had been built in the twenties for the Post-Toasties heiress, Marjorie Post. He has pursued a sheikh-like opulence, emulating the Saudi arms-dealer Adnan Khashoggi. He insisted on having a ninety-foot-long drawing-room in Trump Tower in imitation of Khashoggi's apartment in Olympic Tower; and when Khashoggi was faced with bankruptcy in 1988 Trump bought his luxury yacht, as the ultimate symbol of extravagant leisure. But the appearance of hedonism is largely for show. Trump combines his shrewd bargains with intense personal publicity to increase the value of his properties. He is appealing, he explains, not to old-money New Yorkers who prefer old buildings, but to new-money people including Arabs and Japanese who like their building to be famous: 'we were selling fantasy.'*

His public and private personality have little connection. When I visited him in Trump Tower, I found one wall of his office covered with magazine covers all showing his own beaming face. But they bore no relation with his own sulky style: when the telephone rang, he picked it up crossly and barked out curt replies and instructions to someone who turned out to be his wife. His preoccupation with deals appears to leave little time for relaxation in any of his properties: he does not even have time, he says, to go out to lunch. The deal governs his life. The Post mansion was a bargain, the yacht was a

*Donald J. Trump with Tony Schwartz: *Trump, the Art of the Deal*, Century, London, 1988, p.121.

'steal'; but neither has any visible relationship with his own tastes or habits. He likes deals, as he explains, not so much for the money they make, but for their own sake: as 'my art form'. Once the deal is done, in a blaze of publicity, he moves on to the next.

The flaunting of wealth became part of the style of the eighties. The style has many champions, among them Malcolm Forbes, the seventy-year-old owner of *Forbes* magazine, who is himself said to be a half-billionaire. With highly advertised journeys, with a wide grin and friendly conservative views, he promotes the cause of unashamed wealth. He has a ranch in Colorado, a palace in Morocco, an island in the Pacific and a château in France where he runs a ballooning festival every year, with gimmicks including a huge balloon in the shape of his château. He has a yacht called *Highlander* – the latest of several – on which he sails round the world with two motorbikes and a helicopter inscribed 'Capitalist Tool', and on which he gives lunch parties for famous guests, accompanied by photographers and reporters. His magazine's building in Manhattan has his own museum on the ground floor which exhibits his collection of toy soldiers, toy boats and Fabergé eggs; while his own office is cluttered with personal trophies, gowns of honorary degrees and pictures of himself.

Forbes denies that the rich are either more exhibitionist, or more admired, than before. 'You've got to remember the old days: the Medici or the Church,' he told me in his office which looks like a film set. 'Whoever has what's to be had in big quantities has both attracted interest and had historically undue influence. But it's not new. Wealth simply represents power, and power is consequential to anybody that's around it.' Was it not provocative to flaunt great wealth, I asked Forbes, in the face of so much poverty elsewhere? 'If you aren't guilty for having money, and are grateful, why should you not enjoy it? . . . I don't think it's vulgarity. It's enjoying your money.' The rich, he insists, are compelled by their physical limitations to have a wider purpose than sheer money-values. 'A very rich person only has two eyes, he can only see so much. His stomach doesn't contain any more than somebody with less money. He doesn't have more fingers. He can't steer more cars . . .'*

Many conservative economists agree with entrepreneurs that flaunting wealth is important as part of a dynamic economy. In the words of Sir James Goldsmith, himself a more discreet billionaire:

*Interview, October 18, 1988.

> Vulgarity is to some degree a sign of vigour. It means that new people coming from nowhere are making it. It's the old American dream – anybody can become a millionaire. Now if we don't want vulgarity what is the alternative? Either generalised poverty, which I don't think anybody is seeking, or the protection of privilege so there's no change. The Duke of Northumberland or the Duke of Buccleuch don't irritate anyone; but if we only want people who have had a hundred years to learn to use money to have money, we are clearly precluding change. So if we want change, if we want vigour, we are going to have vulgarity. It's one of the things which irritates, but which is necessary.*

The celebration of wealth was really implicit in the economic theories of the eighties. The shift of balance in favour of the rich had already begun under President Carter, as the Democrats became less concerned about inequality. The backlash against high taxes had started in California in 1978, where the new 'proposition 13' had drastically restricted property taxes. And already in late 1979 the new chairman of the Federal Reserve, Paul Volcker, combated the wave of inflation with monetarist controls which over two years pushed up interest rates to record levels – thus inevitably benefiting creditors against debtors, the rich against the poor.†

But the election of President Reagan in November 1980 brought into the foreground 'supply-side' economics which gave much greater justification to the rich by insisting that lower taxes would stimulate investment and economic growth. Reagan's budget director David Stockman, a late convert to supply-side theory, first followed it with zeal. Reagan announced a three-year programme of tax cuts which, on top of the high interest rates, ensured that the rich became richer. But Stockman himself was soon well aware of the abuses of the new policy. 'Do you realize the greed that came to the forefront?' he said to his friend William Greider in the summer of 1981: 'The hogs were really feeding. The greed level, the level of opportunism, just got out of control.'‡

The supply-side economics were really only a relaunch of one of the oldest economic theories: that the extravagance of the rich automatically benefits the poor. It was specially popular in seventeenth- and eighteenth-century Europe, where the building of

*Interview, October 12, 1988.

†For a full account see William Greider: *Secrets of Temple*, Simon and Schuster, New York, 1988. Specially pp.106, 404.

‡William Greider: *The Education of David Stockman* (updated edition), Signet, New York, 1986, p.55.

huge country-houses with armies of servants was widely seen to be a boon, even a duty, to the masses. The more extreme proponents maintained that extravagance and luxury were essential to economic prosperity; and the theory was popularised by Bernard Mandeville, the Dutch-British satirist, in his polemical poem 'The Fable of the Bees', subtitled 'Private Vices, Public Benefits' (which also had some influence on Adam Smith writing soon afterwards):

> Vast numbers thronged the fruitful hive;
> Yet those vast numbers made 'em thrive;
> Millions endeavouring to supply
> Each other's lust and vanity . . .*

In pre-revolutionary France, where the nobility paid few taxes while the national deficit piled up, this kind of theory was specially attractive. The schemes of the King's financial adviser Turgot to expand the French economy without more taxes were (claims one historian) 'the direct ancestor of supply-side finance'.† In the 1920s the theory was modernised when Andrew Mellon, the Republican Secretary of the Treasury, cut taxes to stimulate investment, while Democrats denounced this 'trickle-down' theory as merely concealing growing inequality. In the 1950s and 1960s the argument was exported to the Third World, where the glaring inequalities in Latin America were depicted as the necessary accompaniment to economic growth. But in the 1980s the theory came back to America with a vengeance. As Stockman admitted to Greider: 'It's kind of hard to sell "trickle down". So the supply-side formula was the only way to get a tax policy that was really "trickle down".'‡

The first two years of the Reagan administration saw a harsh recession, exacerbated by high interest rates and high unemployment. Whole industrial communities closed down and by December 1982 12 million people were out of work. But by the fall of 1982 inflation had been pulled down, and Volcker abruptly relaxed the constraints on the money-supply. By early 1983 the American economy was recovering and millions of new jobs were being created. But the balance of wealth had now drastically shifted. According to the US Census the real incomes of the poorest 40 per cent of the population had fallen by 3 per cent between 1980 and 1984, while the top 10 per cent had increased their incomes by 7 per cent.§ And all over the

*Bernard Mandeville: 'The Fable of the Bees: or Private Vices, Public Benefits', 1723.
†Simon Schama: *Citizens*, Viking, New York, 1989, p.83.
‡Greider: *David Stockman*, op cit, p.48.
§See Greider: *Secrets*, op cit, pp.543,655.

West the stock markets began to recover spectacularly after 1982; in America the Dow-Jones index went up by 230 per cent in the following five years. The booming market was accompanied by a massive new wave of raids and mergers, which in turn helped to push share values up. The much higher valuation of shares did not correspond to any comparable increase in industrial profits or production: it reflected a rush of money which had to be invested, and a higher expectation of capital gains. Higher share prices, higher interest rates and lower taxes all helped to make the rich richer.

The biggest beneficiaries of the boom were nearly all involved in finance rather than manufacturing: the real-estate developers, the investment fund managers, the arbitrageurs who speculated in corporate shares, or the lawyers who arranged mergers. The investment bankers, the traditional grandees of finance, reasserted their power, but with a very different character. Their original dignified chief role of underwriting bond issues had been rapidly overtaken in the eighties by the much more hectic business of trading in securities and arranging mergers and acquisitions. As the traders contributed more of the profits they were able to override the longer-term concerns of the underwriters. The partners became much more individualist and impatient for profits – as emerged from the bitter infighting between the partners of Lehman Brothers Kuhn Loeb which tore the bank apart in 1983, leading to its sale to American Express, which had already bought Shearson two years earlier. Many investment bankers made huge personal gains, but they were now politically highly vulnerable. 'The investment-banking excesses of the eighties did not need economic analysis to expose them,' as John Brooks described them. 'They were clearly visible to the intelligent layman's naked eye, to which they appeared as outrages to common sense.'* It was significant that some of the most successful investment bankers, including Felix Rohatyn and Peter Peterson, the former chairman of Lehman's, were now among the most trenchant critics of the financial revolution.

Moral attitudes to money-making were now going through a major turn, as new prophets of capitalism insisted that people had no reason to be ashamed of pursuing personal gain. Through all the previous post-war decades the support for capitalism had been largely defensive, to counter the critiques of socialists and Marxists. But the new champions insisted that capitalism was essentially benign, interlocked with ancient traditions of exchanging presents and ritual offerings.

*John Brooks: *The Takeover Game*, E. P. Dutton, New York, 1987, p.342.

'Capitalism begins with giving,' wrote George Gilder, one of the more romantic new champions of wealth. 'Not from greed, avarice or even self-love can one expect the rewards of commerce, but from a spirit closely akin to altruism, a regard for the needs of others, a benevolent, outgoing, and courageous temper of mind.'*

The more extreme prophets openly proclaimed that greed was no longer a vice, but the essential motor to the economic machine. They talked like their eighteenth-century forebears, but without the qualifications of Adam Smith. Ivan Boesky, the arbitrageur who was later convicted of insider trading and sent to jail, told business graduates at Berkeley: 'I urge you as part of your mission to seek wealth. It's all right . . . you can be greedy and still be good about yourself.' And his praise of greed was re-echoed in the character of Gekko in the film *Wall Street*, who exhorted shareholders: 'Greed is good. Greed is right. Greed clarifies, cuts through and captures the essence of the evolutionary spirit.' It was a speech which re-echoed through Wall Street (see chapter 9).

The role of greed in reviving the economy was easily oversimplified, for there is nothing productive about greed in itself. 'Unlimited greed for gain is not in the least identical with capitalism,' as Max Weber warned his readers, 'and is still less its spirit.'† A driving passion for money is evident in the most disorganised countries: from the streets of Shanghai, where boys pursue tourists to clamour for dollars, to the souks of Marrakesh where carpet-dealers exhibit as much entrepreneurial cunning as any Wall Street arbitrageur. The problem facing many Western countries in the eighties was not how to stimulate greed, but how to connect it up to the much more difficult task of social organisation for production. As Felix Rohatyn puts it:

> Greed was simply given a broader field of action to play on. People would always rather make a billion dollars than a million dollars. Prior to this decade the only way to really make huge amounts of money was to be essentially very productive. In the eighties you didn't have to be. You could make a billion dollars, as some people did, simply by shuffling pieces of paper, or by helping a raider take over a company and break it up.‡

The new parade of wealth had a more tenuous justification than earlier explosions, being much less closely linked to any productive

*George Gilder: *Wealth and Poverty*, Bantam, New York, 1981, p.23.
†Max Weber: *The Protestant Ethic and the Spirit of Capitalism* (translated by Talcott Parsons), Scribner's, New York, 1976, p.17.
‡Interview, November 17, 1988.

machinery or expansion. The hopeful assumption of supply-side, that lower taxes would increase savings and investments, was soon open to question, as savings reached new lows, while personal debts increased. And it was so much easier to make money from money, rather than from manufacture, that the incentives were inevitably distorting the priorities of a new generation who saw the showman-dealer as their hero.

Were the eighties the beginning of a lasting new phase of individualistic capitalism, or simply part of a recurring cycle? The historian Arthur Schlesinger follows his own father's theory that Americans have alternated about every thirty years between eras of public purpose – under Teddy Roosevelt in 1901, Franklin Roosevelt in 1933 or J. F. Kennedy in 1961 – followed by tides of conservative restoration in the 1920s, 1950s and 1980s. But the contemporary era of conservative individualism, Schlesinger points out, has resemblances to the conservative era after the civil war in the nineteenth century, which lasted over thirty years. The traumas of the sixties may conceivably, like the traumas of the civil war a century earlier, 'have sated the nation's attitude for public action for years to come'. Yet Schlesinger concludes that 'public purpose will have at least one more chance. At some point, shortly before or after the year 1990, there should come a sharp change in the national mood and direction . . .'* And even without a sharp change, the reign of Midas seems unlikely to continue unchallenged, as the social problems accumulate.

The British: Back to Money

The new preoccupation with money was still more striking across the Atlantic – particularly in Britain. For the forty years up to 1980 the British had shown a lack of interest in money-making which puzzled foreign visitors. The retreat from commercialism transcended political divisions: Conservative as well as socialist governments had maintained high personal taxation – up to 75 per cent under Macmillan and Heath, up to 83 per cent under Wilson and Callaghan – and old Tories could be as critical as Marxists of the crude greed of the market-place. The British disdain for money had long roots, going back to the first reactions against Victorian vulgarities, and reinforced by the imperial tradition of service and by two world wars which underlined military and moral values. Behind it lay a fundamental

*Arthur M. Schlesinger, Jr: *The Cycles of American History*, Houghton Mifflin, Boston, 1986, pp.45–7.

resistance to change which may have come from sheer national exhaustion.

The British had seen the industrial revolution come and go; they had avoided political revolutions and military defeats; and they liked to see themselves as more mature in their values than other Europeans. Their aristocrats – even those who remained rich – had cultivated a shabby and unobtrusive style, in which their great houses merged with nature; and they loved to mock American and German money-manias and pursuit of novelty. Intellectuals and academics, who had a strong influence in post-war politics, were insulated from competition and contemptuous of vulgar greed; while many workers suffered what Ernest Bevin called 'the poverty of expectations'. The destruction of the Second World War, in spite of its upheavals and social mobility, never really broke the settled British class structure, or forced industries and cities to rebuild or rethink like their German or Japanese counterparts. To many foreigners in the fifties and sixties the British, from dons to dustmen, seemed stubbornly united in their lack of interest in money.

It was all the more surprising after Margaret Thatcher's election in 1979 to find the British people reverting to a fascination with money and its manifestations – the more eagerly after years of suppression, like a gusher bursting out of the ground. A new generation reacted against their parents' reluctance to talk about money almost as excitedly as the earlier generation talked about sex in the sixties.

Mrs Thatcher, like Ronald Reagan, was committed to supply-side theories and cuts in public spending, while in the mid-eighties the British stock market zoomed up even faster than Wall Street: between June 1983 and May 1987 the *Financial Times* index was multiplied by five. Shares were stimulated not only by more efficient industry, but by the huge increase of financial activity. The rich were liberated from taxes more suddenly than in other countries, as the previous top rate of 83 per cent fell first to 60 per cent and then to 40 per cent. The British now found fewer arguments against money-values, as socialism lost its appeal and the Churches became more interested in fund-raising and justifying their role in the market-place. The signs of money-worship multiplied. Newspapers fattened with business supplements. TV channels competed with money programmes. Banks and credit card companies pressed customers yet more stridently to borrow more money. Tycoons, after years of discretion, became the subject of bestselling memoirs or biographies.

Yet by the end of the eighties Thatcher's incentives had not much changed the traditional hierarchy of wealth. When in 1989 the London

Sunday Times prepared its first annual list of Britain's 200 richest people, it reckoned that over half of them, led by the Queen and the Duke of Westminster, had inherited their wealth, while a quarter of the 200 were landowners, including eleven dukes, six marquesses and fourteen earls. Most of the self-made rich were outsiders who were brought up outside Britain; and very few were connected with industry. Among the nine billionaires (in pounds) the nearest to an industrialist is the German émigré Octav Botnar who had made his fortune as the agent for Nissan cars from Japan. 'Britain's businessmen by now should have seized the commanding heights of the economy, and society,' complained Andrew Neil, the self-made editor of the *Sunday Times*, 'but the old Britain – of Eton, Oxbridge, the land and the Guards – is still secure in its privileges and wallowing in its [inherited] wealth.'*

New money in Britain embraced some of the traditional British style. The eighteenth-century country-house – the central symbol of pre-industrial permanence – renewed its spell as the rich competed to buy mansions which had been unsellable ten years earlier. The British hierarchy of servants could offer a more reassuring and flattering attention than the Americans', while the seasonal rituals of Ascot, Wimbledon or Glyndebourne could tactfully transmute new money into old status. But the Western rich became more alike as they all became more mobile, and as Americans followed the British retreat from manufacturing: and they looked all the more similar in contrast to the collectivism of the Japanese.

The Japanese: Difficult to be Rich

While Americans and British were extolling the advantages of cutting taxes to increase incentives and revive industrial investment, the past Japanese experience had told an almost opposite story. The reforms under the American occupation had forced the redistribution of land and confiscated pre-war wealth, making Japan into one of the most egalitarian countries. The industrial miracle of the post-war decades was achieved with some of the highest tax rates in the world, going up to more than 90 per cent. The big companies, like their counterparts in highly taxed Western countries, had responded by building up a system of perks, cars, golf clubs and corporate entertainment. But the Japanese perks were more directly linked to corporate aims – made easier by the exclusion of wives – and with less obvious abuses

**Sunday Times*, April 2, 1989.

than their Western equivalents; while the tycoons seemed content with relatively modest rewards. The legendary Konosuke Matsushita, the founder of the electronics giant which includes the Panasonic range, who owned 4 per cent of the company, was known as the 'king of the taxpayers', but he travelled by commercial planes, not a company jet.*

Akio Morita, the founder-chairman of Sony who was born into a very rich pre-war family, insists that 'today the idea of wealth seems somehow badly out of place to most Japanese.' The salaries of top executives, he claims, are rarely more than eight times the salaries of new trainees, without stock options or huge bonuses; yet this has been no visible disincentive to harder work. He believes that the most critical ingredient for a successful company is 'a shared sense of fate among all employees. People do not work just for money . . . if you are trying to motivate, money is not the most effective tool.'†

The pattern of the biggest Japanese fortunes appears on the surface similar to those of the West. More than half of the thirty-odd billionaires made their money from real-estate. The huge escalation of city land values in the eighties brought a crop of real-estate Japanese billionaires (in dollar equivalents). One of them, Kiyofumi Moroto, from an old samurai family, owes a large part of his fortune to two acres of central Tokyo where he lives. But most made their fortunes from developing Tokyo land: including Taikichiro Mori who built the Ark Hills skyscrapers; Yoneichi Otani who controls the vast New Otani Hotel in Tokyo; and Shigeru Kobayashi (see chapter 6) who made his money first in the Ginza, and later by buying up prominent American skyscrapers. Other Japanese made their billion from shops and retailing, and only a quarter made it from manufacturing – including Tadao Yoshida, the world's biggest zipper-maker, and Kanichiro Ishibashi, the head of the Bridgestone Tire Company.‡

But the very rich in Japan enjoy far less respect than their Western equivalents. 'I admit it is very difficult to be rich today,' Kobayashi told me, sitting in his vast marble office in central Tokyo. 'There are jealousies among average people.'§ Rich men keep a relatively low profile outside their own office habitat, as a tour of Japanese cities suggests: most of the imposing mansions turn out to be company guest-houses. And the corporate executives are judged more by their

*Ralph Hewins: *The Japanese Miracle Men*, Secker and Warburg, London, 1967, p.339.
†Akio Morita: *Made in Japan*, Fontana, London, 1987, pp.130, 135, 138.
‡For rival assessments of the richest Japanese, see *Forbes* magazine, July 25, 1988 ('The World's Billionaires') and *Fortune* magazine, October 12, 1987 ('The Billionaires').
§Interview in Tokyo, September 20, 1988.

competitive position or their rung on the company ladder than by their salary. There is now much apprehension in Tokyo (see chapter 6) that private greed is growing, and that profits from land are eclipsing rewards of hard work. But a very rich Japanese individual still finds it hard to buy social acceptance through money alone.

The Japanese attitude to wealth remains very different. Individualism is still suspect, and private ambition and rewards are much more integrated within a social and industrial system which can supersede personal greed. But the Asian element is often exaggerated. In many ways, I will suggest, the Japanese attitude has less in common with other parts of Asia than it has with the West in the nineteenth century, and particularly with Victorian Britain, when wealth was more closely linked to production, and ordinary people were more confident that they could all become more prosperous together.

CHAPTER THREE

OVERCLASS, UNDERCLASS

My friends, we are not the sum of our possessions.

GEORGE BUSH, January 1989

The new Midas of the West is very detached from the factory. But he is far from any traditional picture of the decadent rich, of lazy lotus-eaters or sleepy aristocrats. He is busier, and faster-moving than ever before: and it is his hectic activity and mobility, as much as his money, which separates him still further from the poor.

The equation of time and money had transformed the behaviour of the rich: for if time is money, it follows that spare time is valueless. The rich no longer aspire to a life of leisure, and work has become an essential part of their status. But it is work of a rarefied kind, removed from any fixed territory. The favoured status symbols are no longer the elegant house and garden, or park; but the luxury hotel suite, the high-tech yacht, the private jet. Money only really shows itself when it is in motion.

It makes an ironic contrast with a century earlier, when the rich in New York were competing in extravagance and ostentation, with yachts, private resorts or railcars. The new money at that time, much of which came from ruthless and grimy industries, was in search of the kind of status that least resembled its factories; and the sociologist Thorstein Veblen compared the extravagant lifestyles, fashions and entertainment to the honorific elements in primitive societies. Leisured gentlemen needed 'conspicuous consumption' to make them reputable; their wives became 'ceremonial consumers' whose fashions were designed less for beauty than to show off their cost: 'the marks of expensiveness came to be accepted as beautiful features of the expensive articles.'*

New money in the 1880s still aspired to the hierarchies of old money, and the queens of society could act as arbiters and brokers

*Thorstein Veblen: *The Theory of the Leisure Class*, 1899. Republished, Allen and Unwin, London, 1949.

between the two worlds, limiting the encroachments of new millionaires invading from the West. Mrs William Astor's huge ballroom provided a definition of the 'four hundred', the select families who were both rich and respectable enough to invite. The conspicuous consumption remained within a very limited circle: 'A lady should see her name in the papers on only three occasions: the day she's engaged, the day she's married and the day she's buried.'*

The ostentation diminished through the twentieth century with taxes, wars and depression; and by the 1950s Veblen's conspicuous consumption seemed thoroughly outdated. Corporate life was associated with conformity, the 'organisation man' and the 'man in the grey flannel suit'. The sociologist David Riesman explained how the old 'inner-directed' captains of industry had given way in public esteem to the new 'heroes of consumption' including actors and entertainers, and to office managers who were essentially other-directed. Riesman believed that in America (outside Texas) 'the crazy millionaire is dead, and a subdued nonconspicuousness seems to be spreading over our styles in leisure and consumption practices.'†

It was a premature obituary. In the eighties the conspicuous millionaire made a triumphant come-back, riding a new wave of sudden money, with private jets, duplex apartments and ranches in place of the old railcars and mansions. But he shows some fundamental differences from his predecessor a century earlier.

In the first place, money is now itself a much more straightforward yardstick of success. The 'rich lists' compiled every year by *Forbes*, *Fortune* and others, are only one sign of the breaking down of the old taboos against direct statements of wealth. Many of the richest men are glad to spell out the details of their wealth to the compilers, and fortunes can now be more accurately graded – like the acreage of the English rich at the time of Jane Austen. 'Money income as a measure of one's success in life has the drawback,' wrote the economist Tibor Scitovsky in 1976, 'that knowledge of it is seldom in the public domain. Therefore, to enjoy not only one's high income, but also the esteem it can secure, one must make it known through appropriate spending behaviour.'‡ But since then incomes and fortunes have entered further into the public domain: everyone can now know that

*Nelson Aldrich: *Old Money*, Knopf, New York, 1988, p.48.
†David Riesman: *Thorstein Veblen*, Scribner's, New York, 1953, p.170. Also *The Lonely Crowd*, Yale University Press (new edition), 1961, p.209.
‡Tibor Scitovsky: *The Joyless Economy*, Oxford University Press, New York, 1976, p.163. See also S. B. Linder: *The Harried Leisure Class*, Columbia University Press, New York, 1970.

Sam Walton is America's richest man, though he spends very little down in Arkansas.

De Gaulle once said that mystery was the essence of prestige: but much of the mystery has evaporated from wealth, now that a price-tag can be put on every rich man, and on everything he buys in an auction-room. Great wealth, whether from casinos, speculation or junk bonds, is now much easier to transform quickly into social acceptance (see chapter 12). There is still a Mrs Astor who is a kind of queen of New York, as benefactress and charity organiser: but the equivalent of Mrs Astor's four hundred a century ago is now the Forbes Four Hundred, which celebrates the rich, quite simply, for being rich.

But the more striking change is that the rich no longer see themselves as any kind of leisure class as opposed to the working class. Work, which had so long been associated with drudgery, is now essential to importance and status. The cult of leisure has given way to a cult of activity, and spare time is associated with failure and unemployment. Athletics, which Veblen saw as naturally suited to the leisure class since it wasted both time and money,* has become the antithesis of leisure, combining competitiveness and fitness with business deals. 'It was the poor who used to rise at dawn and work till dark,' says Michael Ignatieff. 'Now these orders of time have been reversed: the rich rise at dawn; the poor sleep late.'† Nor does old age provide much remission. Among the 400 richest Americans in 1988, 124 were over seventy, of whom fifty-four were still working full time – including the richest of them all, Sam Walton of Wal-mart Stores, who still visited his stores once a week.

Conspicuous consumption has returned, but now always linked to activity. The wives of the very rich still play the role of ceremonial consumers as Veblen described them a century earlier: the man makes the money, the woman spends it. The haute couture which thrived in American high society in the 1880s, when rich wives went to Paris every year, still performs its social function in the 1980s when a few very rich women compete with 15,000-dollar dresses at charity parties. But the haute couture is now interlocked with a highly publicised and competitive timetable of social activity, in which the dress designers themselves can be masters of ceremonies, often acting as escorts or 'surrogate husbands' to their clients.‡ The richest wives feel obliged to be as busy as their husbands, with their own secretariat and

*Veblen, op cit, p.397.
†*Independent*, January 7, 1989.
‡See Nicholas Coleridge: *The Fashion Conspiracy*, Heinemann, London, 1988, p.69.

crowded diaries. Their day-clothes are no longer designed, like the bonnet or the corset, to make work impossible; like designer jeans, they emphasise both activity and expense.

The work ethic appears to dominate; but it has very little relationship with the old joyless puritan work ethic which was the incentive behind so much Western production. For it is based on a positive dislike of leisure, more than a rejection of pleasure. There have long been groups of people to whom (as Noël Coward put it) 'work is more fun than fun'. Many Japanese have long appeared to enjoy their hard work more than their leisure. But the pursuit of work in the West could now provide a sense of purpose with glamorous surroundings, gadgetry and theatrical style, while avoiding the more depressing surroundings of actual production.

The rich still need to surround themselves with the images of leisure, even if they show an ironic contrast with their own hectic activity. Most ambitious money-men are too busy for social life outside their own work, and may only find time for two quick meals a day. But the leisure-style is still the mark of prestige: and the less time to display it, the more expensive it must look. Veblen's 'marks of expensiveness' are now much more developed; words like 'quality', 'excellence', 'important' (for pictures) or 'exclusive' (for houses), provide new euphemisms for expensive. But the evocation of leisure remains. The Amex Tower, in the World Financial Centre in Manhattan, is the centre of the far-flung empire of American Express which brings together credit cards, banking and international debt, humming with specialised and urgent activity. But on the fifty-first floor the chairman's waiting-room is equipped like a gentleman's library, complete with a telescope, bound volumes of Balzac and Dickens and a book of engravings of Egypt lying open on a desk, all evoking a leisured age of pure fantasy.

New technology encourages the combination of apparent leisure with intense activity: particularly the mobile telephone which provides an ideal status symbol enabling its users to do two things at once. 'When the important call came, I was in the theatre,' says an executive in an advertisement. 'Is it just the successful who get mobile phones?' asks a man in a deerstalker holding a telephone at dawn on the grouse moors. 'Or does success follow the phone?'*

The yacht remains a favourite symbol of wealth, with its associations of glamour, 'away from it all'. But the impatient tycoon no longer intends it for relaxation or idleness. William Astor in the 1880s

*Both from *Sunday Times* magazine, August 7, 1988.

would cruise for weeks off the American coast, with only sporadic contact with the mainland. Today the yacht must be equipped with a helicopter, fax machine and communications centre to provide instant linkage to mainland activity. Jon Bannenberg, the British designer who has devised yachts for many rich clients including Adnan Khashoggi and Malcolm Forbes, insists that his yachts are very hard-worked vessels which put in long mileage; and that the new gadgets enable the owners to enjoy more leisure. But yacht-owners like to be associated with achievement and fame. 'Perhaps it's not an exaggeration,' says Malcolm Forbes in his pamphlet about his yacht, 'to say that from *Highlander* conversations were generated more articles than from any ships since Noah's Ark and Christopher Columbus' wee fleet.'

The new rich still look back to an imagined earlier aristocratic lifestyle, like the millionaires a century earlier. The eighteenth-century English gentleman and his country-house still provide a fantasy role-model, complete with butler, library, servants, art collection and ballroom. But the pressures of time, mobility and efficiency have still further separated the façades from reality. The library is only there to impress visitors waiting to discuss a big deal, with clattering word processors and fax machines in the next room; and the paintings are all costed and reduced to the bottom line. Advertising and mass-marketing have plundered the country estate, the salon, the yacht, promoting the accoutrements to sell cigarettes, raincoats or food. Old money (as Nelson Aldrich puts it) 'is transformed into an upscale feeding pattern, a market with "good demographics".'*

And the rich are as interested in publicity as anyone. Already after the First World War the old fashionable society was being rivalled and undermined by the 'celebritocracy', promoted by Hollywood and radio. Today celebrities – even if they are not rich – can penetrate most of the citadels of wealth, while all but the most secretive rich look for some kind of public acclaim. While the old rich kept their names out of their papers, the new rich try to get their names in – thus transforming the role of journalists who can act as brokers and negotiators between two value-systems.

But what distinguishes the new rich most sharply from their predecessors is their mobility. The rich have always been restless, with the opportunity to escape on to grand tours, cruises or distant estates. But the financiers of the 1980s have become – like their money

*Aldrich: op cit, p. 142.

– much more detached from any single city, region or even nation. The technologies and deregulations which liberated the global markets liberated the money-makers too, encouraging them to detach themselves from any fixed base. Constant movement is often a necessary part of global business; but it can also generate its own sense of purpose. The modern status symbols are linked to easy mobility: private jets, hotel suites or yachts can be rented effortlessly, and agencies can provide entertainment and hospitality round the world. The competition for status and recognition is now on a global scale. Americans compete with Japanese, Australians or Germans for international attention, with the international art auction (see chapter 12) as the ultimate battleground.

The mobility allows the rich to live without any real awareness of any settled community, while highly organised services increase their detachment: servants rented rather than employed, entertainments bought ready-made, apartment-blocks protected like fortresses, stretch limos with darkened glass to avoid contact with ordinary people. The word community itself has changed its meaning, from a neighbourhood to a professional group – an investment, legal or medical community – who may be scattered over thousands of miles: the smaller and more specialised the group, the further they must travel to find each other. The rich can know much more about the lives of their counterparts at the opposite end of the world than about the street-life of people a few blocks away. Manhattan itself has provided one of the most dramatic frontiers, between the glitter and grandeur of the East Seventies and Eighties and the squalor and crime of the East Hundreds in Harlem. It is a frontier not only between wealth and poverty, but between mobility and immobility, time-frenzy and timelessness.

Poverty and Charity

In most Western countries the gap between rich and poor widened during the eighties. In Britain a forty-year trend away from inequality was reversed by the boom and the income tax cuts, half of which went to the richest 10 per cent of the population.* But in America the gap was most glaring – or at least most documented. Among the poorest fifth of the American population (according to the Economic Policy Institute in Washington) the average family income went down by as much as 11 per cent (adjusted for inflation) between 1979

*For an analysis, see Hugo Young: *One of Us*, Macmillan, London, 1989, p.535.

and 1986, while the income of the richest fifth went up by 14 per cent. There are some improvements among the poor, and fewer old people now live below the poverty line. But the median income of black families has declined, and the incidence of poverty among children – particularly black children – is much higher.* 'For the poor and for children, it is something like an undeveloped country,' wrote Emma Rothschild in 1988. 'The poor got poorer, and the young got poorer. Women with children did worse than women without children, and children did worst of all.'†

In New York, as in other American cities, poverty has begun to spill over into the streets of the rich. In the early eighties, the homeless increased so abruptly that they had to be housed in run-down hotels, many of them in the old downtown districts of Manhattan. The new homeless present more problems than the earlier alienated individuals. Most are now families, mostly with women as the heads, and the great majority are black. There is growing evidence of a continuing underclass which is permanently on the dole, outside the social code of the rest of the country. Many of the men are addicted to drugs and many of the women have become pregnant in their teens – a habit that sometimes stretches back over three generations.

There are few bridges across this gap, between this shapeless timeless existence and the highly ordered timetables of the rich or would-be rich. To economists and bankers this underclass appears essentially outside any system. In the words of John Reed, the chairman of Citicorp:

> Maybe 7 million families out of a total of 84 million families are hard core, external to the economic community. They are not so much the product of economic dislocation in the movements of industries as of social dislocation and family problems: problems in getting sufficient education, in providing the kind of environment for education and the disciplines associated with industrial living – the getting out of bed in time to get to a place to get a job and so forth.
>
> It's very difficult to imagine how to bring these people into fuller participation in the modern economy. In the United States this group is very heavily concentrated with women-headed units, who find it difficult to earn a decent living, and also meet the responsibilities of

*Leonard Silk in *International Herald Tribune*, December 17, 1988, quoting Robert Haveman of the University of Wisconsin.
†*New York Review of Books*, June 30, 1988.

> being the head of the family. They have basically gotten on a very destructive treadmill, from which they don't have much of an economic exit. Certainly, society is working and trying to find solutions to this, to date without much help. The financial community is almost irrelevant, these people are living with such limited economic resources . . .*

The underclass has been widely regarded as a new problem afflicting many Western cities: London and Paris have also seen an invasion of homeless, beggars and muggers. But it is partly a reversion to a nineteenth-century condition, in an earlier age of sudden mobility, when large numbers of immigrant or dislocated families were left outside the industrial system. They were often depicted as sub-human, in more brutal terms than any description of today's underclass. Today, as then, the more prosperous communities have no direct economic interest in improving the condition of the underclass, since they do not easily provide reliable workers or servants. And the homeless themselves are very conscious of being outside the system. In the words of Eddie Ward, a thirty-four-year-old graduate in Behavioural Sciences who sleeps in Central Park:

> It sort of amazes me that there's the rich, the super rich, and the underclass and the poor, and we all are part of America, and the rich seem not to care, but the poor and underclass they share amongst themselves; if they see a guy sitting on the side, here's a sandwich, here's a cup of coffee.†

But in at least one respect the contemporary underclass appears unique: it has increased during a boom. In the words of Bob Hayes, the young campaigning lawyer who runs the Coalition for the Homeless in New York:

> People for the first time in the history of this country are living on the streets during a period of general economic prosperity. Before, it was some form of national system-wide economic dislocation, a great depression or financial panic, that hurt everybody. In the 1980s we have managed to just hurt a relatively small proportion of people – but very badly.‡

Economists and bankers see this underclass as impervious to normal economic solutions. 'If you are able-bodied and a reasonably

*Interview, May 9, 1989.
†Interview in New York, November 13, 1988.
‡Interview in New York, November 16, 1988.

aggressive person and have your wits around you,' says Paul Volcker, 'you can obviously find a job in New York these days. And so I think the source of the problem lies elsewhere. I don't think you are going to cure it by bumping up the economies more.'* Many sociologists argue that homelessness is simply part of the wider hopelessness of the underclass, linked to drugs, mental illness, promiscuity and crime. One major investigation found that homeless families also have 'chronic economic, educational, vocational and social problems'.† Yet the visible fact remains that the homeless do not have homes – which many social workers insist are the foundations on which to build any social or psychological recovery. 'There is a three-word solution to homelessness,' says Bob Hayes. 'Housing, housing, housing.'‡

The distribution of housing provides the most visible signs of inequality, as the mobile rich find themselves with several dwellings while the immobile poor have none. The rapid movements of industry exacerbate the problem, leaving empty houses without jobs, and jobs without houses. There is no question that America spent less money during the eighties on housing the poor, and more on housing the rich. Between 1981 and 1987 the federal government's subsidies for housing went down from 30 billion dollars to 8 billion dollars. In New York federally subsidised housing dropped from 20,000 new units a year in the seventies to 5,000 a year in the eighties; while an average of nearly 27,000 new units a year were built between 1985 and 1988 – most of them in Manhattan and mostly far too expensive for the homeless.§ Behind this change lay a fundamental political turnabout as the grand hopes of the Great Society of the Sixties turned into disillusion, and retreated into a narrower, more family-based view. As Hayes sees it: 'We have turned our backs on what had been about a fifty-year tradition of subsidising the creation of housing for poor people in the United States. I see the casualties of that shift in policy on the streets every day.'‖

While the homeless and the underclass grew, the trickle-down theories encouraged the belief that big spending could in itself alleviate poverty by providing more jobs down the line. In the early eighties there was certainly a striking increase in new jobs in America – in sharp contrast with Western Europe. But of 12 million new jobs

*Interview, November 19, 1988.
†Institute of Medicine's Committee on Health Care for Homeless People. See Sue Halpern: *New York Review of Books*, February 16, 1989.
‡Interview, November 16, 1988.
§Sue Halpern: *New York Review of Books*, op cit.
‖Interview, November 16, 1988.

created, 3 million were in very low-wage service industries like shops and hotels, 2 million were in trucking, moving and building, while 2 million were in services to the rich, including finance, insurance, real-estate and the law: and it was these last jobs which were the best paid. The greater part of new building was not of homes, but of shopping centres, hotels, greenhouses and animal hospitals.* Many of the new service jobs were part of a wide pattern of growing leisure, and an increasing proportion of jobs revolved round the spending and patronage of the rich.

The new jobs and wages did not easily trickle down to the underclass and the homeless. The statistics support the impression gained by visitors to America, and caricatured by New York: of a country of increased inequality and separation between rich and poor, in which the poor are more dependent on the rich. It looks almost like a return to the eighteenth-century pre-industrial society, with great houses providing mass employment. But in this more mobile and restless age there is much less personal and long-term commitment. Resident servants have been replaced by a whole network of organisations providing anonymous service at one remove: an industry which largely excludes the underclass. As Felix Rohatyn describes it:

> In New York City we have seen this extraordinary explosion of wealth; and it's all the more noticeable because it lives cheek-by-jowl with extraordinary poverty. This wealth is not terribly modest. I don't think you can blame people for flaunting their wealth if they have worked at making it and they enjoy it. It's there to be seen. But it's a question of degree. And New York City became a city of wealth. The business of New York City was wealth – catering to wealth.†

As the poor became more visible, the rich did show some greater concern. Charity functions or fund-raising galas became far more prominent during the eighties: in New York alone they were reckoned in 1988 to raise a quarter of a billion dollars a year.‡ But there were growing doubts about their effectiveness. Extravagant entertainments which raised funds for the needy were already highly developed in nineteenth-century Britain and America. The 'custom of giving vast banquets in aid of a good cause was peculiarly Victorian,' wrote K. J. Fielding about Dickens' London, 'and it was typically Victorian that

*The statistics are taken from Emma Rothschild's two articles in the *New York Review of Books*: 'The Real Reagan Economy', June 30, 1988 and 'The Reagan Economic Legacy', July 21, 1988.
†Interview, November 17, 1988.
‡*New York Times*, November 21, 1988.

almost everyone realized its absurdity, and yet agreed to keep it going for want of a practical alternative.'* In New York in the late nineteenth century the entertainment for charities became grander and grander: when poverty became fashionable, there was a 'poverty ball' in which guests came dressed in fashionable rags.

A century later the pattern of charity was partly repeating itself, with more visible poverty at a time of continuous boom and diminishing taxes. There was an increase in private funding for the poor and homeless, much of it business-like and systematic, like Hayes' Coalition for the Homeless. But the more showy charities could easily lose sight of their original objectives, as they had so often in the past. In May 1988 the musical *Hair* was staged at the United Nations by the Creo Society – a fashionable fund-raiser dedicated to creative events – which promised the proceeds to Unicef and Children with Aids. The performance took in 830,000 dollars but six months later the organisers, after paying their expenses, had only 9 per cent left for the two charities, and Unicef had still received nothing.†

Felix Rohatyn, whose wife Elizabeth supports many charities, became an outspoken critic of the 'self-perpetuating money-raisers', who acted as vacuum cleaners for glamorous money while ignoring the less glamorous needs of the poor. As he put it:

> New York is a very charitable town, and always has been. But over the last decade there's been a change of emphasis. When you look at the lavishness of the overheads in some of these functions what's called charity here has become a huge business that consists of selling flowers and dresses and fashion magazines and music for causes that are quite defensible but not necessarily charitable . . . and the beneficiaries are very often the providers of those services as much as the institutions that are supposed to benefit.‡

There were mounting criticisms of both the extravagance of charities and their lack of contact with the recipients: some organisers, like Dickens' Mrs Jellaby, seemed more concerned to alleviate the guilt of the rich than to connect up the real needs of the poor. As Eddie Ward complained in Central Park:

> They just tell us: your problem is this. But how the hell do you

*K. J. Fielding: *Introduction to Dickens' Speeches*, Clarendon Press, Oxford, 1960, pp.xxi–xxii. Quoted in Grahame Smith, *Dickens Money and Society*, University of California Press, 1968, p.53.

†*New York Times*, November 21, 1988.

‡Interview, November 17, 1988. See also *Manhattan Inc*, April 1986, for Rohatyn's interview with Ron Rosenbaum.

> know? I have the problem. I think the people that are a real serious part of the capitalist system need to ask the people that live in the street what the problem is, how can they help? But they won't do that.*

There is no simple economic connection between the emergence of an impoverished underclass and a sudden crop of new billionaires. And as Paul Volcker says: 'There is no inherent reason in capitalism why north of 96th street in Manhattan Island is not very prosperous while the rest of Manhattan is doing very well.'† There are plenty of social rather than economic patterns, including drug-addiction, promiscuity and broken homes, which can help to explain the emergence of an underclass in cities across the West.

But the pace of change of the eighties, and the new divisions of wealth, had helped to widen the gulf: people were further separated not only by money, but by speed, mobility and sense of time. The reversal of roles, in which the rich were busy, while the poor were lazy, made the gulf harder to cross. On the one side, those outside the industrial system found it harder to catch up as the system moved faster. On the other side, the rapid financial explosion had left social understanding lagging far behind; and the mobile rich knew still less about the immobile poor. Money certainly provided no easy solutions; yet it was impossible to visualise any remedy which would not require huge public funding.

*Interview, November 13, 1988.
†Interview, November 19, 1988.

CHAPTER FOUR

THE EAGLE AND THE PREY

With no predators you will have a dead industry.

SIR JAMES GOLDSMITH

The most sensational displays of the mobility of money have been in the duels between two kinds of wealth: the corporate wealth of established giant companies versus the personal wealth – or capacity to mobilise wealth – of a handful of individual entrepreneurs and 'raiders' round the world. The long arms of these raiders could suddenly reach out to grab the corporations by their necks, to buy up the shares, to terrorise their boards, to take them over and to turn them upside down. The raids were the most dramatic symptoms of the fundamental economic transformation of the eighties – the globalisation and deregulation of markets, the ease of borrowing, the issuing of new financial instruments. But they were also very human dramas which changed social perceptions of money, and began to alter the political landscape. For the raiders and merger-masters represented the most sudden emergence of personal riches since the late nineteenth century; and they brought back the language of the jungle.

The jungle-view of business had been much in favour in the 1880s, when a few individuals – including Rockefeller, Carnegie and Vanderbilt – had established unprecedented wealth as they merged and monopolised the giant new industries of oil, steel or railroads. The sociologist Thorstein Veblen described 'a gradually advancing wave of sentiment favouring quasi-predatory business habits, insistence on status, anthropomorphism, and conservatism generally'.* These triumphant individuals may (as many historians insist) have been no more than the unwitting instruments of inevitable economic concentration: but they were glad to see themselves as kings of the Darwinist jungle representing the 'survival of the fittest'. The philosopher Herbert Spencer gave encouragement to the jungle-view;

*Veblen: op cit, p.373.

and he proclaimed (in 1882) that for Americans business was the modern equivalent of war. Later the tycoons were mythologised as 'robber barons', vested with all the atavistic romance of pirates and predatory creatures; while historians compared these early industrialists of the 'heroic age' to the buccaneering sea captains of the sixteenth and seventeenth centuries, to Drake, Hawkins or Cabot.*

But the corporations which the rugged individualists founded became gradually stabilised and bureaucratised, while their owners became more scattered and less able to take effective control. James Burnham described in his influential book *The Managerial Revolution* in 1941 how 'the capitalists, the ruling class of modern society, are losing control . . . In the new structure, when its foundations are completed, there will be no capitalists.'†

In the forties and fifties the giant companies like General Motors or the 'Seven Sisters' of oil, competing within prescribed oligopolies, appeared as fixed and self-perpetuating as nations – or even more so, as nations disappeared during world wars while companies thrived. The corporations developed elaborate hierarchies and tiers of management in quasi-military style, but they faced no challenges comparable to war. New giants in aerospace, computers or electronics grew up under dominating tycoons, but their control was soon in turn inherited by managers and technicians with only small shareholdings. Corporations were providing their own form of socialism, or an 'employee society' as Peter Drucker called it; while individual executives appeared less interested in personal display and more interested in corporate grandeur. 'It may not be simply coincidence,' wrote the sociologist David Riesman in 1960, 'that the reaction against conspicuous individual consumption has occurred at the same time that saved corporate wealth is no longer rapidly distributed to stockholders but is retained in depreciation funds or other concealment accounts . . .'‡

Already in the late sixties the peace of some corporations was being disturbed by periodic raids or mergers, led by corporate chiefs who made offers direct to the shareholders. In these 'go-go years' the stock market boom provided new scope to entrepreneurs who were aggressive outsiders. Harold Geneen transformed the telephone company ITT into a global conglomerate; Charles Bluhdorn, the 'mad Austrian', enlarged a car-bumper company into the

*Nevins: op cit, vol 2, p.712.
†James Burnham: *The Managerial Revolution* (paperback reprint): Indiana University Press, 1960, p.97.
‡Riesman: *Thorstein Veblen* (paperback edition), Scribner's, 1960, p.192.

Gulf + Western complex including Paramount pictures; Jim Ling, the school drop-out from a poor German Catholic family in Texas, created Ling-Temco-Vought. The success of these outsiders caused some panic among the traditional Wasp boards of directors, who tried to stimulate anti-trust opposition. But by the recession of 1974 the fears had receded, the mergers had virtually ceased, and the exotic outsiders were soon largely forgotten.

The early eighties saw a new wave of raids on a far broader scale: they were aimed at much bigger corporations, they were frequently hostile and much shorter-term, and they aimed to break up their victims and sell off their limbs, rather than join them to others. Many were launched not by existing corporations but by ambitious individuals, who found they could now borrow billions from banks, from abroad as well as at home. They were encouraged both by a soaring stock market which could quickly push up the value of shares, and by the ideology of the Reagan administration which did not wish to defend traditional corporate power. Richard Darman, the Deputy Secretary of the Treasury, had himself blamed 'corpocracy' for the economy's sluggishness; and the anti-trust laws which could have been used in the companies' defence were held in abeyance.

These raids challenged the whole structure of corporate power, threatening all but the biggest companies. Of the Seven Sisters of oil, one, Gulf, was gobbled by Chevron, while another, Texaco, was crippled after trying to buy Getty Oil, was sued and nearly went bankrupt. The old assumptions about the permanence of corporations and their managerial revolution went out of the window as shareholders rediscovered their power – albeit a very negative one – to sack the directors. Outgoing boards of companies could still defy the shareholders' interest as they departed, by arranging to be paid multi-million-dollar goodbyes which bore little relationship to their worth. But they departed with little dignity; and shareholders, presented with a choice between two kinds of greed, became still more sceptical of the corpocracy.

The small group of raiders personified a renewed and aggressive capitalism. They suddenly and spectacularly increased their own wealth and enriched thousands of followers on whom their expeditions had depended. They welcomed the predatory language and metaphors of the jungles and oceans, hovering like eagles, pouncing like lions, pursuing like sharks. It was a reversion to the 'quasi-predatory business habits' or the 'barbarian animistic sense' which Veblen had detected a century earlier. Business was once again seen in terms of war, and the sudden attacks took on much of the character of a military invasion – or a blitzkrieg – as rival lawyers, bankers and supporters outmanoeuvred, outflanked and outgunned each other with the artillery of money. Dark-suited bankers working through the night loved to talk the language of dawn raids, war-chests, logistics and engagements. While generals had adopted the language of peace, bankers took over the jargon of war.

There was reality behind the war-games. The abstract digits on the screens, the share prices, credit ratings or exchange rates, were the equivalents of armies in terms of their potential to invade other countries, to fortify or demoralise territories. But it was not conventional warfare but guerrilla fighting, of a confusing kind, full of fifth columns and mutineers, in which a whole army could eventually be sold to the enemy. And much of the activity had more to do with the casino than the army.

Conservative politicians and intellectuals were now reinstating the entrepreneur as a romantic hero, as a heroic loner battling against complacent battalions, the reincarnation of the earlier tycoons. George Gilder in 1984 ecstatically explained the lonely make-up and unique destiny of the entrepreneurs:

> Ugly, they wreak beauty; rude and ruthless, they redeem the good and true. Mostly outcasts, exiles, mother's boys, rejects, warriors, they learn early the lessons of life, the knowledge of pain, the ecstasy of struggle. In their own afflicted lives, they discover the hard predicament of all human life, threatened always by the creeping encroachments of jungle and sand.*

Gilder saw American industry being saved by young tycoons leading dynamic young companies, who had broken away from the giants in computers, biotech or electronics: men like Steve Jobs, the founder of Apple, or the motley founders of Micron, the microchip makers in Idaho. 'These firms are full of fighters and fanatics: men with a lust for contest, a gleam of creation, and a drive to justify their break from the mother company.'† And he invested them with a quasi-religious glory:

> Entrepreneurs, though many are not churchgoers, emerge from a culture shaped by religious values . . . Yet more than any other class of men, they embody and fulfil the sweet and mysterious consolations of the Sermon on the Mount and the most farfetched affirmations of the democratic dream.‡

*George Gilder: *The Spirit of Enterprise*, Penguin, London, 1986, p.18.
†Ibid, p.213.
‡Ibid, pp.255–6.

These tycoons certainly had a creativity and courage which was indispensable to new risk-taking industries. And the new industrial revolution had certainly knocked down earlier assumptions that the economic system was an impersonal machine. But their common religious basis was hard to find: the same kind of entrepreneurial qualities were now emerging all over the Far East from right outside the Judaeo-Christian tradition. And the new entrepreneurs seemed unlikely to achieve what earlier generations had never managed: to be loved and respected. 'The prevailing theory of capitalism suffers from one central and disabling flaw:' as Gilder admitted, 'a profound distrust and incomprehension of capitalists.'* Or as the political scientist Peter Berger described it: 'capitalism, as an institutional arrangement, has been singularly devoid of plausible myths; by contrast, socialism, its major alternative under modern conditions, has been singularly blessed with myth-generating potency.'†

It was the raiders who attacked existing companies, rather than the industrialists who built up new ones, who were the chief beneficiaries of the American boom of the eighties. They were primarily interested in making money, not things. With their defiant language of predators and prey, they were beginning to revive the old bogeys of the past, and to reawaken nineteenth-century dread of capitalism as a ruthless force which reduced all relationships to money; as Karl Marx put it in 1848:

> The bourgeoisie wherever it has got the upper hand has put an end to all feudal patriarchal idyllic connotations. It has pitilessly torn asunder the motley feudal ties that bound man to his 'natural superiors' and has left remaining no other nexus between man and man than naked self-interest and callous cash payment.‡

The raiders all cultivated a hatred for existing corpocracies. One of the pioneers of the new wave, T. Boone Pickens – the son of an unsuccessful oilman in Oklahoma – set up as an independent dealer on borrowed money after three years with Phillips Petroleum. After some lucky deals with his own small company, Mesa Petroleum, he developed a contempt for the 'good ol' boys' of the big oil companies. He loved to mock their 'four ps' (pay, perks, power and prestige), and their company planes, yachts and hunting lodges: it was a fitting irony that while they were relaxing by hunting game, he was a real predator, hunting their companies. He soon realised how vulnerable

*Ibid, p.15.
†Peter Berger: *The Capitalist Revolution*, Basic Books, New York, 1986, p.195.
‡Karl Marx: *The Communist Manifesto*, 1848.

these corporations were to raids with borrowed money: 'I decided that we could outthink, outwork, and outfox the big boys, and that would beat all the money in the world.' In his most daring move he tried to buy up Gulf Oil, which then escaped into the arms of Chevron, leaving Pickens with a huge profit. Soon afterwards he made another quick killing by raiding his own former employer, Phillips Petroleum. Pickens never gained control over a big company, but by 1986 he had made 107 million dollars out of buying and selling shares in other companies. He remained the classic loner. He loved gambling with business for its own sake, but had little idea what to do with his money. 'I get a big thrill out of making money, but I don't get much of a thrill out of spending it.' He had turned the virtues of thrift upside down, having always thrived on borrowed money: 'all I have ever known is debt,' he wrote in 1986. 'I owe more money today – $55 million – than I have owed in my life.'*

A more strikingly successful raider was Carl Icahn, from a poor Jewish family in Queens, New York. After studying philosophy at Princeton, Icahn had switched to Wall Street, first running his own trading firm and then raiding successive companies. Unlike Pickens Icahn eventually gained control of a giant company, TWA, and proceeded to reorganise it with apparent success, reaching an agreement with the unions. He nearly ended up with control of Texaco, the oil company already crippled by a court judgment. Icahn was even more contemptuous of corporate management than Pickens: 'Texaco is the quintessence of what is wrong with corporate America,' he told a crowd of analysts. 'We have a corporate welfare state in this country, that is why we can't compete.'† 'Most Chief Executive Officers get their jobs because their predecessors and the directors liked them,' he told *Fortune*. 'They slapped the right backs and laughed at the right jokes. It's reverse Darwinism: once a backslapper gets the top job, he sure as hell isn't going to have somebody better than him as heir apparent.'‡

All the raiders needed the same essential ammunition: large sums of borrowed money; and they soon found an indispensable source of supply in the shape of Michael Milken, the 'grand sorcerer' of Wall Street. Milken had single-handedly developed the new market in junk bonds – the bonds of less creditworthy companies earning high interest rates. He was like the dwarf Rumpelstiltskin who could weave threads into gold until his name and skills were discovered;

*T. Boone Pickens: *Boone*, Hodder and Stoughton, London, 1988.
†London *Sunday Times*, June 5, 1988.
‡*Fortune* magazine, February 29, 1988, p.32.

and for a long time he appeared invulnerable. The son of a prosperous Jewish accountant in California, he was gauche, bald and puritanical: he graduated at the Wharton Business School with flying colours and joined the old but sleepy Philadelphia firm of Drexel Firestone which had once been associated with the great J. P. Morgan, and which was now merged with Burnham. Milken set up his own department in Beverly Hills, specialising in high-interest bonds. With passionate salesmanship and an encyclopaedic knowledge of companies, he could offer huge new supplies of high-interest money which enabled corporate raiders to raise, in a few days, hundreds of millions from insurance companies and investment funds with which to take over their prey. Milken himself remained reclusive, secretive, based in his four-bedroomed house in Los Angeles. He was a classic 'control freak' with an intense desire to manipulate other people, but no idea of how to spend his own wealth. He started work at 4.30 a.m., kept the clocks on New York time, snatched five minutes for lunch on his desk, sometimes made 500 phone calls a day. He controlled his 'disciples' with fear and bonuses, and they in turn treated him as a Messiah. He was charmless and intimidating in his human contacts, but brilliantly eloquent on the subject of money. He provided the ammunition for a new generation of entrepreneurs to raid companies and bring away huge spoils.*

Milken and his colleagues, 'the Drexels', consciously looked back to the captains of industry a century earlier. They talked about the 'robber barons of the future' and described their favourite clients – like Carl Icahn, Henry Kravis, Samuel Heyman, Ronald Perelman or Rupert Murdoch – as 'the new Rockefellers' who were shaking up management and building up empires. They wanted their own stake in the companies they helped to raid, and insisted that owner-managers would have a gut-sense of responsibility which corporate managers did not. In fact, many of the predators who took over companies were soon paying themselves far more in salaries and perks than the previous managers. Nelson Peltz, one of the new breed, was paid 5.1 million dollars in 1986 by his company NPM and explained to the *Wall Street Journal*: 'The industrialists of the nineteenth century were highly paid and highly criticised, and I guess we'll have to bear that burden, too. But those were the guys that did things . . .'†

It was true that already in the late nineteenth century there was

*For details of Milken's methods and lifestyle see Connie Bruck: *The Predators' Ball*, Simon and Schuster, New York, 1988. Also Edward Jay Epstein in *Manhattan Inc*, September 1987.
†Bruck: op cit, pp.145, 245.

a wide gap between 'industrial' and 'pecuniary' employments, as Thorstein Veblen described them. Veblen claimed that remuneration was no longer related to production; the modern captain of industry was preoccupied not with production but with the control of wealth.* But the nineteenth-century entrepreneurs like Rockefeller or Carnegie, however ruthlessly money-minded, were deeply rooted in oil or steel and played central roles in building up their industries. Peltz, Kravis and Perelman made their profits first by raiding, then by relentless cost-cutting. They had little resemblance to the industrialists a century earlier, or to the contemporary Japanese tycoons like Honda, Matsushita or Morita (see chapter 7), who were intimately involved in management and technologies and much closer to the earlier American models.

Most of the new raiders were outsiders. While the tycoons a century earlier were predominantly Anglo-Saxon Protestants, nearly all the new predators – though not Boone Pickens – were Jews. Members of the older Jewish establishment worried that a new downturn or crash could induce a wave of anti-semitism using Jewish financiers as scapegoats. Laurence Tisch, the chairman of Loews and CBS, was reported to have told one of Icahn's colleagues: 'Tell Carl to cut this out. It's not good for the Jews.' An undercurrent of class warfare flowed through many of the raids, not so much between old and new money as between new and newer money. It reached a kind of climax when Michel Bergerac, himself a recent upstart who had risen via ITT to become chairman of the Revlon cosmetics company, found himself threatened and eventually ousted by Drexel's men led by Perelman. 'I'll never forget those twenty or thirty guys coming off the elevators,' Bergerac said afterwards, 'all short, bald, with big cigars!'†

Goldsmith v the Corpocrats

But the most successful of the raiders has a much more aristocratic background, and an intellectual power which he uses to justify and champion his raiding. Sir James Goldsmith is an unashamed predator, but with the style of an eagle rather than a shark or hyena. With a commanding presence, easy smile and soft voice he can appear as a

*Thorstein Veblen: *Industrial and Pecuniary Employments*, Publications of the American Economic Association, Series 3, 1901, pp.190–235. Later expanded in Veblen's *The Theory of Business Enterprise*, 1904. See also Joseph Dorfman: *Thorstein Veblen and His America*, Victor Gollancz, London, 1935, pp.198ff.
†See Connie Bruck, op cit, pp.160, 205, 331.

gentleman-playboy: he flies between his houses in New York, Mexico, Paris and London, with an establishment in each. But his casual style conceals shrewd calculation and planning, and can suddenly give way to a ferocious determination to win.

Like his friend and associate Jacob Rothschild, Goldsmith provides a link with an earlier entrepreneurial age: he is a descendant of one of the European Jewish families who had helped to finance the first industrial revolution. His great-grandfather Benedict Hayum Goldschmidt had set up a banking firm in Frankfurt in the late eighteenth century, with branches in London, Paris and other European cities, through which he raised large sums for railroads, and for Bismarck's Germany. One of Benedict's sons, Adolph, settled into country life in England, where his younger son Frank went to Oxford and became a member of parliament. In the First World War Frank served as a British major in the Middle East: but he had suffered from anti-German hysteria in Britain and after the war Major Goldsmith went to live in Paris, where he took over a group of French luxury hotels, and spent much of his time travelling between them.

Goldsmith was born into this cosmopolitan background and grew up with no fixed abode. He was half-French and half-English; he left France as a child when Hitler moved in, spending the war in the West Indies and Canada. He went to Eton, where he began gambling heavily and left early. He eloped dramatically with a Latin American heiress, Isabel Patino, who died in childbirth soon afterwards. In Paris and London he still gambled, and began his financial career. He had money in his blood, but he was not rich. 'I started as a capitalist without capital,' he says, 'and wanted to re-establish that for reasons of personal satisfaction . . . The drive was need, obviously the appetite recognising the need. Being able to do it meant a lot of luck, a certain amount of skill, and a great deal of fear. I think you need all three.'* Like many other entrepreneurs, including his British rivals Tiny Rowland and Robert Maxwell, Goldsmith's rootlessness gave him a special energy. 'Dynamism is usually the result of disequilibrium,' he once told me in London. 'My disequilibrium comes from the very simple reason that I'm a foreigner over here. I'm a Jew to Catholics, a Catholic to Jews, an Englishman to the French and a Frenchman to the English. I've always been neither one nor the other – which is a very unsettling thing to be.'†

*Interview, October 12, 1988.

†Anthony Sampson: *The Changing Anatomy of Britain*, Hodder and Stoughton, London, 1982, p.327.

Yet the mainsprings of Goldsmith's lonely drive remain something of a mystery even to his closest friends and bitterest rivals. He is quite capable of fear – he had lost his hair in his first business gamble in Paris – but he still feels impelled to re-enter the fray for still higher stakes. He enjoys his money more convincingly than most of his fellow-raiders, with a princely style, an Oriental taste and a powerful sexual drive. He insists that the power of an individual fortune today is very limited: 'It will never be as powerful as it was in the nineteenth century,' he told me, 'nor should it be. It will always be a marginal personal thing compared to the major power of the state.'* But he still seems driven towards some kind of domination, and he relishes the comparison with predators:

> There was some game reserve set up by some well-meaning people, who said it is horrible that these poor animals should live constantly under the threat of predators. Those animals subsequently became degenerate because predators are a necessary stimulant . . . If you eliminate predators in business and just create comfortable bureaucracies and monopolies with no predators you will have a dead industry. The prosperity of the country will shrivel away and your people will suffer infinitely more than by being subject to the constant stimulation of threat and competition.*

Goldsmith soon became a nomadic financier, at odds with the settled society around him. In the sixties and seventies he built up a spectacular financial empire in Britain and France and made an unsuccessful bid for political influence, controlling the French magazine *L'Express* and founding the short-lived British magazine *Now!* But he was exasperated by the European inertia and restraints: 'I have seen European industry, and European freedom and prosperity, destroyed by what I call the triangular alliance, the triangular establishment: big business, big unions, big government, all absolutely throttling out entrepreneurism.'† By the eighties he saw America as providing the opportunity that Europe had squandered, and moved his operations across the Atlantic. He soon made fierce criticisms of the American corpocracy and bureaucracy in general, which attracted many admirers; yet he often seemed to be attacking not just corporate management, but the continuity of society itself.

> I don't believe that there's any difference under the microscope between the bureaucracy of General Motors, the Pentagon, the

*Interview, October 12, 1988.
†Hearings of the House Subcommittee on Monopolies, November 18, 1986.

> Kremlin, the Vatican, or any of these major bureaucracies. They are all the same. They get the same bureaucratic disease and they start looking inwards, and it takes an extraordinarily strong man to cut it out.*

It was clear whom he saw as the strong man. In the United States in the early eighties he made a succession of dramatic raids on big corporations. In December 1982, after a five-year battle, he gained control of the Diamond Corporation, an old match-and-timber company which owned huge undervalued forests. With the help of the 'grand sorcerer' Michael Milken and the Drexels he borrowed 430 million dollars against a revaluation of the forests; and as the American recession turned to boom he began selling off Diamond's assets, paying off the debt and leaving himself with a profit on the deal estimated at 500 million dollars. In late 1984 he began buying shares of another big timber company, Crown Zellerbach: there followed an epic battle with the chairman William Creson who compared Goldsmith – in the now customary rhetoric of raids – to 'the men who pillaged England and Ireland in the ninth and tenth centuries'. Goldsmith was then cruising on the Mediterranean, with calculated sangfroid; but he succeeded in buying more than half the shares, and became chairman: he then sold off Crown Zellerbach's paper-making activities and made another quick profit on the shares.

It was ironic that these two lucrative victories should both depend on buying undervalued forests, which were then sold off for timber. The image of the merchant cutting down trees was deep in European mythology; and it happened that Goldsmith's brother Teddy was a passionate environmentalist, who had founded his own magazine the *Ecologist*, and constantly pressed Jimmy to defend the environment. Goldsmith, having sold off the forests, did become more concerned about ecology: he established a nature reserve in Mexico, took up the defence of Brazilian rain-forests and devised new financial schemes to protect them. While his brother has retreated into a pre-industrial world of organic farming and rural conservation, Sir James still insists that the environment can only be effectively protected in a post-industrial world, by making conservation economically viable. But would he himself ever become part of any settled environment?

It was the old rubber town of Akron, Ohio, which provided the setting for Goldsmith's most controversial raid or siege: a classic

*Interview, October 12, 1988.

case-history of a raider versus corpocrats. Akron had grown rich making tyres for cars in Detroit and had become one of the traditional company towns, a model of corporate paternalism. 'The rubber industry has defined the community of Akron Ohio for a hundred years or more,' said Akron's former mayor and present Congressman Tom Sawyer. 'The rubber companies in Akron have been like families. They have provided recreation opportunities, social opportunities, personal growth opportunities. They have competed for the best and most talented among each new generation. They have been a place where people could invest their lives in the hope of producing a better life for each succeeding generation.'*

But much tougher global competition, particularly from Japan, had already undermined much of the security of Akron. The great Firestone Company had closed plants, and fired tens of thousands of workers. Goodrich had paid off its raiders by buying back their shares: 'greenmail'. Only Goodyear remained as a major all-American company, the only big rubber company still quoted on the New York stock exchange. At its peak Goodyear had employed 5 per cent of the population of Akron and its importance increased as the other tyre companies had been bought up or merged. Goodyear had instilled long family loyalties in its workers. 'Many of us have seen our fathers retire from this facility,' said Tom Seese of the UAW union. 'Our grandfathers, in many cases our mothers, our aunts actually worked at this plant. I would say it's a privilege to live in Akron Ohio and say you worked for Goodyear.'† Goodyear had diversified into aerospace and into an oil company Celeron, which had rashly invested a billion dollars in a pipeline from California to Texas. But the core of the business was still tyres and rubber.

The Goodyear symbol was the blimp, the great rubber airship which proclaimed its name in the sky. 'You could go any place in the world and see the name of your employer on there,' said Tom Seese. 'Everybody related to you if you said you worked for Goodyear.'† Hundreds of blimps had been built in Akron in the past, inside a vast domed 'airdock' – so big, it was said, that clouds formed inside it. In September 1986 Goodyear opened the airdock to the public for the first time for fifty years, for a ceremony to launch the United Way charities campaign and display Akron's social responsibility. It was a spectacular occasion, as the great doors of the airdock opened and 300,000 people converged on the high dome, like a symbol of the

*Interview in Akron, November 28, 1988.
†Interview in Akron, November 27, 1988.

corporate womb.* But the peace of Akron was soon to be shattered by an equally symbolic intruder.

Only six days after the great rally, there were the first signs that someone was buying Goodyear shares, which quickly escalated. The chairman of Goodyear since 1983, Robert Mercer, who had been with the company for thirty-nine years, heard the news on his way back from Japan: he got together his 'swat team' and by the end of October realised that the raider was Sir James Goldsmith, who had bought 12 per cent of the shares. 'I knew the company would never be the same again, as soon as we were attacked,' Mercer said later. 'His strategy was to buy the company, bust it up, and take off with the proceeds. Period.'†

Mercer went to lunch with Goldsmith in his double town-house in Manhattan, refusing to be distracted by the luxuriant style and paintings of nudes. The contrast was theatrical. 'I found Mr Goldsmith to be a very professional man in the obscene business in which he elects to operate,' said Mercer. '. . . I think his acting talent and his histrionics far exceed that of any other raider that we have on the scene. He's just damn good at it . . . But he's in the wrong profession. I'd rather see him on the stage than on Wall Street.' Mercer presented the raid as a classic battle between corporate responsibility and individual greed: 'You can't shoot down a blimp and expect to get away.' He argued that only successful companies were raided: when companies were in serious trouble, like Chrysler in the seventies, no one could find a raider. 'You know a shark doesn't go after dead meat. He goes after live bait.'‡

The Akron people soon painted a picture of an inhuman ogre threatening their livelihood. 'The entire Akron community is in a state of shock,' said Congressman Seiberling from Ohio, who is the grandson of Goodyear's founder. 'I can't recall anything like this since Pearl Harbor.'§ 'He seemed to me a very cold and ruthless person,' said Larry Stump of the UAW after meeting him in Washington, 'someone that didn't care one bit about these families – especially our children.' 'He reminded me of a playground bully as a child,' said Tom Sawyer, who accused Goldsmith of 'consciously attempting to mispronounce people's names as a form of intimidation'.‖ Mercer wrote a letter to Goodyear employees,

*See 'The Goodyear War', Supplement to the *Beacon Journal*, Akron, November 30, 1986.
†Interview in Akron, November 27, 1988.
‡Interview, ibid.
§Hearings on Monopolies, November 18, 1986.
‖Interviews in Akron, November 1988.

explaining how Goldsmith was introducing the corporation 'to a new and not very pretty world'. Goodyear and its PR company encouraged local protest, flew over a copy of a British book called *Goldenballs* and spread stories that Goldsmith had a phobia about rubber bands. Schoolchildren wrote letters to Senators and Congressmen and threw darts at a picture showing Goldsmith with a fat head and mean, red mouth.*

The crisis in Akron quickly reverberated into Washington, where Congressmen were already holding hearings about raiders and corporations. Goldsmith prepared himself for a dramatic star performance which left the Congressmen dazed. He accused Goodyear of neglecting its 'core business' of tyres while it moved into new businesses, including the 'wholly lunatic' oil pipeline. He described how other bureaucratic conglomerates had been liberated by restoring the 'life-giving link of ownership and management'. He explained that his 'not very pretty world' was 'the rough and tough world of competition' in which 'you don't just throw away hundreds of millions of dollars chasing after scatter-brained dreams; a world in which you run a business as a business and not as an institution.' Goldsmith, like the other raiders, made no apology for his personal gains. Congressman John Seiberling accused him of wanting chiefly to make profit for himself. But Goldsmith was undeterred: 'I can think of no other reason for doing business . . . I strongly recommend that the United States, which was built on that idea, remain on that idea. It is very worthwhile.'†

Mercer replied equally carefully, supported by a team of loyal workers in the audience wearing Goodyear caps. He explained that his company's strategies were producing a renaissance in the rubber industry and protested that Goldsmith's arrival had forced Goodyear to abandon its long-term planning, to 'cater to the desire for instant gratification'. He viewed corporate takeovers as 'a method to make enormous profits for the already rich without creating anything new in the way of jobs, products or enhanced competitiveness'.‡ He was backed up in Washington by Sawyer and Seiberling; and in Detroit he was praised by Lee Iacocca of Chrysler, the corporate folk hero, who joined in the attack on the raiders: 'I see billions of dollars tied up in new corporate debt to keep the raiders at bay while research and development goes begging.'§

**Beacon Journal*, op cit.
†Hearings on Monopolies, November 18, 1986.
‡Hearings on Monopolies, pp.323–43.
§Lee Iacocca: *Talking Straight*, Bantam, New York, 1988, pp.92–5.

Goodyear in the meantime had lobbied the Ohio legislature to block the takeover, and Goldsmith was becoming less confident of gaining control. His British allies, the Hanson Group, who had also bought Goodyear shares, wanted to press ahead, but Goldsmith now decided to do a deal, and sell back his shares to Goodyear, at a profit of over 90 million dollars. There was a victory rally for Goodyear at the university's Rhodes Arena, at which Tom Sawyer said, 'we sent that slimy bastard back home.' But it was a Pyrrhic victory. Goodyear had been compelled to sell off its aerospace company, to slim itself down and to borrow more money – much as Goldsmith himself had advocated. 'We've lost maybe 5,000 people who literally hit the streets,' Mercer said afterwards. 'We've downsized the company by about 12 per cent. We've lost our very profitable operations such as our aerospace, our motor wheel operation, our oilfields. And we have a very heavy debt programme . . .'* Goldsmith was amused to watch the after-effects of his raid: 'It has to a large degree happened because of us, but without us,' he explained. 'Because management has adopted our plans . . . Goodyear has become a vital force in the tyre-making business and no longer needs protection . . .'†

In fact Goodyear was still top-heavy with management, and vulnerable to global competition. At the end of 1988 Mercer was succeeded as chairman by his unobtrusive deputy, Tom Barrett, who remained worried about the company's competitiveness. Goodyear was still the biggest tyre company, with 18.3 per cent of the global market, but Michelin was very close behind. Firestone had been finally sold in 1988 to the Japanese company Bridgestone, whose technical skill was giving it a growing slice of the world market. Soon Barrett confirmed many of Goldsmith's objections to the corpocracy. 'There were still too many layers of executives, he said in January 1989: 'We've got to break down the matrix system that's been building at Goodyear over the years. It's safe, but the bureaucratic structure makes it slow in reacting to changes in the market-place . . . It's very difficult to change people's perceptions about the way the company must operate.'‡ It might have been Goldsmith speaking.

In Akron the workers and union leaders still talked, two years later, as if they had been through a war or an earthquake. 'We've been through a terrible time,' said Larry Stump of the UAW:

*Interview, November 27, 1988.
†Interview, October 12, 1988.
‡*International Herald Tribune*, January 26, 1989.

> We've been part of Goodyear for four decades . . . We were part of a family and we were separated from our family, and now we felt that dead men sold us out . . . And we never ever have felt insecure with Goodyear. But now there is no feeling of security . . . There have been reported some separations, and some divorces. As you know, money can help keep a family together and unfortunately they didn't have the money to stay together . . .*

As for Goldsmith, having sold his shares back to Goodyear at a huge profit, he never saw the company again. 'He ran off with 94 million dollars, and for six weeks' work that isn't too bad,' said Mercer. 'It's about twelve times what I've earned in over forty years with the company. And he never got on the payroll.'†

The battle had certainly revealed the extremes of the two kinds of money-power, with dangers on both sides. The Goodyear executives had been far too introverted and preoccupied with empire-building. But Goldsmith had shown little sign of any long-term interest in the company or its employees, or concern for profits beyond the short term. In this raid, as in others, there was little indication of any happy mean. The shareholders who were the true owners remained without any effective power except to make quick profits by backing a raider. And the managers appeared far less responsive to the tough laws of the market-place than their Japanese competitors. As Felix Rohatyn put it:

> The corporate raiders, like all predators, perform some useful functions and many destructive functions. They keep passive or unimaginative management on their toes, but most of the time they have simply gotten financial results. When they have been successful in taking a company over they have stripped it of its assets, run it to pay back debt and squeezed the core out of the businesses.‡

But the battle represented much more than the confrontation between two kinds of ownership. It was part of a wider war during the eighties, in which the bombardments of mobile money were laying siege to settled communities such as Akron, while new communications were overtaking companies which could never hope to be so fast-changing. Was this new force so ruthless that it would cause new revolutions more serious than those in the nineteenth century? I asked Goldsmith:

*Interview, November 27, 1988.
†Interview, ibid.
‡Interview, November 17, 1988.

> Yes, the answer is quite clearly yes. But it's irreversible. We have moved into a new industrial revolution, what they call the communications revolution . . . There are a lot of destructive forces around. We will have to learn to live with them . . . How do you regulate the world? I don't know. I think we will have to live with freedom . . .*

Yet this kind of freedom – to buy and sell corporations across the world, to dismantle their components and lay off employees – was difficult for any society to live with for long. For it involved sacrificing the sense of community, security and long-term social responsibility which was deep in the Western tradition, and it brought back Marx's old bogeys of a world held together by 'naked self-interest and callous cash-payment'.†

Soon after his Goodyear adventure Goldsmith took a well-timed holiday from his raiding excursions. He had seen warning signs on the stock market, and turned most of his investments into cash a few months before the crash of 1987. He appeared to be retreating into philosophical and environmental studies, and began building a huge mansion in Mexico, alongside his own game reserve. But before long he could not resist returning to his real métier, money: and early in 1989 he re-entered the fray – this time in London, through a new company jointly owned with his old ally Jacob Rothschild who had helped to fund his earlier raids.

The raiding activity in Britain had been much less hectic than in America, without junk bonds, with greater individual concentration, and with slightly more anti-trust protection from the Monopolies and Mergers Commission. Back in the fifties, when the financier Charles Clore had first broken the British taboo against takeovers, he had been seen as a jungle monster by both left and right: the Labour Party leader, Clement Attlee, had referred darkly to 'nature red in tooth and claw – particularly Clore'. But takeovers had become thoroughly respectable after Margaret Thatcher came to power, followed by a succession of mergers during the eighties; and they were much more viable in Britain than in other European countries where controls were stricter. And as raids multiplied in America, Britain looked a more promising territory.

Goldsmith and Rothschild were still unsure of how their aggressive venture would be received in British financial and industrial circles. They had a foretaste in March 1989, when Goldsmith starred in a

*Interview, October 12, 1988.
†See p.44.

dramatic debate held in the Bank of England with an audience of leading bankers and industrialists, on the motion that 'this house believes that contested bids tend to be bad for industry'. Two prominent industrialists – Paul Nicholson of the Vaux Group and Sir John Harvey-Jones, the former chairman of ICI – argued against raids and takeovers. They pointed out that raids were most prevalent in Britain and America where industry was in decline, while almost unknown in Japan where industry was triumphant. The City, argued Nicholson, was too short-term and corrupt to be put in charge of industry; and if businessmen ignore their other responsibilities – to workers, customers and the public – they will again face the danger of socialism. Goldsmith replied by reeling off statistics to justify his own raids in America, and claimed that if Britain had permitted more raids in the past her old industries like shipbuilding or motorcycles would not have collapsed. In the following debate many industrialists – including John Banham of the Confederation of British Industries – reluctantly conceded that management needed raids, or the threat of them, to keep them 'under the gun'. Michael Newmarch from the Prudential – the biggest institutional investor in Britain – wished there were less drastic correctives to bad management, but could see no alternative to raiders.

Goldsmith had expected the vote to go against him, but he rallied support with a summing-up which mobilised his eloquent aggression. 'The owner wants value,' he proclaimed, 'the manager wants size.' He championed the contested bid against the agreed merger. 'The best takeovers are thoroughly hostile, but hostile to who? Not to shareholders, or employees or customers – but to a bunch of corpocrats who want to keep their jobs.' The audience voted with a show of hands which showed a large majority supporting Goldsmith. But it appeared to be a show of non-confidence in management (as some participants commented) more than of confidence in the raiders. It was a striking reflection on ageing British corporations that they had to look to such ruthless remedies to shake them up.

As for Milken, the grand sorcerer who had conjured up funds for so many raiders including Goldsmith, he had come up against the full force of the law. It was his obsession with control, more than his greed, which was his danger; for such dominating control was at odds with any view of the free market. And Milken was being closely watched by Rudolph Giuliani, the US attorney for the Southern District of New York, who after helping to clean up the Mafia had become the scourge of Wall Street insider traders. 'The actions of these people can't be explained just by greed for money,' Giuliani explained. 'They've got more than they can ever spend in their lives. There's a point at which their crime becomes habitual conduct motivated by the desire for fame and glory.'* A first warning was sounded when Giuliani arrested Ivan Boesky, the phenomenally successful investor who was then indicted for insider trading; in November 1986 Boesky agreed to pay 100 million dollars and to co-operate with the government in investigating other offenders. Boesky's trail led as far as London, where Ernest Saunders, the chairman of Guinness, was soon afterwards indicted; but more importantly it led towards Milken with whom Boesky had worked closely. In September 1988 the Securities and Exchange Commission alleged that Milken and other Drexel executives had been involved in illegal schemes with other companies, and in March 1989 Milken and two colleagues were indicted on charges of racketeering, with a sensational claim of 1.2 billion dollars on his assets, of which 1.1 billion dollars was made up by his salary for three years. Milken, now guarded by a phalanx of lawyers, said he was confident of being vindicated. The stage was set for a classic confrontation between the power of money and the power of the state.

In the meantime the pace of raids and takeovers showed no sign of slackening. During 1988 there had been mergers in America worth 250 billion dollars – twice the dollar figure for four years earlier – culminating in the record buyout of RJR Nabisco for 25 billion dollars. The sorcerer now had many apprentices. Milken's techniques for generating money through junk bonds had been taken up by the big banks, who were now increasingly depending on fees for takeovers for their profits. Bankers, lawyers, accountants and public relations firms all had a growing interest in continuing mergers, while the pension funds, the dominant investors in American shares, looked to takeovers to provide short-term profits, even though they might threaten the employees whose pensions they provide. Martin Lipton, the lawyer who specialised in defending companies from raiders, complained: 'our major companies are cannibalising themselves through their pension funds.' The takeover fever spread still more dramatically to Britain when in July 1989 Sir James Goldsmith, with his allies Jacob Rothschild and Kerry Packer of Australia, made a bid for the giant British conglomerate BAT, promising to 'liberate the parts to benefit shareholders', and offering the equivalent of 21 billion dollars.

The two versions of capitalism were becoming still more difficult

**Observer*, February 28, 1988.

to reconcile. Companies clearly often needed shock treatment to make them more competitive; yet they were still expected to have social responsibilities, including fair wages, contributions to charity and concern for the environment, which diminished their short-term financial competitiveness. 'However much we want our companies to be lean,' as Lloyd Cutler put it, 'we do not want them to be mean.'* But as existing managements fortified themselves against raiders, they often felt impelled to cut back their commitments and long-term plans, and to borrow as much money – like Goodyear – as the raiders would have done.

The dilemma was made much more serious by the competition from Japan, where corporations combined greater aggression and technical mastery with the kind of long-term security that Western companies had lost since the nineteenth century. 'Japanese management need not concentrate on short-term profit schemes for the sole purpose of appeasing its investors,' said Masaaki Kurokawa, chairman of Nomura Securities International. 'In the US, by contrast, each quarter's profit statement brings around renewed panic or exaltation, as investors concentrate on short-term results rather than long-term profit and investment.'†

The renewed power of Western capitalism, as Goldsmith warned, was a more revolutionary force than anything that had been unleashed since the industrial revolution. But it looked dangerously destructive as it faced an Eastern form of capitalism which was both more dynamic and longer-term in its goals.

*_The Lawyer's Brief_, September 15, 1988.
†Speech, May 23, 1988.

CHAPTER FIVE

THE FLIGHT OF THE BILLIONS

I can calculate the motions of heavenly bodies, but not the madness of people.

SIR ISAAC NEWTON, 1720

Those 400 billion dollars which were floating every day across the world had achieved a life and unpredictable power of their own, watched anxiously by the investors and speculators whose fortunes depended on them. Which way were they moving? Where would they end up? As currencies and markets were liberated and deregulated through the eighties they moved still faster, generating quick gains and profits, but upsetting balances and expectations as they went. Skyscrapers full of highly paid dealers now depended on the floating billions, as they were transmuted from dollars to yen to pounds, for their daily profits. The big banks which had helped to liberate them now watched them with some alarm, like Frankenstein watching his monster: for as the sums got larger their prospects became still shorter-term. John Reed, the outspoken young chairman of Citicorp, did not conceal his concern:

> I always feel that the Gods in some sense are laughing at us up there: because we've become a captive of our own definitions and our own sort of processes . . . We define professionals as being those who produce statistically desirable results. We certainly don't include in that definition a broader, more textured definition of results. We don't have the long-term loyalty to problems and solutions that a less numerically orientated set of investors would have.
>
> I often sit around with leaders of major corporate entities who tear their hair at the fact that they have to become very short-term orientated in terms of their financial results, quarterly earnings and so forth because of the pressures on their stock . . . Of course

the pools of money that are making that concern are their own pension funds which insist on quarterly performance.*

These fast-moving billions have attracted a new breed of global dealers who spend their time trying to catch up with them and make money out of their movements, whose lifestyles have become as hectic as the money. Paul Tudor-Jones is one of the most successful of them in New York: his company manages 350 million dollars of other people's money, and trades about 35 billion dollars a year – a hundred times the value of his fund – across the globe. He set up his own company in 1983 at the beginning of the boom, and adjusted his lifestyle to the global market, sleeping only four hours a night, getting up at dawn, working in front of screens in his luxury apartment or in his office, doing deals on the phone in his car or flying in his helicopter to his country retreat in Maryland. At thirty-four he has a staff of seventy-five and expects to make 100 million dollars a year for himself. He talks non-stop about money-investments in his Tennessee monotone:

> The world right now is globally linked because of the advances in communication. It's never been experienced before. When someone sneezes in Japan, I get a cold here in the United States. I trade all time zones as if they were one, even though I might be trading in Tokyo at night . . . We're not looking at three distinct different ways of trading, we're looking at the same pie, and everyone right now has their finger in it. It's just a function of trying to isolate which way the capital is flowing . . .†

The electronic funds that race across the world, revealing themselves only as blips on the screen, have rushed far ahead of human contact. The advocates of the electronic market-place had long talked about a 'global village'. It has now come about: but it turns out to be a village without a church, or a village green, or a crossroads. It is a market without a place, where every trader is watching every other trader. New communications, like pigeons and telegraphs, have been developed for bankers first, and only much later for the wider political public. Julius Reuter began using carrier pigeons in 1850 to carry news of the money-markets between Aachen and Brussels. The next year he set up his own telegraph agency in London to provide news of exchange rates and money-markets for bankers across Europe; but newspapers were slow to make use of

*Interview, May 9, 1989.
†Interview in New York, November 23, 1988.

his general news service. A century later the story repeated itself, when Reuters made huge new profits by providing an electronic financial news and monitoring service for bankers, leaving its general reporting lagging behind.

The new technology provides still more dehumanised numbers. In 1875, in the early days of transatlantic telegraphs, Carl Meyer von Rothschild first exclaimed 'the whole world has become a city', as he watched share prices falling across Europe. But it was still a city of people who knew each other. The news of the movements of shares, or currencies, was transmitted from one trusted partner to another: the strength of the international Jewish families, like the Rothschilds, Goldschmidts or Sassoons, lay in their combination of quick communications and trust. But the billions which now move every night across the globe are transmitted by quick-firing young dealers who talk between Frankfurt or Tokyo in their minimal language of Hi Hi and Bi Bi. Even the stock markets no longer depend on crowded floors of screaming brokers but on silent screens displaying pure numbers: in the words from Caryl Churchill's play *Serious Money*:

> Since Big Bang the floor is bare,
> They live in offices on screens.
> But if the chap's not really there
> You can't be certain what he means.*

Yet the market is more human than it looks. The huge anonymous sums held by pension funds, multinational corporations, investment trusts or banks may look far too big to be swayed by euphoria or panic. But they are still moved by the most primitive instincts. As Paul Volcker puts it:

> It's a constant conflict between greed and fear. Sometimes the fear is greater and you don't have financial excesses: I grew up in an atmosphere after the depression when in financial markets the fears engendered by depression had made everybody pretty conservative. Now, we've gone through about forty years of really unparalleled growth and prosperity. People take a quite different view towards risk than they did in 1950, and it's been a gradually cumulative process. Now the interesting question is whether we are not getting off on the deep end and borrowing and leveraging again, with very great difficulties as the excesses are corrected.†

*Caryl Churchill: *Serious Money*, Methuen, London, 1987, p.29.
†Interview, November 19, 1988.

These primitive instincts now had the whole world to play upon, including not only stocks and shares but currencies, which were soon showing they could be even more volatile than shares.

Back in the sixties enthusiasts for global deregulation had looked forward to the world's currencies gradually and rationally adjusting their values against each other, as nations with weak exports and economies devalued until they met levels where they became competitive: dollars, yen or pounds would accurately reflect each country's industrial efficiency. When President Nixon disconnected the dollar from gold in 1971, and when currencies began floating independently, no one anticipated the hectic movements which were to follow in the seventies and eighties. Currencies bobbed up and down with each new rumour and expectation. The exchange rates lost most of their visible connection with exports, and by the late eighties the daily movements of currencies were a hundred times the value of actual goods traded. The dollar could change its value in yen by 4 per cent in a day.

Currencies began behaving more like people than numbers – neurotic, distrustful people constantly deceiving and misunderstanding each other. Everyone else watched them, trying to guess what others were thinking, trying to be one, two or three steps ahead in the dance. The dance between Dollar and Yen provided the central drama of finance in the eighties. It was the most unpredictable of all, with swings and turnabouts which alarmed the world which depended on them; while for a long time it concealed the most dramatic development, the shift of wealth and power to the East, until this finally broke through with a near-catastrophe.

The dollar never had a very rational relationship. In the first phase of the early eighties the Reagan administration was committed to a strong dollar – which had helped to bring down inflation by allowing cheap imports, and had attracted foreign investors to finance the trade deficit. But by 1985 the trade deficit was dangerously widening: exports were crippled by the high dollar, and home industries were threatened by cheap Japanese imports. The new Secretary of the Treasury, James Baker, decided that the dollar must come down, to fend off demands for protection; and so began the second phase. In September 1985 Baker met with the four other major finance ministers in New York and published 'the Plaza agreement'. It proposed the 'orderly appreciation of non-dollar currencies' by 'co-operating more closely'. But this cryptic bankspeak really meant that the central banks would now intervene to devalue the dollar – a total reversal of Washington's previous policy.*

The next day the dollar fell from 239 yen to 225.5, or 4.3 per cent – the biggest day's drop in history. The central banks went on driving the dollar down for six weeks until by late October it had dropped by 13 per cent to 205 yen. By January 1986 the five finance ministers met again in London and agreed to let it slip lower, and by September the dollar was down to 153 yen. The fall from 239 to 153 did not accurately reflect the trade flows, or the difference in either production costs or purchasing power. 'What has changed 180 degrees during the recent period,' as Kenichi Ohmae put it, 'is the American government's fundamental belief.'†

In 1987 came the third and most alarming phase. By February Washington worried that the dollar might fall too fast. The finance ministers met again at the Louvre in Paris to try to stabilise the currencies – though still avoiding words like target zones which implied abandoning the market-place. But the dollar went on falling – down to 137 yen at the end of April, the lowest for forty years. It was far lower than Washington had expected, but it was still not correcting the trade deficit with Japan. Governments and central banks were now losing confidence that they could safely manage the currencies. The Japanese now had a surplus of 137 billion dollars; and they were helping to finance the American budget deficit by buying US Treasury bonds. This American dependence made the dollar less stable – still less when the Japanese bought fewer Treasury bonds in the spring of 1987 which forced up the yields.

The weakness of the dollar was all the more worrying because of the uncertainty about what would take its place: for neither Japan nor West Germany wished to take over the role of an international currency. It had a worrying resemblance to the world before the earlier crash in 1929. In the words of Sir Kit McMahon, the chairman of the Midland Bank in London, who had been deputy governor of the Bank of England:

> The whole turbulence of the inter-war period, with the enormous fluctuations in the exchange rates and the high unemployment and the protectionism, was due to the fact that the United Kingdom was no longer strong enough to be top nation, and the United States hadn't realised that it had to be. And I think you see the same

*For a detailed account see Yoichi Funabashi: *Managing the Dollar: From the Plaza to the Louvre*, Institute for International Economics, Washington, 1988, p.288.
†See the *McKinsey Quarterly*, Summer 1988.

> things since the beginning of the seventies, exactly parallel between the United States and now Japan – the same symptoms of fluctuation of exchange rates, high unemployment and protectionism.
>
> The world was very deeply unbalanced, with this very large US deficit, that would need to be financed mostly by the Japanese, week after week, month after month, year after year. There was uncertainty as to how that would happen and whether the exchange rates or the interest rates would have to move. It looked as if the world's leaders were not addressing that problem . . .*

In spite of this instability the New York stock market took a new and inexplicable surge in mid-1987. Through the long boom since August 1982 the Western nations had become accustomed to growing values of shares, which had risen by an average of 300 per cent in the biggest stock markets over five years, surviving several temporary 'corrections'. For most of that time the shares had some relation to company earnings, compared to the yields on government bonds. But after May 1987 shares were looking much more expensive compared to earnings, or to the higher yields on bonds, which showed little sign of going down.†

Yet shares in New York surged forward, further encouraged by Japanese investors who poured 15 billion dollars into American shares in the first nine months of 1987.‡ Through the weird financial summer shares climbed still higher for no obvious reason. Many shrewd investors who were nervous about overvalued shares had lost out before by selling too early, and were coming back into the market. They faced the classic dilemma of the rational man caught in an irrational frenzy, which had been so evident in the South Sea Bubble of 1720: as the banker John Biddulph Martin had put it: 'When the rest of the world are mad, we must imitate them in some measure.' At an early stage of the bubble the great mathematician Isaac Newton had realised how irrational it was, and sold his shares in the South Sea company at a profit of £7,000. But even Newton could not resist the next stage of speculative frenzy and bought more shares, eventually losing £20,000 in the crash.§ And the hysteria was summed up by the poet Alexander Pope:

*Interview in Berlin, September 27, 1988.

†For an official analysis, see Report of the Presidential Task Force (The Brady Report), Washington, January 1988, pp.9–13.

‡Ibid, p.10.

§See Charles Kindleberger: *Manias, Panics and Crashes*, Macmillan, London, 1978, pp.34, 121.

'All this is Madness,' cries a sober sage:
But who, my friend, has reason in his rage?
'The Ruling Passion, be it what it will,
The Ruling Passion conquers reason still'.*

Many investment experts forecast some kind of fall in 1987, but expected it to begin not in New York but in Tokyo, giving them time to sell out before the panic reached America. They were worried that Tokyo had much higher share prices compared to earnings – an average multiple of 58.5 in October 1987 compared to 17.3 in Britain and 19.7 in America – while soaring land prices in Tokyo suggested that too much money was chasing too few assets. They assumed that in a global 'efficient market' Japanese money would behave increasingly like American or European money, and that those high ratios and low dividends could not be sustained. One of the most brilliantly successful investors through the long boom had been George Soros, who had set up his Quantum Fund in New York in 1969 which in eighteen years had multiplied its value by 160. In early October 1987 – while he was promoting his new book *The Alchemy of Finance* – he warned that Tokyo prices were dangerously high. 'I was convinced', he said, 'that the crash would start in Japan.'

Only a few financiers foresaw the coming crisis, and sold their shares. Warren Buffet, the 'Wizard of Omaha', had insisted in the annual report in the spring of 1987 that the stock market was dangerously overvalued. Sir James Goldsmith had written in his French magazine *L'Express* in May 1987, warning that without closer global co-operation to stabilise the markets, there would be a major crash before the end of the year. 'It was obvious to me that the market had gone into a phase of paroxysm,' he said afterwards. 'People had forgotten that things could go down . . . There was a frenzy without any understanding of the major problems and disequilibria, which were not taken into account by the world market-places . . .'†

The Crash and After

In the week of October 12 New York saw some ominous developments, including bad American trade figures. Shares began falling at the end of the week, but without panic. In London on the Friday the great storm closed the market for the day: trees crashed, but not shares.

*Alexander Pope: *Moral Essays*, Epistle 3, lines 151–4.
†Interview, October 12, 1988.

But on Monday morning, October 19, Tokyo began selling shares and dollars while New York was asleep. The selling was taken up in Sydney and Hong Kong. When London opened it soon began dumping American shares, and by the time New York opened the panic had already begun. The rival centres, far from providing alternative judgments, magnified the fear as they reflected it. The New York stock exchange rapidly went into just the kind of general panic it had hoped to avoid. The 'portfolio insurers' had devised computerised programmes designed to protect shares against sudden falls. But it was they who generated much of the panic: three of them sold nearly 2 billion dollars of stocks – 10 per cent of the total sold – in one day. Just a few individual decisions could now demoralise a 3 trillion dollar market-place: 'A handful of large investors,' said the official Brady Report afterwards, 'provided the impetus for the sharpness of the decline.'* The first falls quickly alarmed the whole system. Brokers had expected that in the event of a panic the three main markets – for stocks, futures and stock options – would move separately, thus partly offsetting other movements: if people sold shares, they would buy futures at a discount which could help stabilise the market. As the selling continued, the futures were massively discounted; but that only scared people into selling still more shares. The markets sank together.

By closing-time Wall Street had seen probably its worst single day in history, with a drop of share values of 23 per cent. Other stock exchanges fell even further overnight. Hong Kong, which had proclaimed itself as the freest market of all, faced the worst ignominy. The chairman of the stock exchange, Ronald Li, an autocratic multimillionaire with wide business connections, decided to close the market down altogether for four days. It was a shock from which Hong Kong's confidence would not fully recover: and ten weeks after the crash Ronald Li was arrested and interrogated by the Commission on Corruption, before being released on bail.

The next day in New York began hopefully. Before the market opened Alan Greenspan, Volcker's successor as chairman of the Fed, made an historic statement explaining the Fed's 'readiness to serve as a source of liquidity to support the economic and financial system': in other words the market would not run out of money. Wall Street opened with higher prices, and the day began with a rally. But at 10 a.m. the portfolio insurers once again started massive selling, and the futures market collapsed by 27 per cent in two hours. The shares soon

*Brady Report, op cit, p.41.

followed futures down, into free-fall. There was, said the official Brady Report afterwards, a 'near disintegration of market pricing'.* Then on Tuesday afternoon there was drastic intervention. Major American corporations announced that they were buying back their own shares – at a cost of 6 billion dollars – which quickly rallied their own share prices and others. By the end of the day the Dow index had gained over 100 points since the opening.

The immediate panic was over. But the free-fall of midday Tuesday was the moment of truth. 'It was a very close thing the day after Black Monday as to whether those firms were going to get financed,' said Paul Volcker a year later. 'There were reassuring statements and I think some more personal moral persuasion by the monetary authorities that helped to get us through.' 'It was a very, very close thing,' said Felix Rohatyn. 'It isn't an exercise that I would like to see happen again. We recovered and in the year after the crash the economy kept going and was relatively strong but the confidence in the markets on the part of the individual investor never returned.'†

At first the crash of 1987 seemed to mark the end of an era, like 1929. In the first weeks afterwards New York felt deeply insecure, not just about share values, but about the whole global capitalist system. The five-year stock market boom had come to an end with a bang, and many observers now predicted an end to the high-rolling big-spending style which had accompanied it – particularly in New York. 'People are beginning to see that the five-year bull market of the eighties was a new Gatsby age, complete with the materialism and euphoric excesses of all speculative eras,' wrote William Glaberson of the *New York Times* in a survey eight weeks after the collapse. The historian Arthur Schlesinger judged that 'the collapse crystallized people's discomfort with the unbridled pursuit of self-interest.'‡

The mythology and hagiography of capitalism certainly took a knock. A few financiers, like Goldsmith and Buffet, had got out of the market in time; but several wizards of the markets lost heavily, ranging from George Soros to Boone Pickens, to the Australian Holmes a'Court. *Fortune* magazine had been planning an article on the end of socialism which they quickly abandoned; and their annual list of billionaires, which they had just published, required drastic adjustment and pruning. The richest American, Sam Walton, was reported to have lost 1.8 billion dollars, leaving him with only 6.5 billion dollars.

But over the following year shares gradually climbed up again. The

*Ibid, p.40.
†Interviews, November 1988.
‡*New York Times*, December 13, 1987.

Western economies did not go into recession as they had after the crash of 1929, and much of the doom-talk soon seemed alarmist. 'There was a loss of values,' said Volcker, 'but there wasn't any deep and lasting hurt in the structure of the financial system.'* New York showed little signs of abandoning its big spending, and a new wave of massive mergers and buy-outs brought both new excitement to shares, and huge new fortunes to a few master-financiers. There were a few major sceptics. 'We have no idea how long the excesses will last, nor do we know what will change the attitudes of government, lender and buyer that fuel them,' wrote Warren Buffet in March 1989. 'But we know that the less prudence with which others conduct their affairs, the greater the prudence with which we should conduct our own affairs.'†

The crash – and the pre-crash – had shown up all the irrationality of international finance: global markets, with all their computerised paraphernalia, could be just as emotional as local markets – perhaps even more so. For twenty years investors and economists had been attracted to the theory of the 'efficient market' – promoted by American economists, most notably by Professor Stewart Myers of MIT – which maintained that fluctuating share prices remained rationally related to estimates of companies' future earnings. It was an assumption which had encouraged small investors, and helped to justify surprising mergers.‡

Behind this 'efficient market' lay a broader view of the market-place as the repository of reason. Milton Friedman, the high priest of the school, had insisted that speculation could not ultimately be destabilising, since anyone who buys as prices rise and sells as they fall will lose money, and cannot survive. Charles Kindleberger, having written a history of stock market manias, insisted that this was 'difficult to sustain with any extensive reading of economic history'. And he contended that manias and panics were 'associated on occasion with general irrationality or mob psychology'.§ The mania and crash of 1987 showed many signs of mob psychology; and even Friedman, though he had predicted a fall in the stock market two weeks earlier, conceded that: 'Nobody knows what causes these panics. The causes are psychological and no one understands them. I don't know what caused the Great Tulip Bubble, nor last week's panic.'||

*Interview, November 1988.
†*International Herald Tribune*, March 29, 1989.
‡*Financial Times*, April 5, 1988.
§Kindleberger: op cit, p.28.
||*Independent*, October 28, 1987.

The two-day collapse threw massive doubts over any notions of rational expectations. 'Financial theory can cope with normal ups and downs,' wrote Barry Riley in the *Financial Times*, 'but not with a large discontinuity of the kind that the crash represented.' 'The concept of rational expectation doesn't apply,' concluded George Soros, 'when those expectations relate to events that are themselves contingent on the participants' decisions.'* Six months after the crash a group of economists gathered at the London School of Economics to analyse the lessons. Professor Lawrence Summers from Harvard explained how pension fund managers in a crisis can be overcome by primitive emotions like greed and fear. David Walker from the Bank of England also blamed pension fund trustees. Professor Mervyn King of the LSE explained that share prices had no 'true' value but a wide range of plausible values. And Professor Myers himself recanted: 'the efficient market theory is dead, at least in its simple form.'†

The small investor did not need to be told that the market was not efficient: the crash scared millions away from further dealings with shares. The rarefied world of high finance now looked still more disconnected from reasonable activity – and also very resistant to controls. Three months after the crash the presidential task force headed by Nicholas Brady – later Secretary of the Treasury – analysed the causes of the crash and made recommendations to prevent another, including a single authority to oversee all the markets and requirements for market-makers to show more capital. But the proposals were not followed up, and the system looked still more fragile. 'The single market is a global market,' said the *Financial Times* after the Brady Report, 'and it is only a little less risky thanks to this swift but quite modest correction.'‡

The billions floating round the world now looked still more short-term and volatile, as they turned into one currency after another. There were still deep uncertainties about the relationship between yen and dollar – all the more in mid-1989 when the dollar rushed up again for no explicable reason, to the despair of economic commentators. But what was clear was the continuing strength of Japan.

The crash immediately underlined Japan's advantage. The Japanese stock market, in spite of all Western warnings, proved more stable than the Americans or Europeans – let alone Hong Kong or Sydney. In Tokyo shares fell by only 13 per cent in the day after the crash in New York, compared to 23 per cent in the US. And just after the

* *Wall Street Journal*, January 14, 1988.
† *Financial Times*, April 5, 1988.
‡ *Financial Times*, January 11, 1988.

crash the Japanese telecom giant Nippon Telephone and Telegraph confounded Western critics further by successfully making a huge new issue to shareholders based on a very high multiple. Tokyo recovered much more quickly than other centres, and by mid-1988 it had overtaken its earlier peak.

Many factors helped to prop up Japanese shares, including overlapping investments and the discreet controls of the Ministry of Finance. But the overwhelming reason was cash. The flood of Japanese savings had nowhere else to go, while the Japanese trade surplus provided continuous support for the yen. The Japanese were not much surprised by the outcome. 'The stock market crash was just the tonic the American and global economies needed,' wrote Sam Nakagama, the international economic adviser, a month afterwards. 'By jarring policy-makers out of a course that was producing a dangerous run-up of interest rates, the crash will forestall a recession rather than cause one.'* 'People began to feel that perhaps Tokyo can act as some kind of anchor,' explained Nobumitsu Kagami of Nomura Investments. 'They didn't have any serious difficulty in understanding why the Tokyo market fared better than others: it was simply because the economic fundamentals are so much superior.'†

Gradually Western investors began returning to Tokyo, despite the still higher multiples of shares. They had to admit that Japanese money could continue to behave in a quite different way from Western money, fortified by a unique confidence which immensely increased its power. To many Westerners the shift appeared full of menace. As George Soros described it:

> Japan has, in effect, emerged as the banker to the world, taking deposits from the rest of the world, and making loans to and investing in the rest of the world. It is only a matter of time before the yen supplants the dollar as the international reserve currency . . . The prospect of Japan emerging as the dominant financial power in the world is very disturbing, not only from the point of view of the United States but also from that of the entire Western civilization.‡

It is only once in fifty years or more that the centre of the money-world moves in this way. In the fifteenth century it was Venice which was the magnet for money – and much else. In the seventeenth

**International Herald Tribune*, November 12, 1987.
†Interview in Tokyo, September 14, 1988.
‡George Soros: Afterword to the British edition of *The Alchemy of Finance*, London, Weidenfeld & Nicolson, 1988.

century it was Amsterdam. In the nineteenth century it was London. After the First World War the centre moved uncertainly from London to New York. Each country in its heyday was seen by others as obsessed by money-values, bowing down to the god of wealth. In the mid-nineteenth century England was seen as uniquely commercialised. 'With us, money is the mightiest of all deities,' wrote the English novelist Bulwer Lytton in 1833.* And foreigners agreed more emphatically. 'Why should we be surprised at this people's cult of money?' wrote de Tocqueville in his *Journey to England* in 1835. 'Money is the hallmark not of wealth alone, but of power, reputation and glory.'† 'There is no country in which so absolute a homage is paid to wealth,' wrote the American Emerson in 1856.‡ By the later nineteenth century America itself was seen as the centre of money-mania which subjugated the mind and spirit. When the German sociologist Max Weber first visited America in 1904 he was amazed by the skyscrapers like 'fortresses of capital' compared to the tiny doll's houses of American professors at Columbia: 'Among these masses, all individualism becomes expensive, whether it is in housing or eating.'§

Now in the 1980s financial power was moving from West to East with unprecedented speed. Japan was unlikely to be as decisively dominant as the United States or Britain in their heydays. The financial system would remain pluralistic, shared between North America and Western Europe. But Japan's surplus is likely to remain for several years, and to attract much else, including brains, talent, art, fashion, and the awe of the rest of the world. The Japanese are now the subject of the same kind of fearful accusations as their predecessors, as money-worshippers enmeshed in an inhuman machine. But financial power also brings a sense of confidence, excitement and long-term involvement with the future – which nations in decline so easily lose. Would the Japanese come to be seen as the new cultural centre, as well as the financial centre, of the world? And what would they do with their money?

*Bulwer Lytton: *England and the English*, London, 1833, book 2, chapter 1.

†Alexis de Tocqueville: *Journey to England*, 1835, p.91.

‡Ralph Emerson: *English Traits*, 1856, chapter 10.

§Quoted in *From Max Weber: Essays in Sociology*, ed. H. H. Gerth and C. Wright Mills, London, Routledge, Kegan Paul, 1984, p.15.

CHAPTER SIX

THE POWER OF THE YEN

In trying to internationalise itself Japan tried to adopt an international language, and the language it happened to choose was money.

JUZO ITAMI, FILM DIRECTOR*

The Tokyo stock exchange does not look like the centre of the world. Outside it is dignified enough, a heavy stone building with a long entrance hall like a tomb, with two Ionic pillars at one end and a relief of nubile nudes in the middle. The index of share values in orange digits shines like a mystic number for worship. On the floor above are stalls like a fairground, displaying pictures of the previous stock exchanges, a vivid graph of the soaring share values, and a robot which moves its hands to show the signals which brokers use on the floor.

But the huge room below presents a wild zoological scene, like a screeching aviary, or an aquarium at feeding-time. The dealers – nearly all males under thirty – all have white shirts and black hair, which makes them look like flapping penguins. Only one taller man with brown hair – the solitary American from Morgan Stanley – stands out from the mêlée. At one end layers of men are pushing against a partition desperately outstretching their hands to try to get shares. All round the room men are signalling to each other with fingers, clapping to clinch a deal, then rushing across to each other. Above them gleams the four-figure index, with its decimal points constantly changing.

The Japanese prefer this face-to-face market-place to working on computers in remote offices; and it looks like a caricature of unbridled free enterprise. Yet behind the apparent confusion and chaos there are calm, solid forces. Groups of huge corporations own interlocking blocks of each other's shares; the kind of 'insider trading' which is illegal in London or New York is part of an inherent understanding between Japanese companies; and the government intervenes more

*Alan Stanbrook: 'Tokyo's New Satirists', *Sight and Sound* (London), Winter 1987/8, p.57.

decisively to ensure that the market will be harnessed and controlled. The vigour of the room still expresses the dynamism of the Japanese economy as both corporations and individuals pour in cash from their savings, which flow pushes prices higher and higher. And this pressure of new savings, more than any conspiracy, provides the fundamental strength of Tokyo compared to London or New York.

It is still hard to comprehend that this frantic floor is now the centre of the financial universe. By 1986 the shares traded here were worth more than all the shares on the next-biggest exchange, in New York. The Japanese stock market, backed by the continuing trade surplus, represents an unequalled money-power, whose long hand can reach out across the world to buy up buildings, land and companies, which can make or lose jobs and transform people's lives. And on present trends Japan is likely to be the dominant economic power for the rest of the twentieth century.

But this sudden accumulation of wealth raises new questions about the power of money and what can be done with it. It is the first time that the money-centre has shifted away from the West, away from American and European traditions and networks. And for the first time this money-power is not connected to military power. How effectively can the Japanese use their money abroad without guns or armies to protect it?

In the nineteenth century few Westerners in the Far East would have imagined that Asians could ever challenge the Anglo-Saxon mastery of money. Confucius' emphasis on respect for elders, for tradition and the family, was blamed for much of the incompetence and decadence of the Chinese mandarins who treated Western merchants with such disdain; while Buddhist monks were associated with the contemplation of eternity and the withdrawal from the temporal world. And even after the Japanese began to show their strength in the late nineteenth century, they appeared as a military power of modernised samurai, rather than a financial power.

Both the monks and the samurai were deceptive. Already in the late eighteenth century the Japanese popular educator Toshiaki Honda was explaining that 'to all outward appearances this country is ruled by the warrior class, but in reality it is ruled by merchants.' The nineteenth-century Zen monk Shosan Suzuki was later seen as the man most responsible for developing capitalism in Japan. He advised merchants:

> Throw yourself into worldly activity . . . Your activity is an ascetic exercise that will cleanse you of all impurities . . . If you

> understand that this life is but a trip through an evanescent world, and if you cast aside all attachments and desires and work hard, Heaven will protect you, the gods will bestow their favour, and your profits will be exceptional.

His philosophy, says the contemporary scholar Shichihei Yamamoto, 'like the Protestant ethic, has led to the equation of thrift with secular asceticism'. Yamamoto, noting how contemporary Japanese salesmen in Africa have been likened to pilgrims, suggests that 'they are following Shosan's admonition to treat commerce as an ascetic exercise, like a pilgrimage.'*

Buddhism in Japan today does not seriously interfere with money-making, and many monks are shrewd capitalists themselves. Religion is largely disconnected from everyday Japanese lives, as in most Western countries, while the ascetic tradition is most visible in encouraging hard work and its most obvious yardstick, money. The Japanese still turn to Buddhism for funerals, for blessing new houses or in family crises; and some Buddhist monks continue to preach eloquently against money-values. I went to the Toshaido monastery at Nara, the ancient capital of Japan, to talk to the eighty-five-year-old abbot, Mr Morimoto, who is periodically consulted by Japanese corporate chiefs. With a small wizened head and a body encased in saffron, he sat cross-legged beside a harmonious Buddhist garden. He spoke passionately against the current rush of Japanese materialism, occasionally bursting into a guffaw. 'Buddha said that the materialistic view won't suffice for the happiness of human beings. The more material we have, the less blessed spiritually we will be; and there is no limit to people's greediness. What Buddha said about 2,000 years ago is particularly true of the contemporary Japanese.' It was a persuasive homily: but it was hard to see much connection between this eloquent monk in his exquisite garden and the hubbub of modern Japan a few miles away.

When Japan first made its impact on the Western world in the last century, it was as a military not a financial power; but its mastery of Western finance was the basis of its military success. The first major contact between Japan and the Western system came from the American navy, which sailed into Japanese waters and compelled Japan to open itself up to overseas trade; but it was British trading companies and banks who were the dominant Western influence until the end of the century, not the Americans who were preoccupied with their

*Shichihei Yamamoto: *The Spirit of Japanese Capitalism*, Tokyo: Kobunsha, 1979, chapter 1, translated in *Entrepreneurship* magazine by Daniel R. Zoll.

own continent and opening up their own West. The commercial interaction was quick: by 1863 William Keswick of Jardine Matheson introduced four Japanese friends to the City of London; nine years later one of them, Ito, after visiting America, established a regulatory system for Japanese banks. Already by 1873 Japan had its first modern bank, the Dai-Ichi (which still survives). By 1870 Japan had raised its first loan, to build a railway, from Schroders in London. By 1871 it had its own proper currency, the silver yen, in place of the Mexican dollar. By 1880 the Japanese government set up the Yokohama Specie Bank (now the Bank of Tokyo) to finance foreign trade in place of the Hong Kong and Shanghai Bank, and by 1884 it had its own branch in London. The old military class was beginning to face competition in status from bankers and businessmen: when the young Shibusawa Eiichi visited Paris he was surprised to find a colonel treating a banker with deference; but Eiichi went on to become the respected father-figure of the Japanese business community, connected with founding 500 companies, including the predecessor of the Dai-Ichi Bank.*

Japan was already setting a pattern quite different from other Asian or Latin American countries trading with the West. It wanted to borrow money and skills from the West, to build railways, ports and factories, but not to allow foreign investment or control. 'In all dealings with the outside world the aim of the Japanese was to establish and safeguard national independence,' wrote Sir Fred Warner, the former British ambassador in Tokyo, in his study of Japan's financial links with Britain. 'From the very beginning, they determined to create as quickly as possible an independent industrial base and an independent military power.'†

The obvious signs of Japan's effectiveness remained its military and naval build-up, after it won the war against China in 1895 and against Russia in 1905. But a few bankers were aware of the unusual financial skills of the Japanese: Lord Rothschild in 1906 wrote that they 'are just as proud about good financial measures as they are about successes on land and water'.‡ In the First World War they were able to export textiles, chemicals and ships to markets which had been dominated by the West, and they built up sufficient balances in America to provide bonds for the British Treasury, denominated in yen. But the post-war inflation and the earthquake of 1923 set back their prospects; and by the thirties the depression and the Manchurian War had cut

*Yamamoto, ibid, chapter 10.

†Sir Fred Warner: 'Japan and the City of London', Richard Storry Memorial Lecture, no 2, St Antony's College, Oxford, 1988, p.3.

‡Ibid, p.12.

them off from the West. The Americans and Europeans associated Japanese industry with cheap toys and textiles imitating their own goods. The brutalities of wartime, and the weirdness of Japanese kamikaze pilots, the jungle-fighters or prison-camp guards, tended to obscure the commercial mastery which, like the Germans', underlay the military victories.

It was not until after the Second World War that Japan's commercial dynamic made its full impact on the world. There has been endless debate about the underlying secret of Japan's success in capturing world markets. But there was always one initial and overpowering incentive: the desperate need to earn foreign currency. It was this harsh necessity which distinguished East Asians from Latin Americans and Africans. Akio Morita, the son of a rich industrialist, had his own insight when he set up the electronics company which later became Sony:

> We didn't have enough rice and we had no energy, so really we were desperate how to survive. We knew that unless we made it our business to acquire foreign currency – with which we could buy what we need – we could not live . . . So that's why Japanese people started to work together. Also I think Japanese people are skilful: when we hit the wall then we suddenly started to work hard to break through this wall. When a crisis comes all Japanese people get together.*

But whatever their special skills, the Japanese had to admit that it was the drastic reforms of the American occupation which did most to increase their commercial effectiveness – in ways that are full of irony in today's United States. For the Americans were very harsh on the rich in Japan, as Morita well knew: 'The occupation forces changed our tax laws and the government imposed the highest income tax on high-income people, and the lowest income tax in the world on the low-income people. Then we became an egalitarian society, which completely broke the class feeling, so that everybody felt in the same class.'†

'Have you acquired the American dream, more than the Americans themselves?' I asked Morita.

'Maybe. Maybe we are fortunate that we are a homogeneous people and that our education system is good.'

The Americans gave Japan another crucial commercial advantage

*Interview in Tokyo, September 20, 1988.
†Interview, ibid.

when they forbade it to have armed forces outside its own country, a ban later endorsed by its own constitution. Japanese industrialists soon began to see the benefits. 'In a defence industry if we achieve a target we don't have to pay too much attention to that cost,' said Morita. 'But in a consumer industry we have to create new products at a reasonable cost. So we need more creativity than the defence industry.'*

Commercial ambition in Japan could now occupy most of the vacuum left by military ambition. The Japanese sublimated their aggressive energy into industrial competition, and gave decisive priority to production and salesmanship, with a directness which was first mocked and then copied by the West. At the KYG management training school below Mount Fuji, young managers and salesmen are put through a 'hell camp' like a marine platoon, shouting slogans, memorising rules and learning how to laugh. The school has often been depicted as typical of Japanese conformity; but it has now set up a branch in California.

The merchants in Japan had more openly taken over from the samurai. The highest new Japanese status was being given not to generals or even bankers but to industrialists. Manufacturing companies could attract the brightest graduates from the University of Tokyo, banks the second-best. The battles between corporations, both within Japan and outside it, became the equivalents of military campaigns, and the precepts and principles of war could be transferred to commerce. The classic *Art of War*, written by Sun Tzu in the fifth century BC, became essential reading for many corporate chiefs who looked to it for an understanding of strategy and guile. 'All warfare is based on deception,' wrote Sun Tzu. 'Hence, when able to attack, we must seem unable; using our forces, we must seem inactive; when we are near, we must make the enemy believe we are far away; when far away, we must make him believe we are near.' With such tactics the new generals of industry marshalled their forces and took successive competitors and countries by surprise.†

Money, rather than military prowess, became the measure for success; but money was channelled and harnessed to the productive machine. Japan gave such overriding priority to industrial production that its financial power was late to show itself. When its exports first spread across the world in the sixties and seventies the yen was kept low enough to give them an advantage. The Japanese could still feel

*Interview, September 20, 1988.
†For an account of military parallels see Douglas Ramsey: *The Corporate Warriors*, Grafton, London, 1987.

themselves relatively poor and insecure, which maintained their drive. Even in the early eighties Japan was still reeling from the second oil-shock which had redoubled the price of oil, causing a new bout of insecurity and worry about raw materials. It was not until 1983 that a further surge of exports, together with continued high savings and low government borrowing, enabled Japan to begin exporting long-term capital. And it was not until after the Plaza agreement of 1985, when the yen went from 240 to 170 to the dollar in seven months, that the Japanese found themselves dominating the world financial scene.

By 1986 Japan was already the world's biggest creditor nation – the position that America had occupied in most of the twentieth century, and Britain in the nineteenth century – and after the crash in October 1987 the yen was stronger than ever. Japan remained an immensely successful industrial power; it was now also a major financial power.

The Japanese still felt insecure. Their industrialists feared that the high yen would make their products too expensive abroad and at home – with some reason. Cheaper textiles began to flood in from neighbouring countries like Korea and Taiwan, and by March 1986 one of Japan's oldest textile factories, Yamato Spinning, had to close down. But the Japanese companies surprised the world – and often themselves – by their response to a commercial challenge, and by their quick redeployment of forces, which made Western companies look like old-fashioned infantry. They cut labour costs with the help of robots, automation and streamlined production, and when necessary they cut wages. They moved still more rapidly into high-tech industries where costs mattered less. And they rapidly set up many more factories in East Asia, America and Europe, to take advantage of cheaper labour abroad.

In the meantime the high yen, together with the deregulation of Japanese finance, had given huge opportunities for financial gains on top of industrial profits. The Japanese bankers and dealers were quick to master a global technology. The new trading-room of Sanyo Securities in Tokyo claims to be 'the largest continuous open work space in the world': a single, self-contained room under a curved roof fifty feet high, where 750 traders buy and sell stocks and bonds from all over the world, each with a computer terminal and three video screens, facing a single vast screen where orange and blue graphs reshape themselves through the day. More than any other financial building, it looks like a lay cathedral, dedicated to money-worship.

But the industrial corporations were also turning to the money-game, or zai-tech, the new word for financial engineering. By 1988 many of the biggest Japanese companies, including Toyota and Sony, were making more money out of financial operations than from manufacturing. Toyota, with liquid assets of 20 billion dollars, was now making higher financial profits than all but the biggest banks. And the strength of the Tokyo stock exchange allowed Japanese companies to raise new money with great ease, replacing debts with capital and financing massive new research and development for the future, even when their profits were declining – a complete contrast with the American pattern. Like Wall Street they were making money out of money: but they were constantly ploughing the money back into production.

The Japanese corporations now emerged still more triumphantly, as the richest and most effective machines for mobilising production and technology that the world has ever seen. Like Western companies in earlier decades, they are immune to raids and takeovers, protected by their cross-holdings of shares. They are not troubled by quarterly earnings or shareholders' protests about low dividends: they are more concerned with increasing their market-share over their rivals than with immediate profits. Their cash hoards and low interest rates enable them to invest in long-term projects and research for decades ahead, keeping new car engines or computers under wraps until they are ready for battle. Their wealth is the key to their power, but the money is channelled and controlled into the corporate purpose: they have a clutch which can link money and production. Their smooth working depends as much on their social and aesthetic sense as on their financial dynamic. 'Business is an art rather above architecture,' said the founder-chairman of Matsushita, the electronics giant which includes Panasonic. 'Business has to be built like a block. All the elements have to be pure and faultless and all must harmonise. The arrangement is a thing of beauty and the art is much more complicated than that required to build a building.'*

The wealth of the Japanese corporations was now still greater compared to the government's. It was they, not the government, who held huge surplus funds and could take bold long-term decisions. And their financial clout was very evident in its impact on politicians.

There was a long tradition of bribing Japanese politicians, but the flood of money in the eighties had multiplied the stakes. Members of parliament had to step up the traditional gifts to voters at weddings or funerals – the going rate was equivalent to 150 dollars per wedding

*Hewins, op cit, p.334.

– while rich and ambitious tycoons, impatient of the bureaucratic controls, looked to bigger bribes to ease their path. One of them was Hiromasa Ezoe, a lean-faced outsider who in 1960 had founded his own small publishing company, Recruit, which grew into a conglomerate with 12,000 employees. By the late 1980s Ezoe was earning the equivalent of over 10 million dollars a year, but he still felt excluded from the political inner circle, and he scattered favours to cabinet ministers, civil servants and other businessmen. It was in the time-honoured tradition of 'money-politics', but Ezoe in his impatience had overstepped the mark, and by 1988 the prosecutor was on his trail, uncovering a succession of distinguished recipients. By early 1989 the finger was pointing clearly at the Prime Minister Noboru Takeshita, who first denied the charges and then apologised, while his popularity slumped and the stock market suffered. Finally in April Takeshita resigned in disgrace and shares went up by 1 per cent in a day: the climax to the biggest Japanese financial scandal for forty years.

Western critics played up the specifically Asian element. But the scandal was not so unlike nineteenth-century America, where the huge new corporations led by Standard Oil were generously bribing state legislatures to ease their expansion across the continent. Nor was it really a scandal about private greed: the money was used for electioneering rather than personal spending, and the Japanese appeared to be less personally greedy and corrupt than American Congressmen or British MPs. What was more disturbing was the overwhelming economic power of the Japanese corporations which had no real parallel in other countries.

Takeshita's resignation produced a wave of anguished discussion about the relationship between cash and politics in Japan. 'This is more than a leadership crisis,' said the political scientist Yoshikazu Sakamoto. 'It's also a crisis of ideas. We have money but we don't know how to use it.' 'But it's just recycling money back to the community,' one editor in Tokyo assured me. The contrast between corporate wealth and the political poverty was more worrying in the context of a nation rapidly emerging into a global role, and some Japanese saw it as a sign of their country's immaturity in the face of American military power. 'Leaders indulge in teapot power struggles,' said the political adviser Jun Eto, 'in which tremendous amounts of money are thrown about as the principal weapon.'*

The political scandal was comically offset by a more domestic

**International Herald Tribune*, April 26, 1989.

money-mystery, after a chicken-seller found wads of rotting yen notes in a bamboo wood outside Tokyo, worth about a million dollars, which he reported to the police. In the following gold-rush a labourer found another 700,000 dollars' worth. Intense public excitement followed, like a whodunit: eventually the notes were traced to a mail-order businessman who admitted that he had abandoned the money after he had been worried about friends' business deals which had led to murders and suicides. The explanation remained mysterious: it was, said the *Yomiuri Shimbun* which had led the story, 'like a very bad end to a detective story'. But the bamboo wood had provided a kind of fairy-tale about the new Japanese confusion of money. 'The average Japanese cannot play the money game,' said the *Yomiuri Shimbun*. 'When these worlds collide as they did in the bamboo thicket, public interest is immense.'*

The Japanese were becoming aware with some bewilderment that they were now the money-centre of the world, as another island-nation, the British, had been a century earlier. There were many resemblances to Victorian Britain, which had the same ability to combine monarchy and ritual with dynamic innovation, the same national self-containment and homogeneity, as its confident new middle class spread round the world, keeping close-knit. The Victorian public schools, like the Japanese schools, put team-spirit and conformity above individualism, kept women in second place and respected regimental virtues rather than the entrepreneur who could never buy prestige and status. The Victorians had the same enthusiasm for mechanised factories where (as Taine described it): 'man is an insect and it is the army of machines which holds the attention.'† And the Victorians had the same sense of excitement with the future, planning new institutions, systems and projects with an optimism and confidence which later British generations lost.

By the 1980s the British, like the Americans, were constantly referring to a Japanese conspiracy: to 'Japan Inc', which subjugated the individual, and spread secretive networks across the world. But most of these accusations had been made a century earlier by foreigners observing the Victorian British who had their own racial exclusiveness and patriotism. And much of the rhetoric against the Japanese had been delivered against any successful nation – the

International Herald Tribune, May 23, 1989.
†Hippolyte Taine: *Notes on England* (translated by Edward Hyams), London, Thames & Hudson, 1957, p.222.

Dutch, the Venetians or the Americans – as they reached the peak of their money-power.

Certainly most Japanese would agree that they had a less individualistic attitude to money than Westerners. Nobumitsu Kagami had worked for several years in London before becoming the managing director of Nomura Investment Management in Tokyo, where I talked to him in 1988:

> The main reason is probably social. Western people are perhaps more individualistic: they feel they have got to live on their own and money is something with which you can acquire some degree of independence. Also, perhaps, because money as motivation is an important element of capitalism, which in the Western world has developed far more than in Japan. The Japanese are generally more group-oriented: whether you are secure in the group you belong to is probably more important than how much money you have. From that point of view, money as a source of motivation is probably less important in Japan.*

But would the Japanese retain this corporate attitude to wealth, in a specifically Asian way? Or would growing prosperity bring with it a burst of individualism and personal assertion, as it had in earlier Britain or America?

Certainly the rapid rise of the yen, and the soaring stock market, generated a surge of money-consciousness in Japan, as everyone began playing 'the money-game'. Money became a favourite subject for satire and comedy, particularly in the films of Juzo Itami: *A Taxing Woman* showed a woman tax-collector who saw her work as a substitute for sex, and *The Funeral* showed the preparations for a Buddhist funeral constantly interrupted by obsessions with money: the Buddhist priest himself arrives in a white Rolls-Royce. Other films showed a nostalgia for a more leisurely and innocent Japanese life: the popular series about Tora-san – the endearing drop-out who sells trinkets at carnivals and pursues beautiful women who reject him – has been through forty instalments over twenty years since 1969. 'In the beginning Tora-san's way of life wasn't abnormal at all,' said the director Yoji Yamada. 'Now he looks like a relic from the ancient past.'†

Housewives joined in the obsession with money-technology, or zai-tech. Women's magazines have begun devoting columns to

*Interview in Tokyo, September 14, 1988.
†*International Herald Tribune*, March 7, 1989, and *Japan Times Weekly*, January 21, 1989.

zai-tech instead of slimming. A book called *Stock Investment for Women* became a bestseller. Miniature calculators showing share prices, yields and interest took the place of knitting at home. Yuriko Koike, a lively woman journalist, presents a nightly zai-tech programme on television: and she sees the new money-making as rapidly strengthening the role of Japanese women. 'Japanese women dominated domestic finance historically,' she explains, 'and many husbands were given their allowances from their wives. Now that the Japanese family becomes much richer, people start to think how to make money from money . . .'*

How much will they save? What will they buy? As a new generation of Japanese wives rush into luxury boutiques and travel agencies, carrying Louis Vuitton bags and festooned with designer labels, the prosperity of whole nations depends on their choices. The government committed itself in 1988 to improve housing and living conditions, as one official explained, 'so that the public can enjoy a quality of life befitting Japan's image as an economic superpower'.† But sellers of luxuries still complain that they refuse to relax. 'We have more money than we know what to do with,' says Keizo Saji, the billionaire who has controlled Suntory whisky for a quarter-century. 'We must make efforts to spend it and enrich our lives.' He cannot even persuade his own executives to drink at lunch: 'We have been putting free beer on their table for ten years, but nobody touches it.'‡

The rush of money rapidly internationalised the appearance of central Tokyo. The districts of Roppongi and Shinjuku turned from horizontal to vertical: tall self-contained islands of corporate wealth now stare at each other, almost indistinguishable from their American equivalents. The shopping canyons of the Ginza glitter with English slogans and French and Italian designer names; McDonalds hamburgers and Dunkin' Donuts shine out from hoardings; Western musicals led by *Cats* and *Starlight Express* are played in huge tents; five orchestras in Tokyo compete in performing Western classical music.

Yet the surge of national wealth does not make much difference to the lifestyles of many ordinary Japanese – even those who are now dealing with huge sums of money. Mr Shukuzawa, working in the Sumitomo Bank, the second-biggest bank in the world, told me that he gets up at six, leaves home at seven, reaches his office at eight and works until seven in the evening at the earliest. He takes only one

*Interview in Tokyo, September 22, 1988.
†*Japan Times Weekly*, November 12, 1988.
‡*Financial Times*, October 15, 1988.

MONEY AND DEATH. In the sixteenth century Hans Holbein the Younger depicted the miser in the *Dance of Death*, facing the inevitable retribution.

THE DEALING-ROOM AS CATHEDRAL. In the headquarters of Sanyo Securities in Tokyo 750 traders can buy and sell stocks and bonds across the world, in front of a vast screen which dominates the room like an altar.

THE PREDATOR. Sir James Goldsmith is the most articulate and persuasive of all the raiders of companies in his attacks on incompetent 'corpocracy'.

THE GUARDIAN. Paul Volcker, the chairman of the Federal Reserve for most of the eighties, was resolute in cutting back inflation – at some human cost.

MONEY FOR LUNCH. In a Houston restaurant share prices and time-zone clocks ensure that its customers never forget that time is money.

THE BANKRUPT AS HERO. John Connally, former governor of Texas and Secretary of the Treasury, borrowed and speculated too rashly; but emerged from his bankruptcy still larger than life.

WHERE DOES JAPAN FIT INTO ASIA? Vice-Minister Toyoo Gyohten, at the Ministry of Finance in Tokyo, explains that Japan, like King Midas, has many problems in becoming so suddenly rich.

'THERE'S NO LIMIT TO GREED.' Morimoto, the Buddhist abbot of the Toshaido monastery, laments the materialism of contemporary Japan as he sits beside his exquisite garden.

JAPAN BUYS WESTERN CULTURE: 1. Akio Morita, the chairman of Sony, shows off a cover-picture of himself with Cyndi Lauper, a star of CBS records – which Sony bought for 2 billion dollars.

JAPAN BUYS WESTERN CULTURE: 2. Yasuo Goto, chairman of the Yasuda insurance company in Tokyo, explains why he bought Van Gogh's *Sunflowers* for £24.7 million.

CHINESE AND MONEY. Fang Li-zhi, the dissident astrophysicist in Beijing, insists that Marxism is dead and economics are the same everywhere.

CHINESE AND MONEY. Rong Yi-Ren, the heir to a huge Shanghai textile company, became a Communist official and now runs China's investment group, CITIC.

A CAPITALIST IN CHINA. Malcolm Forbes, a believer in conspicuous wealth, cruises back to Shanghai on his yacht *Highlander*, arguing that the Chinese need to see how well free enterprise works.

CAPITALIST YESTERDAY. The Peace Hotel in Shanghai was the grandest hotel in Asia in the thirties, the showpiece of the Sassoon family. Now proletarian Chinese practise exercises on the Bund in front of it.

出納

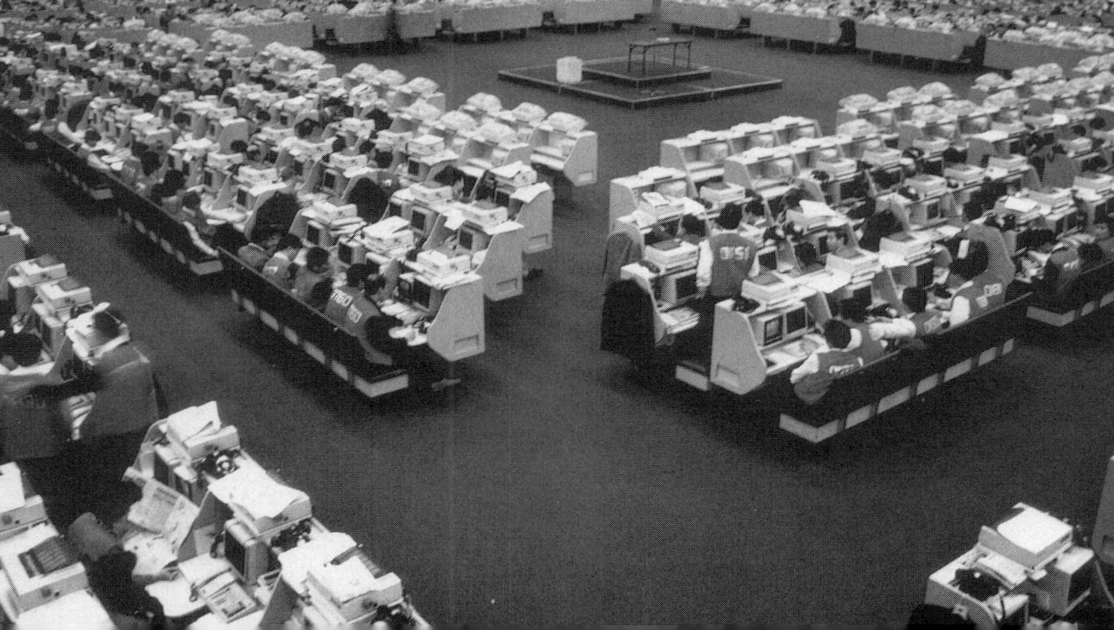

The Shanghai stock exchange looks more like an old shop: there are only a few bonds to choose from, and business is not very brisk.

The new Hong Kong stock exchange is immaculate and highly computerised: but it has become subject to still more extreme surges of panic.

RIVAL MONEY SYMBOLS. The new Bank of China skyscraper in Hong Kong, designed by the Chinese-American I. M. Pei, represents the financial power of mainland China.

The skyscraper of the Hong Kong Bank, designed by the British Norman Foster, represents the power of expatriate Chinese and their highly mobile capital.

THE HEIR TO A DEBT-MOUNTAIN. In Argentina Carlos Menem, with his famous sideburns, electioneered with populist policies like his heroes above him, the Peróns. But once he became President he warned his voters there would now be 'surgery without anaesthetic'.

Ghana used to be called the Gold Coast, a legendary centre of riches in Africa: and some Ghanaians still hope to make fortunes by panning for gold.

'Money is a religion,' says Kwasi Ntansah of the foreign exchange business 'In God We Trust' in Ghana. 'If you do it in a stream it becomes dangerous.'

IN GOD WE TRUST FOREX BUREAU LTD.
GOD WE TRUST FOREX BUREAU LTD.
IN GOD WE TRUST FOREX BUREAU LTD
P.O.BOX 30, NIMA-HIGHWAY. TEL.
TELEX: IGWTFB
U.S. DOLLAR
C.F.A. FRANCS
DEUTSCHE MARK
IN GOD WE
FOREX BUREA

The great banker Pierpont Morgan by Edward Steichen, who captured his terrifying dark eyes and his bulbous nose – on which the world's financial system was said to depend.

THE PATRON'S PARADISE. Botticelli's *Adoration of The Magi* has traditionally been thought to represent members of the Medici family: with Cosimo (kneeling before the child) and his son Piero (kneeling beneath the Virgin) who is looking at his brother Giovanni, next to whom is Cosimo's grandson Giuliano and (on the far left) Lorenzo 'the Magnificent'.

Andy Warhol was advised to paint money because that was what he loved more than anything. And his paintings of money now fetch more and more money.

week's holiday a year. He dines at home only once or twice a week. He and his family look back with some nostalgia on their time in London, where they had an apartment close to Primrose Hill which was twice the size of his Tokyo apartment.

Some feel themselves worse off than before. By 1987 the land values in central Tokyo had multiplied so rapidly that no one today who does not already own an apartment has much chance of ever owning one, unless by inheritance (and death duties remain high). For the first time since the war, the Japanese are talking about a class system, divided between those who own property and those who do not. Opinion polls have repeatedly shown that about 90 per cent of the Japanese regard themselves as 'middle class'; but the numbers calling themselves 'lower middle' have been increasing – up to 30 per cent in 1987. 'There is some justification,' wrote the marketing analyst George Fields, 'in seeing this as the beginning of the breakdown of a sense of community in the Japanese culture, the most obvious being the rise in land prices.'* Certainly the sudden wealth from property, as in so many other societies, has raised questions about the fairness of earnings. As Kagami of Nomura puts it:

> Japanese society has always valued the asset or wealth that you earned through hard manual work. And all of a sudden you find that the price of land on which you live goes up three or four times more than your annual income. People begin to question what they are really doing in their work. I think this breeds some kind of social discontent, particularly among young people who do not possess any particular property: they are probably becoming more desperate about their future . . .†

Many Japanese are concerned that the new money-mania is beginning to strain the consensus. 'This individual greed in some respects is really undermining the traditional virtues of our society,' said Toyoo Gyohten at the Ministry of Finance. 'There is a growing concern about that.'‡ 'People are becoming more individualistic,' says Kagami. 'Society is beginning to change: for example, the life-time employment system in the company is probably in the process of breaking down gradually. Families are probably breaking up. Therefore more people feel that they have got to live on their own: and in that kind of situation money is important.'§

**Japan Times*.
†Interview, September 14, 1988.
‡Interview in Tokyo, September 8, 1988.
§Interview, September 14, 1988.

More fundamentally, the surge of wealth is changing attitudes to the nation itself. As Gyohten puts it:

> When there is a very strong collective wish among people to make their country stronger and wealthier it is easier to mobilise a national consensus to work together. [Now] I think it will be a very difficult task for any nation to maintain a good nationalistic sense . . . But what is nationalism in this world? Economies are so interdependent now, and one country cannot survive without making others also better. The recognition of this interlinkage among different countries will certainly modify this basic concept of nationalism.*

Kenichi Ohmae, the highly articulate engineer who runs the management consultants McKinsey in Tokyo, and who flies constantly between Japan, America and Europe, is very sceptical about the future of Japanese patriotism:

> Money is a very rational being. Money knows no national boundaries. Where it makes sense it keeps moving. There is no nationalism associated with money. This is the reason why lots of money is flowing out of this country. Rather than re-investing in Japan we are buying real-estate in the United States, Australia and Europe . . . If you sell a piece of land in Japan that is six foot by six foot in the centre of Tokyo you can buy an estate in Canada, a really beautiful home in the United States. Now why should you then keep this piece in Tokyo?†

What can the Japanese do with their money? However much more the families consume, however many Gucci shoes, Louis Vuitton bags, bottles of Johnny Walker whisky or McDonalds hamburgers they buy, they are very unlikely to use up the massive surplus that Japan builds up year after year from its exports. In the meantime, like America or Britain in their heyday, Japan has to lend and invest the dollars, pounds or Deutschmarks which it earns abroad. As John Reed, the chairman of Citicorp, sees it from his vantage-point in New York:

> Japan is to savings a little as Saudi Arabia is to oil. They simply have a large pool of this valuable commodity. If the Saudis could only consume their oil within Saudi Arabia it wouldn't have much value because their needs are infinitely small as compared to their

*Interview, September 8, 1988.
†Interview in Tokyo, September 22, 1988.

> resources. That is true also of Japanese savings. The value of savings in Japan, if they must be used only within Japan, is close to zero, because there are more savings than uses for that money . . . The benefit to Japan is only the utilisation of those savings outside of Japan.*

As the yen went higher American companies and property became still cheaper to buy. But the Japanese faced a new risk of political unpopularity abroad, and new worries about protecting their investments. In America Japanese-owned skyscrapers, office-blocks and luxury hotels became the symbols of the growing power of the yen and the Japanese 'money-weapon'. The Japanese bought property mainly in a few highly publicised centres, particularly Manhattan and downtown Los Angeles, which exaggerated the trend; while Hawaii, where Japanese owned most of the beachfront at Waikiki, provided a caricature of the invasion – a new Pearl Harbor attacked not by bombers but by yen.

In Tokyo I went to see the biggest buyer of American real-estate, Shigeru Kobayashi, the exuberant president of the Shuwa Corporation, who is already a dollar billionaire. He works from the top of one of his buildings, the 'Tokyo Business Residence', a bright white building surrounded by multinational headquarters. He has two immense office-rooms with white marble floors, full of Californian kitsch and mementoes of Japanese-American amity, including a framed thank-you letter from Nancy Reagan and several American eagles. On a table is a model of a projected Tokyo skyscraper with a miniature King Kong gorilla waiting to climb up it.

Kobayashi began buying houses in the Los Angeles suburbs with the help of his son in the late seventies; but they were hit by high American interest rates. Then the yen began shooting up in 1985 and transformed Kobayashi's prospects: 'I was more than surprised. I was absolutely amazed.' He began buying skyscrapers, borrowing money at low interest rates in Japan which provided high yields in America. By 1988 the Shuwa Corporation owned thirty-six buildings in America worth over 2 billion dollars, most of them very visible landmarks on prime sites, in Los Angeles, San Francisco, Boston, Chicago, Washington and New York; the biggest is the Arco Plaza in Los Angeles which Kobayashi bought for 600 million dollars in cash. His current target (he told me in 1988) is to buy half a billion dollars of real-estate a year in America; but he finds it so easy to borrow that he has no real limit.

*Interview, May 9, 1989.

The skyscrapers provoked some fierce criticism from Americans who saw Japanese investments as a threat to their regional autonomy or sovereignty. But Kobayashi betrays few worries. He had been assured by the US Treasury, he told me, that they had no objection to his buying provided it was orderly and not speculative; and he promised them that he regarded the investments as permanent. He sees himself as providing a stabilising force. 'Japan has been accumulating the dollars from every corner of the world through the trade surplus. And naturally we have to return the surplus to where it is needed. The best way to return it to the US is to make investment in real estate.'*

Property was only part of the fast-growing Japanese investment abroad: the biggest securities firms, led by Nomura, are now awash with funds needing to be invested, some of which has to overflow across the world. It was a bewildering realisation for a traditionally self-contained people. As John Reed saw it:

> The Japanese financial institutions feel quite uncomfortable operating outside Japan with other than Japanese customs . . . They are not large in terms of business activity around the world. To the best of my knowledge the Japanese institutions do not aspire in any dramatic way to change that: they are primarily oriented towards their role in the domestic economy.†

'We feel a bit worried by the gap that exists,' said Kagami of Nomura, 'between the amount of money we can handle and the knowledge and expertise to do that . . . We know that at some point we have got to go abroad: do we know enough about what's going on in the rest of the world, just sitting here? I don't feel we know enough.'‡ For the time being the Japanese banks are very hesitant to wield their full clout: but they will inevitably increase their direct involvement as their knowledge caught up with their wealth.

Were these investments really safe? The flood of Japanese buying and lending abroad – from the building of plants to the financing of American Treasury bonds – inevitably raised questions about their security. Unlike the previous financial powers with massive surpluses, America and Britain, the Japanese had no military forces which could protect them. As trade relations between Tokyo and Washington became more strained, Japan's dependence on American military strength looked more precarious.

*Interview, September 20, 1988.
†Interview, May 9, 1989.
‡Interview, September 14, 1988.

There were plenty of alarming scenarios offered by military experts. Japan could once again be threatened by her two huge neighbours, Russia and China, over whom she had little financial leverage. China – according to some experts, including the influential historian Paul Kennedy – could become a major military power. Japan could be destined to follow the fate of the Phoenicians in the ancient world, the trading nation eventually crushed by the military power of Rome. If Japan seriously challenged the United States, or began withdrawing its loans, Washington could respond by removing its military umbrella from Japan, thus forcing it to devote far more of its wealth to defence.

The Japanese still retained much of their familiar sense of insecurity, in spite of (or because of) their wealth. Could their money-power abroad provide an alternative form of security to military power? Or would they eventually look to their own armed forces to protect their investments and their domestic security? Japanese leaders in different spheres gave very varied replies.

'If we were constantly to be thinking about military force then I suppose the right thing would be to stay in Japan,' said Kobayashi, recalling that he was a soldier in the Second World War. 'But nothing could be further from my thoughts,' he went on with a chuckle. 'I don't think that military power has anything whatsoever to do with this business.'*

'I know we need a sort of defence force,' said Akio Morita, whose Sony Corporation has factories all over the world. 'But nowadays we have such a good communications system all over the world – computers, television, telephone. Through this communication system we can exchange our ideas any time instantly. Under these circumstances I won't expect any big war between countries.'†

'We haven't really reached that stage yet,' said Kagami, who is involved with huge investments through Nomura. 'Although we have been investing abroad, the amount of investment still is relatively small, and the majority of people simply do not feel it necessary for us to do something to defend it.'‡

Kenichi Ohmae, like Morita, is confident that information and communications can avoid future wars:

> People say that no empire in history has been built without military power. I think they are wrong because today, unlike many years ago, we have this power of information. The information goes to

*Interview, September 20, 1988.
†Interview, September 20, 1988.
‡Interview, September 14, 1988.

> ordinary people; and they know what's best. They know what kind of life they ought to protect. If people have accurate information they don't want war: they don't want the government to emphasise military force . . . Military power today is of little value. We all know that . . . If you look at the prosperous countries today, they are very similar to Japan, without natural resources: Singapore, Taiwan, Korea, Switzerland are countries with only people. I think it's marvellous that we are finding we can achieve this prosperity without natural resources, and perhaps without military power.*

'Certainly in today's world money can play a variety of roles,' said Toyoo Gyohten, 'which may in some areas be comparable with the military power. But basically the objective of military power is destruction while the objective of economic assistance is construction. There is still a very fundamental difference between the military relationship and economic co-operation.'

'But don't the Japanese feel frustrated,' I asked Gyohten, 'having worked so hard and made so much money, that they cannot spend it without creating resentments?'

'I think it's the same with any individual human being,' he replied. 'If you have money, that will cause both pleasure and agony. Yes, I think King Midas had the same experience.'†

This sudden concentration of wealth still raises uneasy questions for the West. Can money-power remain divorced from military power, and extend round the world without trying to dominate it?

Japan in the past has been almost uniquely determined to maintain its national identity, to bring home the world's ideas and technology, and to harness them to its own purpose and wealth. Now it has succeeded in transferring its military skills and ambitions into economic achievements, with sustained team-work, while it maintains the habits of high savings and corporate loyalties which have dissolved in the West. Many Westerners dread that this corporatism will threaten not only their companies but also their liberal individualist tradition, compelling them to become more like the Japanese.

But Japan's collective attitudes to money, I suspect, are less specifically Asian than most Westerners believe. Much of the corporate dynamism and loyalty has more to do with an earlier stage of capitalism – with a combination of optimism, insecurity and communal purpose which Europeans and Americans have now left behind

*Interview, September 22, 1988.
†Interview, September 8, 1988

as they develop more individual and less productive ambitions. Japan's wealth is already diluting its purpose. A new generation of widely travelled Japanese are acquiring more individual and international tastes, more interest in leisure and variety. Japanese executives return from abroad with a more cosmopolitan and less conformist view, sometimes even with Western wives who have different ideas about the role of women and bringing up children. And the influence of overflowing money is itself widening the outlook of the Japanese as it changed the British and Americans before them. The more money they send abroad, the more they become interdependent and interlocked with the interests of other countries; and the more they need to create a stable and prosperous world to operate in.

The Japanese still face a unique challenge: to use their wealth to create economic rather than military security. They rightly see modern communications as the constructive alternative to weapons – to provide the knowledge, feedback and political awareness to avoid confrontations and to safeguard their own wealth and future. But they will need inspired political leadership to make that challenge appear as exciting and rewarding to their grandchildren as the military challenge appeared to their grandfathers in the past.

They face the most obvious but difficult opportunity among their neighbours. They have invested huge sums in East Asian countries, extending their economic influence as far west as Thailand, as far south as Indonesia and Australia, as far north as the top of China. But these natural trading partners are precisely those countries which were occupied or threatened by Japanese troops in the Second World War. And nowhere is Japan's challenge greater than in dealing with its giant and complicated neighbour, China, which has had such violent swings in its attitudes to both foreigners and money.

CHAPTER SEVEN

SEVEN FACES OF CHINA

To get rich is glorious.

CHINESE SLOGAN, *c.* 1980

Shanghai, the biggest city in China, can look back to more extreme swings in its attitudes to money than any major centre in the world. Its old people can look back to seven contrasts over half a century, all the way from unrestrained capitalism to the obliteration of all private profit. And now once again it faces another reversal. Can it ever find a stable relationship with the world's economic system?

When I visited it in 1988, it looked as if Shanghai was beginning to come full circle, back towards some form of capitalism. The city was still full of ghosts of the thirties. The famous skyline of domes, cupolas and towers along the waterfront or Bund, more completely preserved than any Western equivalent, still evoked its heyday as the centre of Asian capitalism. I stayed at the once-grand Cathay Hotel where my father stayed fifty-five years earlier, now called the Peace Hotel, still the centrepiece of the Bund. It now had many proletarian touches, including a rowdy restaurant at the top and advertisements for bicycles in the windows, but it cultivated a profitable nostalgia for the thirties: most of its delicate decor is untouched and it preserved the original elegant suites in German, Japanese or English style. When I stayed there, Japanese and American tourists packed into the old Horse and Hounds Bar to listen to 'the Old Jazz Band'. A Shanghai architect showed me round the palaces of the Bund, pointing out the architectural details of the thirties and describing the strict rules for their preservation. Only the spacious suburbs where my father had once stayed were almost unrecognisable: the Tudor-baronial houses are now inhabited by eight families or more, rooms crudely partitioned, walls and ceilings caked with dirt. And all over Shanghai the seething crowds seemed to be demonstrating that no economic system could ever now contain them. But there was a sense of hope everywhere, that Shanghai was at last emerging from its long and wretched isolation to become once again a world port and financial centre.

Shanghai has always been the exposed Chinese frontier with Western capitalism, ever since British troops captured it in 1842. Foreign merchants then established their own 'International Settlement' virtually independent of Chinese control, run by a municipal council elected by the foreign taxpayers with its own extraterritorial laws. By the late nineteenth century the foreigners were allowed to build factories and Shanghai became a major industrial centre. Chinese workers seethed into the international settlement to work for Western companies; while Chinese entrepreneurs, beginning as agents, soon built up their own banks and factories and became a powerful financial group in their own right, freed from their own government's patronage and control.

Westerners continued to see the Chinese as having a hopeless lack of understanding of money. As H. G. Wells described China in *The Outline of History*: 'This great empire was still carrying on most of its business on the basis of barter like that which prevailed in Babylon in the days of the Aramean merchants. And so it continued to do to the dawn of the twentieth century.'* In fact until the industrial revolution the Chinese economy was much less backward than it appeared: later calculations reckoned that in 1800 the standard of living (measured by gross national product per head) was actually higher in China than in Western Europe. It was not until the industrial revolution was under way that the Westerners clearly showed their economic ascendancy,† which remained until the late twentieth century. China had long had a sophisticated system of coinage and exchange, in which the 'tael' or unit of account varied in measure in different parts of China; but foreigners saw this variation (says a recent historian of the biggest Western bank) as 'characteristic of Chinese deviousness, lack of progress, possibly even absence of true religion'.‡

But the Chinese – even the Shanghainese – remained inhibited by the traditional aversion to money-making. The Chinese Emperor and his court in Beijing regarded merchants with disdain. The classical four ranks of Chinese society put the scholars first, then farmers, then artisans and then the merchants. The Mandarins, as the historian of

*H. G. Wells: *The Outline of History*, 1920, revised edit. Cassell, London, 1951, p.577.

†$228 in China, compared to $213 in W. Europe and $266 in North America; though by 1860 the Chinese figure had declined to $204. See Fernand Braudel: *The Perspective of the World*, Harper and Row, New York, 1984, p.535, and p.656, note 93.

‡Frank H. H. King: *The Hongkong Bank in Late Imperial China 1864–1902*, vol 1, Cambridge University Press, 1987, p.36.

Chinese science Joseph Needham described them, 'had the effect of creaming off the best brains of the nation for more than 2,000 years into the civil service. Merchants might acquire great wealth yet they were never secure . . .'* The Chinese Mandarins came to be seen as the prototypes of subsequent anti-commercial castes, from civil servants to academics. The Emperor and his courtiers looked down on the British and other Western traders – the 'foreign devils' – who were trying to do business with them. As one court official described them: 'they looked upon trade as their chief occupation and were wanting in any high purpose.'† It was only after rebellions, reprisals and revolution that China was compelled to allow foreigners to trade through 'the treaty ports', of which Shanghai soon became far the most important.

In the late 1920s and 1930s Shanghai became the most spectacular boom city in Asia. To some Chinese businessmen it seemed a miraculous transformation. In the words of T. C. Tao, a prominent businessman in Shanghai in the 1980s whose father was a member of the imperial court before becoming a capitalist there in the thirties:

> I think that this period of Shanghai could be considered as one of the best times in Chinese history . . . Shanghai was able to change from a traditional, agricultural and village-like town, into a modern, Western-like cosmopolitan city. Shanghai was able to produce a special layer of people who could act as an interface between the really modern lives of Western society and of the traditional Chinese one.‡

But it was a ruthless transition, ruled over by an ugly alliance between politicians and gangsters. After the nationalist leader Chiang Kai-shek took Shanghai in 1927 he turned against his communist former allies and killed many of their leaders. He then used the 'Green Gang', the chief underworld organisation based on opium, dominated by Tu Yueh-sheng, to compel the Shanghai financiers to contribute to his funds by kidnapping and terrorising them. The worlds of crime and government were interlocked through the top families: T. V. Soong, Chiang's finance minister and brother-in-law, had family connections with Tu, who became a director of the Bank of China and chairman of the Commercial

*Joseph Needham: *The Grand Titration*, p.39. Despite his own leanings towards communism and his admiration for Soviet science, Needham was compelled to conclude that 'the rise of the merchant class to power, with their slogan of democracy, was the indispensable accompaniment and *sine qua non* of the rise of modern science in the West.' Ibid, p.150.

†Ibid, p.184.

‡Interview in Shanghai, January 11, 1989.

Bank of China.* It was Shanghai's 'age of confusion' which provided the harsh schooling for many future international Chinese entrepreneurs. The young An Wang – who later founded a computer company with the help of Shanghainese friends – was a mathematical prodigy at school in Shanghai in the twenties. 'For some educated Chinese this period was like the European Renaissance,' he wrote later, 'but for most of the poor, the times were more like the Dark Ages. Europeans read about the Dark Ages in textbooks as ancient history. The Age of Confusion is a living, terrible memory to those who suffered through it.'†

But the international settlement in Shanghai felt misleadingly secure, reassured by its cosmopolitan sophistication and protected by its own police and laws. The flow of money and cheap Chinese labour enabled Europeans and Americans to enjoy a legendary lifestyle, living in big houses in the suburbs full of Chinese servants; while the city-centre became famous for its night-clubs, Russian hostesses, bars and brothels. The divided police allowed the Shanghai criminals to control the streets and make their own bargains with foreign businessmen; and the background of violence seemed quite tolerable so long as it left the Westerners unharmed. Jim Ballard, the author of *Empire of the Sun*, was a schoolboy in Shanghai in the thirties and he recalls:

> We took for granted that it was a violent city, like Beirut today. It had scope for every known imagination and ambition, unrestrained entrepreneurial venture capitalism at full blast. If you wanted to do anything you could do it. There was constant political violence. We could drive out in chauffeur-driven cars to see dead soldiers and horses and walk round the battlefields. But I was brought up to feel that as a Western community we were safe from any danger.‡

The foreigners had built up the city with confidence in spite of obvious threats to the future. The huge profits from textiles and other industries encouraged further investment, and Shanghai had become one of the most imposing cities of Asia. Along the Bund the bankers and traders competed with rival palaces of Venetian grandeur. The most powerful Shanghai businessman, Sir Victor Sassoon – a descendant of the Jewish trading family from Baghdad – dominated with panache: in 1929 he opened the Cathay Hotel, where he enter-

*Parks M. Coble: *The Shanghai Capitalists and the National Government 1927–1937*, Harvard University Press, 1980.
†Dr An Wang (with Eugene Linden): *Lessons*, Addison-Wesley, Reading, Mass, 1986, p.16.
‡Telephone interview, April 14, 1988.

tained in his own grand suite on the eleventh floor – still lovingly preserved. The dangers were very close to hand. My father wrote home in 1932 to describe the 'Shanghai incident' when he watched the street-fighting between the Japanese and Chinese from the hotel. 'When I woke it was to hear machine-guns rattling and bombs dropping.' But the Western investment continued. The centrepiece of the Bund, the massive granite headquarters of the Hong Kong and Shanghai Bank – the 'Honkers and Shankers' – was opened as late as 1935 with the same kind of optimism which marked Hong Kong fifty years later.

The next phase was the Japanese domination. The Japanese were already increasing their influence in the late thirties after they had occupied Manchuria, when Japanese textile companies were determined to weaken the competition from Chinese: by exerting pressure on Chiang's nationalist government – which needed their help in fighting the communists – they forced them to reduce the tariffs in order to extend Japanese imports. After Pearl Harbor, the Japanese took complete control over Shanghai and the Chinese hinterland was opened up to Japanese exports and industrial development. The Chinese suffered from many military atrocities and humiliations; but the more lasting trauma was the knowledge that the Japanese held the keys to industrial as well as military organisation. The Chinese confusions were no match for the Japanese sense of unified patriotic drive.

The next contrast came after the war. When Chiang Kai-shek returned to power in 1945, Shanghai soon appeared more prosperous than war-torn Europe, with an atmosphere of 'riotous abundance' stimulated by a new surge of Western money, including large grants from aid organisations. But corruption and inflation played havoc with Shanghai's prospects, and the gap between rich and poor grew wider as the value of money could halve in a week. The Shanghainese kept up their optimism and faith in the future, what they called 'Maskee'. There was a song which went:

> Me no worry,
> Me no care,
> Me going to marry a millionaire;
> And if he die,
> Me no cry,
> Me going to get another guy.*

*Noel Barber: *The Fall of Shanghai*, Macmillan, London, 1979, p.36.

The millionaires' days were numbered, and the scale of corruption outraged not only Shanghainese but many Western businessmen, like David Middleditch who arrived as a young executive in 1948 with the British trading company Jardines. 'It was believed that pretty well everyone could be bought and sold,' he recollects. 'Shanghai was an extremely corrupt city and that of course was one of the reasons for the downfall of the nationalist government. Nobody regretted their passing for that reason alone.' The communists saw Shanghai as their birthplace; and financial chaos made them all the more popular with their promise of enough food for everyone. The devalued 'gold yuan' became still more useless: the rich delivered carfuls of notes to buy jewellery and gold to take out of the country. Middleditch remembers how he was sent by the office to collect the petty cash: 'I went round in a five-ton truck with three coolies. We collected in crates something like 50,000 million gold yuan. It was worth peanuts.'* As the communist army approached Shanghai in 1949, much of its wealth was visibly leaving the city. Ships loaded textile machinery to carry it to Hong Kong or Taiwan; and one correspondent, George Vine, woke up in the middle of the night to see the gold from the vaults of the Bank of China being loaded on to a ship to be carried to Taiwan.† Owners, managers, entrepreneurs and criminals, left with as much money or gold as they could, pulling the plug on a great industrial city.

Yet when the communists arrived, many businessmen thought they would remain indispensable. As Middleditch recollected:

> Most people in Shanghai had been through Chinese civil wars, the period of the warlords, the Japanese war with China, the Japanese war with the West. They were used to troubles and turmoils.
>
> When the communists came, I don't think people regarded this as a total disaster. The general belief was that they would be very pragmatic . . . They would feel that it was important to maintain business to earn foreign exchange, to look after the economy. Even after the liberation it took a year or two before people realised that it wasn't going to be like that, and that political considerations were going to override economic considerations.‡

In fact the communists rapidly collectivised industry and abolished the remaining entrepreneurial energy of Shanghai and the rest of China. They commandeered the capitalist strongholds. The Hong

*Interview in Shanghai, January 10, 1989.
†Barber, op cit.
‡Interview, January 10, 1989.

Kong and Shanghai Bank became the local party headquarters. The Shanghai Club became a seamen's hostel, still with the longest bar in Asia, but now dispensing tea and cheap meals. The Cathay Hotel was used by visiting party delegations. But their political attitudes were less different than they appeared from Chiang's nationalist government, which had established itself in exile in Taiwan. As Professor Wong Siu-lun of Hong Kong describes it:

> There were certain basic similarities between the Chinese communists and the previous nationalist government. Both had the official attitude of being hostile to private business. They believed entrepreneurship was intrinsically bad, so they would create monopolies. They were concerned about raising revenue from industry, and they regarded the industrialist as cunning and evading taxes. The difference is only in the degree to which they pushed it. In 1949 the private entrepreneurs felt that this tendency had become intolerable and they must leave for Hong Kong rather than follow the nationalists to Taiwan.*

And behind this resemblance lay the deeper tradition of contempt for merchants. As T. C. Tao, who later became a Shanghai businessman, puts it:

> The Chinese traditional concept has the idea of despising people who make money for their own benefit. So merchants are considered as the lowest class in the whole society. This concept certainly has a lot to do with our extreme socialist idea which we had ever since the founding of this new republic in 1949. There is an inseparable relationship between the traditional Chinese concept and the modern socialist concept. And we just cannot cut off the new from the old.†

By 1966 Shanghai was facing yet another change as it bore the brunt of the horrors of the cultural revolution, which had gained much support from the Shanghai radicals and intellectuals. The young revolutionaries were determined to obliterate all links with capitalism and international business, to an extent which was only later fully revealed. In 1988 I sought out one of the industrial veterans, He Jin Tang, a quiet, reflective man in his sixties, who had studied textiles in Britain and had run a Shanghai textile factory before the war. 'They took my house and everything, including my money,' he said.

*Interview in Hong Kong, January 27, 1989.
†Interview, January 26, 1989.

'They made me clean lavatories and live in two rooms with my family of seven. I was half starved. I didn't dare speak a word of English. You couldn't imagine such things happening in the twentieth century.'*

The cost of the cultural revolution was doubly deadly: it cut off the Chinese from any understanding of world money for a decade. But it was not just an extreme teenage form of Marxist anti-capitalism; it was taking to an extreme the earlier contempt for merchants and money-makers. While the Western world was speeding up and opening up, China was turning back into itself.

Then in the eighties Shanghai experienced yet another turnabout. After the death of Mao, Deng Xiaoping in Beijing was determined to move towards a more liberal economy, to release money incentives and to open up international trade. Deng proclaimed that it was now correct 'to make some people rich first, so as to lead all the people to wealth'.† But he insisted that he was still practising socialism, with special Chinese characteristics. There was more truth in Deng's insistence than his Western admirers realised: for he was never prepared to match his economic liberalism with political freedom. There were soon intense arguments about Marx and money. An elderly Beijing economist Yu Guang Yung, who was president of the Society for the Study of Marx and Lenin, created a furore when he complained that Karl Marx never gave practical advice about money, and insisted that the future is money – playing on the sound 'qian' which means both future and money. The debate continued. Some attacked Deng for abandoning Marx, others attacked him for not abandoning him totally, not facing up to the new global realities of money.

Deng's new policy achieved spectacular success among the peasants who were now able to make profits from crops and invest in equipment; but it fared less well in the big cities and factories rooted in state ownership and centralised pricing. As the old capitalist bogeys of the thirties began to show themselves again – corruption, inflation, prostitution – Marx's original *Communist Manifesto* was quoted back at the leaders, with its warning that all human relations would be reduced to cash. The courageous astrophysicist Fang Li-zhi was ousted from the Communist Party after stirring up students in 1986; but he rallied to Deng's defence two years later: 'Our present adverse tide of behaviour,' he insisted in 1988, 'is not due to the liberal policy advocated by Deng . . . It is an abrupt manifestation of the poisonous

*Interview in Shanghai, May 1988.
†Orville Schell: *To Get Rich is Glorious*, Pantheon, New York, 1984, p.14.

legacy of feudalism . . . Yes, capitalism places emphasis on earning money, but exorbitant gain cannot last, because of the element of fair play in equal competition.'* But Fang was intensely critical of the corruption. As he put it in January 1989: 'There are two reasons. The first is the link with the one-party government: no one can check officials. The second is that now we have two systems in the economy. So it's quite easy to take some money from the public ownership to use in the private ownership – to make a wrong cycle.' And Fang insisted that: 'Marxism is dead in China. This year is just forty years since the foundation of our republic. The other countries which forty years ago were in about the same situation as China have become developed or near-developed countries. But China is still undeveloped.'†

As money-making came back into favour, Shanghai seemed to be coming full circle. Foreign businessmen were coming back, not to the old baronial mansions but to hotels or special apartments – still quite separate from the Chinese. Shanghai was rediscovering its own entrepreneurs who quickly tried to take advantage of the opening-up. T. C. Tao, one of the most prominent, formed his Shanghai Industrial Consultants in 1979 to represent many Western companies. But he remained keenly aware of China's limitations, as he explained in Shanghai in early 1989:

> China has got a problem. We haven't got the necessary incentive and the motivation, as in a capitalist society, nor can we go backward to the old way of management. So it is rather a state of undecidedness . . . One of the important things we can do here in China is to learn from our neighbours, what has been happening in Hong Kong, Taiwan, Singapore, South Korea. If we can really learn something good from these countries in the region I think China will finally be able to find a way to get rich . . .
>
> After more than thirty years of rigid control, China is now allowing a small part of the people to get rich. But we can already see the bad effects of such a driving of people to earn money: we have already achieved an imbalance between the intellectuals and those people who are money-driven because we have not got the corresponding checking mechanism.‡

Rong Yi-ren has been one of the most remarkable survivors through every Chinese turnabout. The son of one of the Rong

**Ming Pao Monthly*, Hong Kong, July 1988.
†Interview in Beijing, January 15, 1989.
‡Interview, January 11, 1989.

brothers who founded a textile empire in Shanghai, he stayed there after 1949 with his children and became a keen supporter of the communists. He became vice-minister of the textile industry and an influential politician in Beijing. He kept a low profile during the cultural revolution but then reappeared in 1979 as president of CITIC, the China International Trust and Investment Corporation, which became the showpiece of China's new move towards free enterprise, with a share in the Cathay Pacific airline. He still insisted in early 1989 that capitalism and Marxism can be reconciled:

> Before the liberation, with our unequal status, capitalism had a severe effect on the Chinese economy. Chinese industry and agriculture could not develop. Now, this country is our own. We are in charge of our own destiny, so foreign markets treat us equally and consequently this isn't such a big problem now . . . Before the liberation, I was myself organising a capitalist enterprise. But today, I am involved in a socialist enterprise. I believe that this business can achieve even better development. Marxism has not ceased to progress, but will develop along with this society.*

The Shanghainese seemed confident that they could combine the benefits of capitalism with the structures of Marxism. In 1984 Wang Daohan set up a tiny but much-publicised stock exchange which began issuing a few bonds which were mainly bought by employees of the companies. He found that people were 'not very clear about the concept of shares'. Five years later it was still on a small scale, still nervously controlled: 'Our hope is not that it will develop freely,' Mr Wang explained, 'but under guidance, with rules and regulations.' He insisted that he was following Marxist principles: 'We are continuing to absorb those parts of capitalism – methods, technology, management – which can benefit our socialist construction.' And he seemed confident that Shanghai had 'already established close links with the international market-place, and should become an international city'.†

Could Shanghai, which had swung between so many extremes, at last reach some equilibrium in its attitude to money? Could it welcome free enterprise and foreign capital without turning its people once again against corruption and exploitation by foreigners? In the summer of 1988 I asked many Shanghainese, young and old: most then seemed touchingly optimistic. 'Young people today don't want to

*Interview in Beijing, January 16, 1989.
†Interview in Shanghai, January 20, 1989.

discuss socialism versus capitalism,' I was assured by Han Zihui of the Shanghai Journalists' Association. 'They know that that kind of analysis is useless for development. We just want to develop faster. Ten years of chaos under the cultural revolution has made everyone believe in reform – unlike the Russians.' 'We don't say exploitation nowadays,' said He Jin Tang the texile manager. 'Mao always talked about it, but now you never see the word in the papers. We know we don't have the money and things to compete with the rest of the world, like Hong Kong.'*

There were some signs of success. The textile factories were expanding, exporting cheap shirts and dresses to Europe and even to Japan – in reverse of the thirties. The city planned to develop Chong Ming Island as a new industrial zone. But all the high hopes dissolved in the snarled-up communications, the traffic jams, the congested river and inadequate docks. The harbour was too shallow. The telephones did not work. Taxis were hard to find. Shanghai had the second-lowest growth rate in China, next to Tibet. The population of the central city per square mile was among the densest in the world – far denser than Hong Kong.

There was no lack of greed. Visitors were pursued by boys desperate to buy foreign currency; advertising was returning to the streets; Shanghai teachers were reported to make money out of selling hard-boiled eggs at the gates of their schools. Shoppers crowded into the gold and jewellery shops which had gone underground during the cultural revolution. The glitter of money and gold – gold decoration, gold teeth or simply gold hoards which had long fascinated the Chinese – returned to the surface. Chinese officials as well as shopkeepers were trying to make quick gains from foreigners, to drive a hard bargain. But they were deeply ignorant of the real world market-place, all the more isolated by the wasted decade. Greed was no substitute for intricate planning and patient knowledge of global markets which were the secrets of real industrial advance.

The Shanghainese were now once again becoming aware of the success of the foreigners – particularly the Japanese, whose cars, trucks and machines outnumbered other imports. The only bright lights which shone over the Shanghai waterfront at night were the neon signs for Casio and NEC ('they're our new army and navy,' one Japanese friend joked). But the Japanese were also the most aloof of the foreigners: they lived in the brand-new Hilton or JAL Hotels, or in the Hongqiao Villa apartments near the airport, while most of their companies were

*Interviews in Shanghai, May 1988.

in two new Japanese-built blocks, the Union and the Ruijin building. The relations between the Japanese and Chinese remained formal, often uneasy. I asked Mariko Seiki who looked after Japanese businessmen at the Hilton. 'Some Chinese want to be friends with me,' she said, 'but I usually find it's because they want to buy currency on the black market. I like friendship to be pure.'

The two ancient rivals of Asia remained mutually uncomprehending. The older Chinese, like An Wang the computer tycoon, could not obliterate their memories. 'Having both observed and experienced Japan's economic aggressiveness,' he reflects, 'I am led to the conclusion that they learned little in World War II. Instead of tempering their imperial ambitions, they are merely pursuing their goal in the economic arena rather than the military one.'* But young Shanghainese knew they could not do without Japanese investment and management, while the Japanese needed cheap Chinese labour and mass markets of the future.

The contrast between the poverty and chaos of Shanghai and the wealth and effectiveness of the foreign visitors was more extreme than in the thirties, with obvious dangers. Yet the party leaders seemed remarkably unworried. As it happened I saw the contrast in caricature, when the American publisher Malcolm Forbes, the exuberant prophet of global capitalism, arrived in Shanghai in his luxury yacht the *Highlander*, complete with its helicopter on the top deck proclaiming 'Forbes: Capitalist Tool'. He had been cruising through East Asia with a motley shipload including Mrs Thatcher's son Mark, Gerald Ford's son Jack and the King of Bulgaria. Forbes invited a group of Chinese dignitaries, journalists and visitors including myself to a lunch party on the yacht while it sailed through Shanghai harbour. The Chinese guests included the ex-mayor, Jiang Zemin, the Vice-Minister of Culture Ying Ruocheng and Deng Pufang, the crippled son of the party leader, who was carried on his wheel-chair to be shown Forbes' two motorbikes. It was a genial party. Forbes introduced his Chinese guests by quoting with his wide grin the motto of his yacht: 'Age and treachery will overcome youth and skill'. The vice-minister (now best known for playing the prison governor in the film *The Last Emperor*) responded enthusiastically. 'This is an eye-opening experience,' he said in smooth English. 'I've just been into some of your bedrooms and it *is* eye-opening.'

As the *Highlander* sailed back to the Bund I argued with Forbes:

*Wang: op cit, p.213.

wouldn't the Chinese react once again against capitalism if it went too far, too fast, as in the thirties?

> I don't think so. Today the central government has real power, centralised power, which can control any excesses: the age of the warlords has gone, like the old days of feudal barons in Europe. And when China acquires Hong Kong it can become a real asset to the industry of Shanghai – provided the government doesn't create apprehension by insisting on all the trimmings of sovereignty in Hong Kong. With the help of the expatriate Chinese, the potential for Shanghai is enormous.

And Forbes later described how his visit had generated goodwill for Western capitalism:

> It was kind of fun to see the leaders of Shanghai and twenty people from the Beijing government including Deng's son go down off the *Highlander* holding 'capitalist tool bags' . . . I don't think it created resentment. What kind of country is it where private citizens can create a business, can come on a trip without government permission and can spread the word about a free enterprise system? I hope it did make an impact.*

Already a few months later there were warnings of trouble. Students all over China had revolted in protest against the leaders' corruption and nepotism and the lack of democracy. Deng himself was under fire, and his crippled son was fiercely denounced on wall-posters for benefiting from a corporation in Hong Kong which held funds, which foreigners had raised, to help Chinese cripples.

But no one was prepared for the climactic reversal, in the summer of 1989. Massive students' demonstration in Beijing brought to the surface all the hidden resentments of corruption, while Gorbachev's visit ironically provided a focus for desperate demands for democracy. Deng was confronted by all the dangers of providing greater economic freedom without political freedom. The students were tragically confident of the power of protest and publicity which was played round the world; but Deng remained above all a military leader, and like his master Mao he knew that power grew out of the barrel of a gun. In the ruthless crackdown that followed, the old arguments for economic growth were swept aside. The astrophysicist Fang Li-zhi who had been a hero of the students took refuge in the American

*Interview, October 18, 1988.

embassy. The army, which was recruited mainly from peasants who had done well out of Deng's reforms, was pitted against the young generation in the cities who were again depicted as corrupted by foreign influences.

Shanghai was once again in the front line, as a centre of student revolt. The students seethed into the Bund, taking control of traffic and blocking surrounding streets with buses. They barricaded Fudan University and made speeches on the campus. They blocked the railway line with their own bodies until a train roared over them, killing six and provoking others to burn carriages. Thirty thousand marched on the town hall, with a petition of optimistic demands including a free press. The mayor, Zhu Rong Ji, for a time placated the students, calling them patriots and sympathising with their protests. But as the crackdown spread to Shanghai, the students were as helpless as those in Beijing. The supposed ring-leaders were tracked down and then displayed on television, hands tied, with traditional public humiliation and shame. The police took back control of the streets. The horrors of the cultural revolution no longer seemed buried in the past. And in Beijing the former Mayor of Shanghai, Jiang Zemin – who had been a jovial guest on Malcolm Forbes' yacht a year before – was appointed as the hard-line new Secretary of the Communist Party.

The Shanghainese were now looking at yet another face of China. It was both the newest and the oldest – the ancient face of central power which saw its own authority as the overriding priority, which could not tolerate dissent, which distrusted foreign influence and business, and which dared not allow the individual freedom on which wider economic prosperity would depend. The crackdown dashed the hopes of many of Shanghai's new entrepreneurs. T. C. Tao, who had already been building up his overseas contacts, now based himself in California, like so many other Chinese exiles, finding new energies outside his home country. Shanghai's hopes of challenging Hong Kong as a financial and trading centre now once again looked forlorn; while Hong Kong itself faced terrifying new doubts about its future safety.

CHAPTER EIGHT

THE FIRE OF THE EXILES

The fallen leaves return to the root.

CHINESE PROVERB*

The end of capitalism in Shanghai in 1949 had been followed by the development of a much more dynamic Chinese capitalism across East Asia. It revealed a total contrast of attitudes to money: for the Chinese who had failed to make any economic system workable at home proved brilliantly successful in making money abroad.

It was Hong Kong which was the most spectacular beneficiary. As a well-organised British colony it had always provided a striking contrast with the disorganisation on the mainland; but it had been seen as essentially a British achievement. Two years after the British had occupied it, the Colonial Treasurer wrote in 1844 how there was 'not one respectable Chinese inhabitant on the island . . . there is, in fact, a continual shifting of a Bedouin sort of population, whose migratory, predatory, gambling and dissolute habits utterly unfit him for continuous industry.'† As Hong Kong prospered many mainland Chinese were persuaded that only Europeans had the special ability to organise business. 'I began to wonder how it was,' said the Chinese revolutionary Sun Yat Sen, the son of a Christian missionary who had been educated in Hong Kong, 'that foreigners, that Englishmen, could do so much, as they had done, for example, with the barren rock of Hong Kong within seventy or eighty years, while in 4,000 years China had no place like Hong Kong.'‡

But in the 1940s Hong Kong was somnolent compared to Shanghai. In the words of Sanford Yung, who came from Shanghai and is now chairman of the accountants Coopers & Lybrand in Hong Kong:

*Quoted by Nien Ching: *Life and Death in Shanghai*, Penguin, London, 1988, p.533.
†Colin Crisswell: *The Taipans*, Hong Kong, Oxford University Press, 1981, p.101.
‡Address at Hong Kong University, 1923, quoted by Maurice Collis: *Wayfoong*, Faber and Faber, London, 1965, p.117.

> Those who came from Shanghai had thought Hong Kong no comparison to Shanghai in her heyday. Hong Kong in those days was a sleepy, slow southern port: hot, damp, humid, just an entrepot. In those days we didn't have the entrepreneurs that suddenly arose in the sixties . . . By tradition or by nature, Hong Kong people did not speculate, did not gamble too much except in horse racing. The Shanghainese are entrepreneurs, and take risks. They would spend a lot of money, build a factory, develop housing and local people followed. You can't watch your neighbour get rich very easily every day and not do anything about it. Hong Kong people have learned a lot from the Shanghai entrepreneurship.*

It was the refugees from communist China in 1949 who transformed Hong Kong. They came from many Chinese cities; but the most vital energy and wealth came from Shanghai. The Shanghainese made up only 4 per cent of Hong Kong's population but they soon owned 80 per cent of the cotton mills, and they built factories and established themselves in world markets with a speed which devastated their competitors abroad. The Shanghai entrepreneurs had the advantage of employing refugee workers who had little choice but to work long hours for low wages; but they had also acquired a deep knowledge of textile technology through Western connections: the Tang family had studied at the Massachusetts Institute of Technology for three generations.

The rich Shanghai families showed a spectacular global mobility. The two Rong brothers who had founded the huge Shen-Xin textile company in the twenties had spread their families wide. The elder brother, Rong Zong-jin, emigrated to Hong Kong and all his children later left China – for America, Hong Kong or Brazil. The younger brother, Rong De-sheng, stayed in China, but his sons emigrated to America, Bangkok and Australia; only his fourth son, Rong Yi-ren, stayed in Shanghai, and now runs China's most important capitalist concern, CITIC (see previous chapter).

The Shanghainese who came to Hong Kong after 1949 already had international connections: they could soon borrow heavily from the banks; and as family firms they could plough profits back into new machines which became among the most modern in the world. Many economists and conservative politicians have depicted Hong Kong as the triumph of unrestricted free enterprise, risk-taking, profit-maximising and experimenting. But Professor Wong of Hong Kong

*Interview in Hong Kong, January 25, 1989.

University gives a different picture in his recent scholarly study: of family-based firms with close-knit Shanghai connections which could exclude newcomers, thus allowing them to invest heavily in equipment for long-term profits.*

The contrast between Hong Kong and Shanghai was soon the reverse of the old relationship. In Hong Kong the old waterfront palaces were knocked down and replaced again and again with still taller skyscrapers, their offices keeping pace with each new global fashion and plugging in still more closely to international technology. Hong Kong was turned outwards as emphatically as Shanghai was now turned inwards, with no hinterland to restrain or confuse its driving ambition. Behind British colonial façades, rituals and discipline, the local Chinese capitalists as well as the Shanghainese were soon outdoing their ex-masters. The Hong Kong and Shanghai Bank was still formally run by British expatriates, but it became the citadel of Chinese money – with not too many questions asked – providing finance for the booming factories and the trade with the mainland. The British and Chinese businessmen remained socially very separate, each fortified by their own kind of arrogance. But the Chinese were gradually taking over the financial heights, from the stock exchange to the racecourse.

Hong Kong was soon to produce some of the richest men in the world, including dollar billionaires. As a young man Yue-Kong Pao had been educated at Shanghai University and began his career in banking; then in 1949 he left for Hong Kong and began investing in ships. Within a few years he had established his own World Wide Shipping Corporation and was spreading into banking and real-estate. The Hong Kong and Shanghai Bank eventually recognised his financial power by making him vice-chairman, and in 1976 he was knighted by a British (Labour) government. When I visited him in 1980, polite, smiling, reserved, he seemed to express all the global confidence of Chinese capitalism, as he lamented Britain's decline and gestured hopefully to a photograph of his new heroine Mrs Thatcher beside him. Li Ka-shing, who came from Canton, gained control of the Hutchison Whampoa trading company in Hong Kong, and was eventually to become a billionaire with huge overseas interests now partly based on Vancouver. Run Run Shaw had left Shanghai in 1927 for Singapore, where he began buying cinemas and making films; after the war he moved with his brother Runme to Hong Kong

*Wong Siu-lun: *Emigrant Entrepreneurs*, Oxford University Press, Hong Kong, 1989, pp.167–9 (to which I am indebted in this paragraph).

where he built up hugely profitable film studios churning out horror and Kung Fu movies. Like many other exiles, he found money a more important yardstick than culture: when asked which films he most liked he replied: 'I particularly like movies which make money.'

It was not only Hong Kong which was transformed by the Chinese exiles. All through East Asia the refugees from mainland China were impinging on earlier Chinese communities, providing new dynamism and networks of money, revealing a mastery of finance which contradicted any theories about Chinese commercial backwardness. As far west as Thailand, as far south as Indonesia, the Chinese communities were strengthened by the new refugees from Shanghai, Canton and other mainland cities.

Taiwan, where Chiang Kai-shek established his exiled government, became the most phenomenal success-story. First with American aid, then on their own, the Taiwanese soon achieved one of the largest growth rates in the world, developing from the earlier state-controlled system into a freer capitalism. Today Taiwan has the biggest foreign reserves of any country. Taiwanese businessmen from Shanghai and other Chinese cities began exporting round the world. Y. Z. Hsu, who had a small knitting company in Shanghai, left for Taiwan just before the communists moved in; in Taiwan he and his family built up the Far Eastern Textile Company, with their family share now worth at least a billion dollars.*

Singapore developed from an industrial to a financial centre, servicing its neighbours Malaysia and Indonesia and rivalling Hong Kong. Its Chinese families showed a mastery of banking. The head of the Kwek family, Kwek Hong Png, had left China in 1928, and built up a massive business in rubber trading, finance and property. Lee Seng Wee with his family founded the Overseas Chinese Banking Corporation (OCBC), which for a time became the most powerful bank in Singapore. In Malaysia Chinese families were almost equally powerful, including the Kweks' cousins, confusingly called Quek. Even Indonesia, despite its strong anti-Chinese resentments and purges, still had powerful Chinese financiers led by Liem Sioe Liong, the close friend of President Suharto, who controls the Bank of Central Asia.

Like earlier Jewish refugees to Europe and America, the overseas Chinese had financial skills and family networks which enabled them to move money swiftly, secretly and confidently across the world – sometimes to the despair of bank regulators who sought to oversee

*For estimates of wealth, see *Forbes* magazine July 25, 1988.

the funds. The fast-moving Chinese billions became an important part of the East Asian industrial miracle. In Kuala Lumpur, Bangkok, Djakarta, and even Manila, overseas Chinese businessmen and bankers played a central role connecting the countries with each other, speaking the same language and sharing the same values. While the Japanese supplied investment and technology, the Chinese added their own mix of entrepreneurial energy, speculation and rigorous attention to the details of money.

The dynamism and prosperity of the overseas Chinese became still more contrasted with the confusion and desolation back in China. It was much more than the ideological contradiction between capitalism and communism. There was the difference between a people at home – with all the constraints of their society, families and the weight of the past – and in exile, where they were compelled to work hard and make money to survive. The commercial dynamic of the overseas Chinese, like that of other exiles, seemed to depend on a narrowing of purpose, on being cut off from their culture and roots. 'Confidence is sometimes rooted in the unpleasant, harsh aspects of life,' says An Wang, the computer tycoon, 'and not in warmth and safety.'*

The scope and ambition of Chinese entrepreneurs was rapidly unleashed after their separation from traditional constraints. As Professor Wong puts it:

> In traditional China and even in modern China, the ultimate protection of wealth is to have power, and authority. Therefore, successful families have to send the talented sons into officialdom as protection. Not so in Hong Kong. The colonial government is less heavy-handed in dealings with private businessmen so they can concentrate their efforts to pursue wealth. And wealth can be readily translated into social prestige and gain official recognition – to enter the legislative council, or get various titles directly; whereas in China wealth has also to be converted into political power before you can have secure status. In Hong Kong and in other overseas Chinese communities it is that removal of the attraction of power that lets the economic skills of the Chinese entrepreneurs flourish.†

Many of the Chinese exiles still looked back with some longing towards their homeland. Could the two strands of Chinese, exiles and natives, ever come together? Through the cultural revolution the

*Wang, op cit, p.12.
†Interview, January 27, 1989.

exiles' relations with the mainland were dangerously strained, and Hong Kong went through nerve-racking times as Beijing tried to intimidate and terrorise the colony. But with the coming of Deng and his new economic policies they saw new possibilities of a rapprochement.

There was much more interchange between the Chinese abroad and at home, with still more flights between Hong Kong and mainland China, to fly Chinese exiles to see their families or try to do business again. There were poignant encounters between cousins who had developed quite different attitudes to families and money. I. M. Pei came back to China to design a hotel (the Fragrant Hills) in Beijing. Sir Y. K. Pao the billionaire founded the airline, Dragonair, in Hong Kong to fly to mainland Chinese cities: he began revisiting his home town near Shanghai, to which he presented a hospital; he gave a hotel to the Chinese government in Beijing; and he even began dropping his Sir.

But the Chinese at home and abroad still have the fundamental difference between people still rooted in their own ancient society through all its upheavals, and those who had got away to find all the new motivations of money, without any real home. The Chinese exiles could graft projects, hospitals, schools and foundations on to their old country; but they could not so easily reconnect with the attitudes of their cousins who were still enveloped in their own pride and insulation – all the more since the great leap backwards of the cultural revolution – and who could not share the same language of money.

For Hong Kong the relationship was a question of life or death as they faced the prospect of being absorbed in 1997 into the Chinese state under the control of Beijing. The colony still forged ahead: by 1989 its changing skyline was crowned by two spectacular skyscrapers, symbolising the rival powers. The hi-tech building of the Hong Kong and Shanghai Bank, representing the power of international capital, was now being overshadowed by the new building of the Bank of China which represents the power of Beijing (and which is designed by an American architect I. M. Pei, who comes from Canton and whose father was the president of the Bank of China).

Could Beijing really tolerate a free-wheeling capitalist alternative in the midst of a system still supposedly Marxist? The rich Hong Kong Chinese were very doubtful. Already over three decades their billions had moved in and out of bank accounts across the Pacific, or to New York or London. The mobility of their money was legendary. To quote William Purves, the chairman of the Hong Kong Bank:

> Money is free to move. It moves sometimes ahead of the people, and it moves to where it can be employed attractively but with safety. Safety and the value of money is all-important . . . Confidence is very important to Hong Kong. Money is volatile. If there's no confidence money goes very quickly; there's no exchange control here. It will go to where it seems to be a safer place, to be employed at some later date in a different way.*

Many rich sons and daughters in Hong Kong had acquired alternative domiciles and nationalities, or had become virtually placeless as they flew through the new air-networks connecting the Chinese communities. But the prospect of 1997 sent a new exodus from Hong Kong. They spread out not only to East Asia, but increasingly to Western cities – like Sydney, Vancouver and Toronto and Los Angeles. There had long been Chinatowns in the West, established in the nineteenth century with their own self-contained communities, cuisine and tradition of diligence: a statue of Confucius stands over the main square of New York's Chinatown. But the new exodus, first from China, then from Hong Kong, gave them a new dynamism, leadership and ambition.

The host countries became rapidly aware of the entrepreneurial skills of the overseas Chinese. In the United States they were rising to the top in business and the professions; and the success of Asians at American universities – particularly in mathematics – was so marked that some were introducing quotas. In Los Angeles a Chinese won a Nobel Prize for a discovery which was later developed by the Japanese. In December 1988, Feng-hsiung Hsu, a twenty-nine-year-old Chinese graduate student from Taiwan, designed the first computer to win a chess contest with a grand master. The Canadians and Australians now competed to attract the richer, more qualified Chinese, with the Canadians winning out: Vancouver, pioneered by Li Ka-shing, now has its own 'Hongcouver' across the Pacific.

Through most of the eighties the exiles retained the hope of closer links with the mainland. The Beijing government encouraged Hong Kong to think it could retain its own system intact, with an eye on later embracing Taiwan, too. Hong Kong's businessmen had invested heavily in factories inside China, where labour was much cheaper, in the belief that Hong Kong itself would become increasingly a financial rather than an industrial centre.

When the Chinese students began demonstrating for democracy

*Interview in Hong Kong, January 23, 1989.

in May 1989 the young in Hong Kong showed their own enthusiastic support, joined by many mainland Chinese who were working or studying in the colony. Western businessmen watched hopefully; and the two oldest trading companies, Swires and Jardines, were both confident that Deng would follow a conciliatory policy towards the students. No one foresaw the ruthless crackdown which followed. The most plausible explanation was the most worrying: that Deng felt so insecure that he was terrified that the students could actually bring down his government; and that China was on the brink of becoming once again ungovernable.

The effect of the crackdown on Hong Kong was devastating. The stock market fell by 20 per cent in a day. Bank of China customers queued to collect their deposits. Every business relationship with China now seemed threatened, and potential foreign investors rapidly retreated. The tourist business to China collapsed and planes to the mainland flew almost empty. Much more serious, Hong Kong's prospect of joining China in 1997 changed from a hope to a nightmare. The obvious rivalries in Beijing increased the possibility of the worst scenario: a return to chaos in China, a new 'age of confusion', torn between rival warlords who would fail to understand the need for a capitalist stronghold. The whole identity of Hong Kong was back in question. The residents desperately petitioned the British government to grant them citizenship, without much success: and they faced once again the prospect of being permanent exiles, more cut off from their homeland than ever.

The Tigers' Secret

The dichotomy between the two kinds of Chinese was only an extreme case of the contrast between other Asians at home and abroad in their attitudes to money. The fatalistic, other-worldly Hindus in India seemed a world away from eager, money-minded Indian shopkeepers in London or New York. The helplessness of Bangladeshis, Vietnamese or Cambodians in their own country could turn into dynamic activity in Los Angeles or London. Once outside their home territory they left behind their restraints, obligations, obscure loyalties and traditions and focused their identity and ambition in money as the source of security, achievement and recognition: the yardstick by which all others could instantly judge them.

Refugees had always acquired a special preoccupation with money: particularly religious refugees who retain their discipline and separateness. Jewish refugees could stimulate the economies of whole countries. The Huguenots, the Calvinists who fled from France in 1685, established their financial networks abroad. The Parsees, the Persian followers of Zoroaster who emigrated to India in the eighth century, have retained their separateness and commercial dynamic ever since, strengthened by their sense of probity, social conscience and emancipation of their women. Their families have helped to transform India, including the Tata family who set up its biggest steel company and Air India.

Even voluntary exiles acquired a new dynamic. The Europeans who emigrated to the New World in the last century rediscovered a driving interest in money and America seemed able to turn any nationality into money-makers. Even the British, however disdainful of money at home, could acquire a restless commercial ambition after emigrating to America and the Commonwealth. In the post-war decades a succession of expatriates, including Roy Thomson from Canada, Rupert Murdoch from Australia, Michael Edwardes from South Africa, and Ian MacGregor from America, returned to their native country from which they made fortunes.

But it was now the East Asians who had the Midas Touch: not only overseas Chinese and other exiles, but whole nations. By the eighties the Japanese miracle had become the East Asian miracle from Thailand to Indonesia. 'The fire of Prometheus' – as David Landes called the industrial take-off – had flared up in one country after another, generating a high economic growth which had no precedent in their own history. As Europeans a century earlier had stimulated and reinforced each other's industrialisation and trade, speeded up by railroads and telegraphs, the East Asians were now growing together, connected to the great engine of Japan but increasingly establishing their own motors. The trade was now accelerated not by railroads or steamships but by telecommunications and air-routes which were multiplying faster in East Asia than in any other region: the new Asian airlines like Singapore, Cathay Pacific or Japan Airlines had become growth industries in themselves.

These countries owed little to natural resources: their wealth had emerged from rugged and unpromising territories, and they forced Westerners to change their own views about the wealth of nations. For centuries Europeans had seen wealth overseas in terms of treasure: gold or precious metals mined under the ground; booty from ships; jewels or spices. The word gold-mine, or the names of Klondyke or Golconda, were synonymous with sudden riches. Even in the late nineteenth century a whole country, South Africa, could be built on gold. In the mid-twentieth century the oilfield took over from the gold-mine as the sudden bringer to wealth, as impoverished sultans or sheikhs found themselves transformed into billionaires by accidents of geology.

The limitations of treasure, it is true, had long been apparent. In the sixteenth century Spain had turned its rich inheritance of gold and silver into disastrous inflation and unproductive indulgence. Adam Smith pointed out that, 'It was not by gold or silver, but by labour, that all the wealth of the world was originally purchased.'* As the industrial revolution raced through Europe and America it revealed much more clearly how countries depended on work and skills rather than on natural resources – all the more as transport became cheaper and oil and electricity could carry energy anywhere. But the people with the skills were nearly all Westerners, who needed the developing countries for their minerals, oil or crops, not for their people.

By the 1980s all those attitudes had been painfully reversed. Richly endowed countries like Argentina (see chapter 10) were falling still further behind. The OPEC countries which had seemed to be cornering the world's wealth in the seventies were rapidly losing it by the eighties. But East Asia was revealing more rapidly than Europe had done the relationship between wealth and highly organised labour, as first Japan and then smaller countries achieved their phenomenal growth rates with few advantages other than their own skills.

It was Korea which was the most unexpected, particularly to the Japanese who had once occupied it and who had not concealed their contempt. The Koreans had been seen as the Irish of Asia, more easy-going and jovial than the Japanese, incapable of seriously competing. But their bitter resentment of Japanese oppression had given them a more powerful motivation than the Irish against the British. Their post-war experience was even harsher than that of the Japanese, as their country was partitioned between communist and anti-communist systems, and then thrown into one of the most brutal of all civil wars. The North Koreans were much more industrialised than the South and nearly defeated them before the UN troops fought them back, leaving much of the South destroyed.

But the destruction laid the basis for the most sudden industrialisation in the East. With the help of American aid and Japanese technology the Koreans first followed in the wake of Japan's textiles, shipbuilding and steel, but were soon seriously competing with them.

*Adam Smith: *The Wealth of Nations*, 1776, Book 1, chapter 5.

Like the Japanese they had a highly educated elite who explored global markets and future technologies. When I first visited Seoul, already a skyscraper city in the mid-seventies, I was surprised to find Yale-trained technocrats talking a far more international language than British industrialists and politicians, realising how their nation's survival depended on understanding the future. They could not look back on the past, with its miseries, frustrations and grinding poverty. But I always noticed a sadness when I asked the question, 'What have you lost?' for in transforming their cities and communities they had lost most of their continuity with their proud ancient culture. They seemed almost like exiles in their own country.

The 40 million Koreans were the most serious rivals to Japan's industrial power among the 'Four Tigers', the 'chopsticks countries' who became the legends of the seventies and eighties. But the very smallness of the others – Taiwan, Hong Kong and Singapore – provided another lesson in money-making. Like the old city-states of Italy they had benefited from their compact, authoritarian governments and concentrated skills to adapt to each change in world demand and opportunity. Cities without hinterlands had advantages, as Singapore discovered when it separated from Malaysia: and Beijing looked with envy at these compact states without a billion people to share with. Lee Kuan Yew told me in 1980 that when Deng Xiaoping visited Singapore he said on leaving: 'If only I just had Shanghai.'

When I travelled through the Tigers I asked the same question everywhere: what was their common secret of commercial success? Westerners had many political and economic explanations – particularly that they had all embraced capitalism and foresworn socialism, and turned to free enterprise rather than centralised planning. But inside, the countries reveal very different political patterns. Taiwan had begun as a highly autocratic regime run by Chinese nationalists who were highly sceptical of free enterprise.* Singapore's government under Lee Kuan Yew had a highly centralised economic plan. Hong Kong was still supervised by a colonial government which had little room for democracy. 'The East Asian evidence,' says Peter Berger, 'falsifies the idea that a high degree of state intervention in the economy is incompatible with successful capitalist development.'†

But one common experience overrode all the differences: the endurance of misery and danger which had compelled them to work together to make money in order to survive. The defeated Chinese

*See p.98, Wong Siu-lun.
†Berger, op cit, p.158.

nationalist army and followers who took refuge in Taiwan; the South Koreans who were nearly destroyed by the civil war; the Chinese refugees who swam over to Hong Kong; the Singaporeans who were isolated and terrified of a hostile Indonesia; the Japanese themselves who were starving and destitute in 1945: they all had to turn away from their past and find ways to earn foreign currency through exports. Whatever the economic system they chose, that original shock provided the essential psychological dynamic. However harsh and disciplined their process of industrialisation, it was far less harsh than the misery which preceded it.

As these countries now compete with still more devastating efficiency against Americans and Europeans, Westerners are still more inclined to look towards specifically Asian explanations, particularly to a collective capitalism which is rooted in commercial attitudes to wealth and achievement, and which combines the security of collective socialism with the dynamism of capitalism. To many Western businessmen this capitalism appears fundamentally different in its beliefs and workings from the Western orthodoxy – like a schism in the global faith. And certainly there are obvious common Asian characteristics, including strong corporate loyalties, a powerful work ethic and small living spaces. But the most powerful thrust, I believe, comes from the break with the past, and the corresponding excitement with the future. It is the lack of historical clutter, of settled corpocracies, institutional structures and rigid work-practices which differentiates these countries most sharply from Europe and America; and their optimism, adventurousness and corporate spirit contain more echoes from nineteenth-century Europe and America than from their own Asian past.

CHAPTER NINE

THE MIDAS PLAGUE

Everybody in Vanity Fair must have remarked how well those live who are comfortably and thoroughly in debt; how they deny themselves nothing; how jolly and easy they are in their minds.

THACKERAY: VANITY FAIR

Beautiful credit! The foundation of modern society.

MARK TWAIN

Of all the contrasts between Eastern and Western capitalism the most far-reaching has been the different attitude to saving and spending. Japan and the other Asian industrial countries had acquired a double financial strength, both personal and national. Their industrial corporations had originally owed much to the high rates of personal savings which had financed their investment. Now many of them were building up their own huge surpluses, while the families were continuing to save.

The reasons were psychological rather than economic. The savings, as in other countries, were closely related to a sense of insecurity; but the insecurity persisted long after the first causes. The Japanese in the early seventies already had a very high ratio of domestic savings of 16 per cent; it then went up sharply to 24 per cent after the first oil shock in 1974 – even though the surge of inflation was undermining the value of savings – and stayed high until the mid-eighties when it returned to about 16 per cent – still far higher than any Western country. By the mid-eighties the Japanese had reason to feel more secure than at any time since the Second World War, with low oil and commodity prices, and high exports as well as a high yen. Yet their savings remain strikingly high; and their accumulation, together with the industrial surplus, was now changing the face of global finance. For these great pools of savings could flow all the more rapidly into a Western world which was accumulating still heavier debts, and desperately needed capital both to pay them off, and to invest in the future.

While the East kept on saving in spite of greater apparent security, the West kept on spending in spite of the dangers. In America the personal tax cuts which were supposed to increase savings and thus investment had, on the contrary, encouraged more spending and borrowing; and by 1987 Americans were saving only 3.2 per cent of their disposable incomes. And both the personal and national debt seemed to reflect an optimism which was no longer well founded. As Paul Volcker put it in November 1988:

> There is a willingness to buy now and pay later, whether you are public or private . . . driven partly I think by the feeling the economy is going to grow, because it's been growing so there'll always be something out there in the future to pay with . . .
>
> It's not the government itself – by world standards – that is in such big deficit. It's the combination of the deficit with a very low savings rate. We are at the bottom of the world league among industrialised countries and probably among almost any kind of country and our rate of savings has unfortunately been declining instead of increasing.*

Other critics were fiercer in their denunciation of debts. In the words of Peter Peterson, the former chairman of Lehman's Bank and ex-Secretary of Commerce:

> We've been consuming much more than we've been producing, we've been borrowing more than we've been saving and we've been brought up to believe in an ethic of entitlement rather than a work ethic. And the government has been a very willing co-conspirator in this concept through the pressures of certain specialist interest groups, who thought of our economy as a kind of vending machine that turns out goods. Who produces these goods, who creates the wealth, was somehow left to others. The result of it all is, I think, that we've been led into a wonderful land of Oz in which all our dreams come true . . . To a large extent we were doing this on borrowed money from foreign bankers and foreign lenders who were quite willing to lend us all kinds of money in record amounts.†

It was through debts and loans that the true power of money was showing itself round the world. Money became an instrument of control as soon as those who were without it depended on those who

*Interview, November 19, 1988.
†Interview in New York, November 22, 1988.

had it. The Western hemisphere in the eighties – with a few exceptions like Switzerland – had acquired greater debts with remarkable casualness. But the real cost of them was gradually becoming much more evident – whether for individuals, companies or nations. At each level debts were subtly but inevitably restricting independence of action.

Debts had lost most of their traditional moral opprobrium, their associations with social disasters or unscrupulous moneylenders. The change was visible in the language. Banks and credit cards offered to make bigger loans to small customers in terms of reorganising or rationalising their finances, discreetly implying they were getting something for nothing. Corporations were invited to add to their 'gearing' or 'leveraging', to 'roll over' their debts, or to make use of 'financial instruments' which were all ways of increasing or stretching out debts. Debtor nations were presented with a dictionary of reschedulings, restructurings, securitisations or extended facilities, all concealing additional borrowing. Bad loans became impaired assets. 'New money' meant old money at higher interest rates. Words could become weapons in the hands of the creditors, as Professor Michael Faber described them in his analysis of debtspeak: 'The strong have appropriated the language and, at times, have perverted it further to strengthen their position at the expense of the weak.'* The old words like debt, owe and ought were full of moral resonance, expressing both financial and moral obligation. The German word *Schuld* means both guilt and debt. But new words, and the attitudes behind them, had distanced the lenders and borrowers still further from a sense of obligation and involvement. And the financial instruments in the eighties, as the economist Henry Kaufman pointed out, diluted still further the strength of the original promise to pay, so that America was moving towards a financial system in which 'credit has no custodian'.†

Yet debts, whether personal or national, were becoming much more perilous. In the seventies, high inflation had encouraged both individuals and nations to borrow, whether to maintain spending, to stimulate growth, or to stave off misery. But in the eighties debts were working their revenge: their victims were losing more control over their own lives, narrowing their choices, and mortgaging their future.

*Michael Faber: *Beware of Debtspeak*, Institute of Development Studies, Sussex University, 1988.

†Henry Kaufman: *Interest Rates, the Markets and the New Financial World*, Times Books, New York, 1986, pp.22–6.

It was individual borrowers whose attitudes had most changed, all across the Western world. Traditionally, European bankers were restrained from the open encouragement of lending: their forbidding style was in striking contrast to American banks which advertised loans in the windows and displayed their bank-safes through plate-glass. But by the seventies the lifting of credit restraints and the competition between banks and credit cards had made Europeans more like Americans, selling loans as openly as soap. And all through the West the moral and social objections against debts had been heavily undermined by the years of inflation. Anyone who had borrowed heavily to buy a house in the early sixties was rejoicing in the eighties, after the five-fold inflation had wiped out most of the debt while multiplying the value. Businessmen found debt equally desirable as the means to successful investment and profits, and many success-stories, like that of Boone Pickens, had depended on the bold accumulation of debts. The prudence of the thirties had become the timidity of the eighties.

In America debts had always been much more acceptable in personal and business life: the opening up of the West had been built on mortgages and debts – for land, houses, farm machinery or factories. The harsh discipline of mortgages was as much part of the American work ethic as the puritan conscience. The great crash and the depression revealed the full cruelty of the relationship between lenders and borrowers, as investors were bankrupted and banks foreclosed on farms; and the next generation of bankers and individuals had an instinctive prudence and dread of debt. But by the sixties that generation had retired or died off; and the way was open for a new borrowing spree, particularly for houses. The American savings and loans associations, the 'thrifts', multiplied their mortgages for houses, which in turn multiplied their value. The house became increasingly not only the family home, but its chief investment. Incomes, house prices and mortgages all went up together, with reassuringly few bad debts.*

The growth of credit cards in the sixties and seventies blurred the distinction between convenience and debt. Credit cards were an obvious boon, a built-in accounting system which became almost indispensable for travel: they provided travellers with a new sense of security and identity – which the advertisements emphasised – as their magic card was recognised by outlandish foreigners who spoke only the language of money. The global computerised networks of

*See Tim Congdon: *The Debt Threat*, Basil Blackwell, Oxford, 1988, pp.173–4.

today's credit cards, linking millions of customers to shops, hotels and services round the world, represented all the magical mobility of money. Their enticing names, like Visa or Access, carried none of the old associations of frowning bank managers saying no to a loan. With all their benevolence they could easily conceal their role as an extra overdraft with an abnormally high interest rate. Many borrowers turned to credit cards to maintain their spending; and by the mid-eighties personal bankruptcies and defaults on credit cards were rapidly increasing. Credit cards accounted for much less debt than house mortgages or hire-purchase on cars; but their constant invitations to spend freely were changing the whole environment and psychology of money. On the one hand they offered customers infinite private choice and opportunity, to go anywhere, buy and eat anything. On the other hand they caught them in an inescapable net of discipline and scrutiny, recording all their intimate shopping and spending. As one philosopher puts it: 'in the credit card world we feel private but in fact the whole world, all of time and fate, collapses down on us, pinioning us in place.'*

MasterCard, the biggest credit card network, based in New York, controls its 'electronic highways' in 170 countries and territories with intricate technologies, handling millions of transactions and billions of dollars every day. Pete Hart, the chief executive of MasterCard International describes how: 'It's fascinating to watch these various marriages consummated – satellite, fibroptics, computing, the whole array of telecommunications alternatives – enabling us to move financial transactions with far greater certainty, security and complete integrity.' Hart denies that his magical network has encouraged any laxity towards debt: 'My conscience is completely clear. We don't seduce anyone to use credit irresponsibly.' But like many bankers he has worries about changing public attitudes to money. He thinks that America does not educate its young people about the dangers of debt, and that too many have to learn 'through the hard knocks of reality'. Does he not think that banks and credit cards have encouraged greed?

> I think that Gordon Gekko's statement in the movie *Wall Street* was probably one that snapped all of us to attention. When he stepped up and said 'greed is good', I think it caused all of us to look inward and say: gee, is that really the case? Should greed ever supersede basic human values? I think the answer that 99.9 per cent have come up with is no, absolutely not. We are seeing

*David Bodanis: *Web of Words: The Ideas Behind Politics*, Macmillan, London, 1988, p.101.

> a re-examination of our values as they apply to the market-place and the world at large, and I think that's a very healthy sign.
>
> Perhaps here in the United States people have been somewhat self-indulgent during the eighties. There's been a tremendous growth in confidence with a tremendous job expansion. We've had an explosion of two-income families which have given them a sense of comfort that perhaps this country didn't enjoy before. And so we have perhaps been somewhat self-indulgent. But I don't think greed is an appropriate term.*

By the early eighties the virtuous circle of lending and borrowing was turning vicious. The recession and very high interest rates rapidly endangered hundreds of thrifts which had provided mortgages at much lower rates; while the value of houses went down instead of up. Many borrowers faced a moment of truth which they preferred to postpone.

Texas magnified the problem as it had magnified so much else. In the mid-seventies the quadrupled oil price had caused a boom in the two confident Texan cities Houston and its rival Dallas. Not only oil companies, but other industrial giants moved their headquarters to Houston which spread out across the flatlands while the big banks lent with enthusiasm. The redoubling of the oil price in 1979, which precipitated a recession in other states, produced a new boom in Texas: and the banks, full of oil money, lent freely for massive new building.

Then in 1982 came the sudden drop in the oil price which rapidly undermined the basic security of the banks; but with hardly credible rashness the banks continued to lend for property which was intimately linked to the oil price. 'I can't quite explain the degree of real-estate speculation that took place . . .' Paul Volcker said afterwards. 'Promptly as the economy recovered, they went off on a binge of real-estate lending based upon an analysis that said that a lot of those loans wouldn't be good unless [energy] prices went up.'† Much of the new property was making losses on its rents, but the buildings still increased their value. 'The net result in Texas was a sort of financial perpetual motion machine,' wrote the Dallas broker Frederick Rowe. 'Development profits encouraged more development, which led to absurd levels of unleased space.'‡

By May 1985 Dallas had as much empty office space – 34 million square feet – as all the office space in Miami; and when the *Dallas*

*Interview in New York, February 24, 1989.
†Interview, November 19, 1988.
‡*Fortune* magazine, August 1, 1988.

Morning News revealed the amount the slide began. The fantasy-Texas remained almost unaffected by the reality below the surface: the TV series *Dallas* was meanwhile making the city famous round the world as a big-spenders' paradise. 'I think people are getting confused because they don't see that series addressing itself to the problems which the real Dallas and the real Texas are experiencing,' said John Connally later. 'We've been through a major trauma in this state . . . Oil and gas, agriculture and real-estate were the three legs of the stool of prosperity on which the Texas economy had been built. Now all of them were in trouble at the same time.'* Many Texan multimillionaires on whom the TV mythology was based faced precipitous falls. By 1987 two of the richest, Bunker Hunt and Clint Murchison, had lost their fortunes from over-borrowing; and in July 1987 John Connally, one of the most stylish and celebrated of all Texas governors, went bankrupt.

John Connally now provided a new kind of American folk-tale, of ambition turning to humiliation, then resignation. In the seventies he had epitomised all the Texan virtues: fine-looking, outgoing and generous, he could make people feel more confident with a single hard handshake. He was self-made, one of seven children who had, he explained, 'walked barefoot behind two mules pulling a horse-drawn plough'. He was three times elected governor of Texas, and eventually rose to be Secretary of the Treasury under President Nixon. Back in Texas he had borrowed, invested and prospered until he had 126 horses, 500 cattle, and five houses, including a house in the hills above Austin where he kept his treasures and entertained lavishly.

In 1981, at the height of the oil boom, Connally joined his friend Ben Barnes, a former lieutenant-governor, in an ambitious real-estate company which soon became involved in projects worth 300 million dollars, including a fourteen-storey condominium on South Padre Island. 'We moved too fast, we borrowed too much money: we probably at one time owed close to 300 million dollars,' he said afterwards. 'For a couple of poor boys that was a lot of money. And then we hit the downturn . . .' By 1987 Connally was compelled to file for bankruptcy, listing debts of 93 million dollars against assets – mostly real-estate – of 13 million dollars. 'It was a very humiliating and embarrassing situation,' he explained. 'I never expected to go through anything like it. We did what we felt we should do; we basically sacrificed everything that we had acquired in our lifetime of marriage to try to pay off as much of the debt as we possibly could . . .'†

*Interview in Texas, December 1988.
†Interview, Ibid.

Connally endured failure with as much panache as success. In his bedroom he put an embroidered pillow saying 'It's not a sin to be rich any more, it's a miracle'. He sold off four houses and then watched his treasures being auctioned in front of TV cameras, with many of his rich friends bidding-up the prices. Eventually in June 1988 he was discharged from his debt, owing 50 million dollars to unsecured creditors who hoped to receive about 10 cents in the dollar. He remained philosophical:

> I don't want to worry about possessions any more to the extent that I have in the past. One lesson I learned out of this bankruptcy is that not only fame is fleeting but so are possessions . . . I'm not going to do anything that's not fun. All my life, even in the practice of law, I have been reacting to other people's needs and requirements. From here on my life is going to be my own, and I'm going to control my life . . . The greatest luxury in the world is the luxury of time to think and occasionally do what you want to do.*

Not all Texans got off as lightly as Connally. The earlier euphoria had misled almost everyone, including the banks, which had all been too optimistic, too influenced by their own directors' friendships and patronage. By early 1988 three of the five biggest Texan banks had had to be rescued by banks from other states. By the summer the biggest, FirstRepublic Bank, was taken over by a North Carolina Bank, NCNB, with the help of 4 billion dollars in federal assistance. In October the last of the five, MCorp – considered the best-managed and most cautious – had to appeal for help to the Federal Deposit Insurance Corporation.

The greatest potential disasters were the Savings and Loan banks whose other name, the thrifts, now sounded sarcastic. Hundreds of them all through America had ceased to be solvent as the prices of houses and land had collapsed, but the insolvencies were most serious in Texas. The federal government ultimately guaranteed their deposits which led them to still further rashness; and eventually the Bush administration in 1989 had to bail them out at an estimated cost of 100 billion dollars, in return for stipulating strict capital requirements in the future – which became less strict after relentless lobbying from the thrifts.

Texas had survived its worst crisis as the eighties were ending, with a recovery of the oil price and some adjustment to other industries.

*Interview, ibid.

But like other debtors it had paid a heavy price in terms of autonomy: for its major banks were now controlled from outside Texas, and the great pools of oil-money on which its long confidence had been based were now dissipated.

As individuals and regions had become circumscribed by debt, so had American companies. Through the seventies and early eighties most of them had maintained a cautious 'debt-equity ratio' – their debt compared to the stock market's valuation. But in the boom of the mid-eighties corporate debt was increasing by 150 billion dollars a year.* The debts were rapidly increased after corporate raiders began using junk bonds to buy up vulnerable companies (see chapter 4), and they escalated further with the spread of 'leveraged buy-outs' (LBOs), which substituted more debt for equity. In late 1988 the LBOs reached a new climax when Kohlberg, Kravis Roberts (KKR) made a bid of 20 billion dollars for the giant tobacco and food company RJR Nabisco which left it saddled with far bigger debts.

The language became still more misleading. Leverage, which implied greater strength, caused much greater weakness. Junk bonds which sounded as harmless as junk mail were in fact a ruthless means of securing short-term control at great cost to the future: the high interest rates could often only be repaid by rapidly selling off assets and foregoing plans for long-term investments. Debts were once again restricting freedom of movement; and corporations became easily distracted by the manipulation of their borrowing. When I was invited to speak to a conference of airline executives I soon realised it had nothing to do with planes, routes or passengers: it was devoted to explaining new financial instruments which would load the airlines with still heavier debts.

The ease of borrowing gave thrilling opportunities to daring entrepreneurs who could persuade the banks that they had a sound record for generating profits, and who could thus rapidly expand while retaining full control. The most spectacular global empire-builders – particularly the Australians like Rupert Murdoch, Alan Bond and Kerry Packer who had a tradition of aggressive gambling – were able to borrow rapidly on their personal reputations and commit banks to sharing their risks. The triumph of the individualists in the eighties fitted naturally with the bankers' competitiveness – all the more after their loans to developing countries had turned sour. But these bold partnerships had built-in dangers: for the entrepreneurs were constantly tempted to acquire still more compan-

*Lawrence Malkin: *The National Debt*, New American Library, New York, p.77.

ies with more borrowed money in order to sustain their record of rapid growth; and once they overreached themselves the burden of debt increased the hazard, threatening to turn their whole empire into reverse.

But the most spectacular of all borrowers was the federal government; while its national debt was the most difficult for the public to understand. The idea of a government borrowing money by issuing bonds had always been morally confusing, ever since it was implemented three centuries ago. Governments were accused of profligacy and setting a bad example; but wars always required rapid funds which could not be raised fast enough by taxes; and citizens soon proved quite willing to buy government bonds in peace as well as war. 'A national debt, if it be not excessive will be to us a national blessing,' said Alexander Hamilton in 1781.

Through most of the years since the Second World War Western governments kept their national debt reasonably under control. In the fifteen years until 1960 America reduced the proportion of its debt to its gross national product from 100 per cent to 50 per cent.* The ratio began to increase in the late sixties, with the growing costs of both the Vietnam War and social security; but the high inflation of the seventies made it much cheaper for governments to borrow from their people – who paid a high price for their patriotism.

But in the eighties, as inflation went down and interest rates went up, the Reagan government was committed to increased defence spending, to reducing personal taxes, and to maintaining social services. Since it could not do all three, it began to borrow much more rapidly. By 1986, Reagan's budget director, David Stockman, was facing a cumulative deficit, over five years, of 700 billion dollars – 'nearly as much national debt,' he recorded, 'as it has taken America two hundred years to accumulate.' It was an indulgence which happened with remarkable ease; and the federal and personal borrowing binges appeared to be part of the same basic mood. In the words of Pete Hart of MasterCard:

> There is a correlation between personal debt and the national debt here in the US. The runaway inflation of the late seventies encouraged people to buy now and to repay with cheaper dollars . . . The mental set that permits the individual to spend excessively permits his or her government to spend excessively as well. We think there's going to be a correction not only in the US but world wide.†

*Congdon, op cit, p.53.
†Interview, February 24, 1989.

Over half the American personal savings went to financing the government's borrowing. But this was not enough; and increasingly the Treasury bonds, which were the main instrument of Washington's borrowing, were not bought by Americans at all, but by Japanese. The national debt was no longer a national affair: it was a debt to foreigners. And once America was borrowing heavily from abroad, it faced awkward questions about choices and sovereignty. John Connally, having been both Secretary of the Treasury and a personal bankrupt, had seen the problem of debts at both levels. As he put it in November 1988:

> Whether you talk about a family or a city or a state or a nation there are certain economic rules that govern all of us. None of us can live beyond our means for too long a period of time without getting into deep, deep trouble. This is what worries me about the United States. We have lived beyond our means, we have run up an incredible debt now, of about 2.8 trillion dollars . . . the largest debt that's ever been incurred by any nation on earth. We can't continue to do this.*

Or in the words of Paul Volcker:

> We're borrowing about 3 per cent of the GNP from abroad. I'm told we are borrowing from abroad about 20 per cent of the savings of other developed countries. So we are taking a pretty good chunk of what other people are saving to satisfy what has been a consumption drive . . .
>
> We in the United States have gotten ourselves in the position where we are so dependent upon borrowing from Japan. I don't think it is healthy in the long run, indeed, that Japan has this great, enormous excess of savings available to the rest of the world . . . I don't think it bodes well for American leadership in the world, not just economic, but in a lot of directions.†

The debt to foreigners was bound to be wounding to American pride and psychology, for it set a limit to choices ahead. Like imperial powers before it, the United States had become accustomed to living beyond its means. As Britain had borrowed from America in two World Wars, or as France had borrowed from Holland in the eighteenth century, so America was compelled to borrow from Japan. Yet it was hard to maintain a moralising stance. For many economists

*Interview, December 1, 1988.
†Interview, November 19, 1988.

were concerned that the world was saving too much, and spending too little. If Americans stopped spending, without a corresponding increase by Japanese (and by West Germans and other surplus countries), the subsequent American recession would hit all exporting countries. If the Japanese were happy to keep financing Americans by buying their Treasury bonds, companies and real-estate, why should they not continue? And Americans could well argue that they were doing a crucial favour to the rest of the world which required more and more consumption to maintain their exports.

Nearly forty years ago the science-fiction writer Frederik Pohl had written a prophetic fantasy called *The Midas Plague*.* It visualised a future America in which most of the population were forced to maintain high consumption through ration books which condemned them to live in huge houses, drive big cars and eat elaborate meals. Only the elite were allowed to live in small flats with bare rooms and to work long hours in austere offices: work had become the greatest luxury in the world. The story foresaw the value which would be put on work in the eighties. But the Midas Plague was also revealing itself in the relationship between spendthrift Americans and thrifty Japanese living in small rooms and working long hours, yet depending on American extravagance for their economy. After the crash of '87 had exposed the weakness of the American economy, the rest of the world was still more aware of the dangers of an American recession. The Japanese were content to continue lending to the Americans who provided both an outlet for their savings and a market for their products; while the Americans continued consuming imports, including Japanese cars and electronics. Midas had after all spread his plague, and only the Far East appeared immune to it.

*Frederik Pohl: *The Midas Plague*, Galaxy, 1951. Reprinted in Spectrum, selected by Kingsley Amis and Robert Conquest, Gollancz, London, 1961, pp.13–67.

CHAPTER TEN

THE DEBTORHOLIC'S DECLINE

Let us live in as small a circle as we will, we are all debtors or creditors before we have had time to look round.

GOETHE

The developing countries suffered a much harsher punishment for their debts in the eighties: which was the more bitter because they had to make their repayments to a country which turned out to be the biggest debtor of all.

The same combination of high interest rates with low inflation, which had undermined American home-owners, caused much more serious suffering for people in the Third World who had far less political power to protect them. The big Western banks had first begun massive lending to Latin American and other big debtor countries in the mid-seventies when the bargains they offered the Ministers of Finance seemed too generous to refuse. The banks were flush with funds from the newly rich OPEC countries, and the developing countries, which were faced with far higher oil bills, were desperate for money – which the banks were offering at interest rates which were frequently lower than the rate of inflation. The keenness of the banks to lend without asking questions was in comical contrast to any traditional picture of bankers' prudence. In 1928 the Canadian humorist Stephen Leacock had written a story comparing the difficulty for an individual of borrowing a few dollars with the casualness of a country borrowing a hundred million: 'the process is quite easy, provided you borrow enough.'* But this lending of billions far exceeded his comedy. The global bankers had never really worked out how the debts could be repaid; and they appeared unconcerned that much of the money was leaving the countries as fast as it came in.

*Stephen Leacock: 'How to Borrow Money', from *Short Circuits*, 1928.

So long as dollar inflation continued and commodity prices were high, the countries could repay their interest without too much pain. But the Latin Americans faced a heavier crunch than Americans after October 1979, when Paul Volcker in Washington determined to cut down inflation, at the cost of higher interest rates and a gathering recession which also cut back commodity prices. The countries now had to pay back much more, with lower exports with which to earn it. And their governments' political stakes were far higher than Washington's: for many of them were just re-emerging from dictatorships and juntas to democratic elections, and their governments now faced all the political unpopularity of having to repay heavy debts to foreign bankers. The ultimate risk was the failure of democracy.

The foreign bankers rashly continued to lend even more money through 1980 and 1981, while the Latin Americans faced deeper problems and much of the new capital flowed straight out of the countries. 'Up to perhaps about 1979 it was necessary and sensible,' said Sir Kit McMahon, the chairman of the Midland Bank in London which was then one of the biggest lenders to Latin America. 'After that it was not sensible, and excessive. It's probably the excessive bit that's given us all our problems.'* By 1981 a crisis was predicted by many observers and critics outside the banking world, including myself.† In the summer of 1982 the crisis happened: Mexico announced it could not meet its mounting interest payments, and the whole international banking system was in jeopardy, until it was rescued by Washington and the International Monetary Fund.

Most Latin American countries had a long history of borrowing and defaulting in roughly fifty-year cycles since their independence in the early nineteenth century. Americans and Europeans were inclined to attribute their unreliability to Latin characteristics, to a 'mañana' philosophy and to the legacy of the Spanish empire (the ex-Spanish Philippines in the opposite hemisphere showed a similar tendency). The carelessness of the debtors was now matched by the carelessness of the lenders: 'mañana' was spreading across the Rio Grande. But the Latins were facing a much more immediate retribution than the Americans, as they felt the full force of the bankers' discipline. While Texan investors had safety-nets maintained by political pressure, and their thrifts were kept solvent by federal funds, the workers and peasants of Latin America paid a much more immediate price.

How did so many Latin American countries get caught in such

*Interview, September 27, 1988.
†Anthony Sampson: *The Money Lenders*, Hodder and Stoughton, London, 1981.

dangerous debt-traps? They each had unique problems, but it is useful to take one of them, Argentina, as a kind of caricature. It certainly is not typical: it had more abundant natural resources than the others, few racial problems, and an almost all-white population of immigrant families from Italy, Germany and Britain as well as Spain. Yet its white population – to the chagrin of racists – was the heart of the problem. Other Latin countries liked to tell a joke about God scattering his treasures round the world. He began pouring all kinds of riches on to one territory until someone told God: 'Stop! Why are you giving everything to Argentina?' God replied: 'Wait till you see the people!'

Argentina showed the clearest symptoms of a debtorholic country which had wrecked its own future through excessive expectations and lack of discipline. Bankers saw it as a case-history of how not to run an economy. As Paul Volcker put it:

> Argentina used to be one of the richest countries in the world, before World War Two, and they've gone in relative terms steadily downhill. They have suffered from their relative wealth. They could carry out policies that were not good for industrial growth, without killing themselves, because they are such a basically rich country.*

Or in the words of John Reed of Citicorp, who was partly brought up in Argentina and whose bank is one of its biggest – and sternest – creditors:

> Argentina is immensely wealthy by any definition: people, education, land, natural resources. And yet the per capita income has been reduced over an extended period of time, probably forty to forty-five years. Why? One reason of course is that if you're immensely wealthy you have the capacity to continue to live well without necessarily growing. And they do not have a rapidly growing population. A country like Brazil which adds a million workers each year to the workforce had better create a million jobs. Argentina doesn't have that discipline and has not had the problem.†

Yet, as elsewhere, the rashness of the borrowers was matched by the rashness of the bankers; and Argentina can look back on an extraordinary history of double illusions, which it is important to try to see through the eyes of the Argentinians themselves.

*Interview, November 19, 1988.
†Interview, May 9, 1989.

From the time of its independence in 1816, Argentina had presented an attraction to European investors and lenders, as it glittered as a potential new America; and its financial future soon became interlocked with the most powerful bank in Britain, Baring Brothers, with disastrous results for both. Already in 1824 Barings had raised £700,000 for Buenos Aires (then a separate entity) to build a port: though British investors were wary – with good reason, since Argentina soon afterwards went to war with Brazil, and then defaulted on the interest. Barings tried repeatedly to reach a settlement for the bondholders, while the dictator Juan Rosas offered odd payments in kind – first two frigates, then part of Patagonia, and then in 1843 the Falkland Islands (which the British were already occupying). But Barings wanted money, and the British government provided no help in the form of gunboats or even diplomatic pressure. Argentina took thirty years to resume any payment to bondholders, but Barings were soon making further loans, at very high interest rates. In 1866 they raised £1.25 million to finance Argentina's war with Paraguay, which once again left them with unsold stock. Why were those cautious bankers so persistent? 'The fact was that Argentina enjoyed immense natural wealth,' writes Barings' official historian Philip Ziegler, 'and that though incompetence, corruption and political instability might from time to time put foreign investors at risk, in the long run their profit was likely to be secure.'*

But Barings' investments were far from secure, and they remained over-optimistic. After 1880, when the new President General Roca integrated Buenos Aires into Argentina, the country began a spectacular boom. British investors poured more into Argentina than into the United States: by 1889 Argentina took more than 40 per cent of all British foreign investments. Barings agreed to finance a massive expansion of waterworks for Buenos Aires, of which British investors were again rightly wary. In 1889 the whole Argentine economy was in trouble under the new President Celman, and Barings belatedly realised the full corruption and incompetence of the waterworks. The next year the Argentine government defaulted on its quarterly payments and the President fled. Barings were hopelessly over-extended, and by the end of 1890 they faced immediate bankruptcy. They were reluctantly rescued by the Bank of England, with the help of Rothschilds and others, but they were never the same again. Argentina had effectively broken the bank which had been known as

*Philip Ziegler: *The Sixth Great Power: Barings, 1762–1929*, Collins, London, 1988, pp.103, 111, 233–4.

the 'Sixth Great Power'. Yet after a few years of financial chaos Argentina regained its attractions. The British banks remained cautious, and their loans were heavily restricted after 1914; but they were replaced by ambitious American banks, most notably National City Bank (later Citicorp). The symbiosis between rash lenders and borrowers resumed.

When the Argentinians came to the end of their first spectacular expansion, they could not easily face up to the limitations: they were set in a pattern of optimism. It was a psychological as much as an economic condition; and contemporary Argentinians look back on that early experience as the cause of their subsequent problems. In the words of the economist Dr Guido Di Tella:

> We grew at about 6 per cent per year when good countries were growing at 1 per cent, 2 per cent. This kind of development was impossible to continue: all the new countries of the last century had a problem when the frontier closed. Argentina tried for two or three decades not to be aware that the frontier had closed, but that path was not viable any more.*

Or in the view of the banker Arturo O'Connell:

> The prosperity of Argentina before 1930 owed a lot to mining the 'top fertile layer'. It was an economy much closer to today's oil-producing countries. It was to be expected, with the benefits of hindsight, that Argentina would get into great difficulty once that fertile layer started to become exhausted. And we faced competition from some of the most powerful countries in the world that started protecting their own agricultural producers.†

A people accustomed to easy wealth from the land, backed by easy loans from abroad, found it hard to face the need to create wealth through industry and exports. They had been close to self-sufficiency, and preferred to ignore the rest of the world, including the rest of Latin America. In the words of Rodolpho Terragno, the former Minister of Public Works:

> There's something psychological in our problems. I think that the Argentine society has been secluded in this part of the world. Our political problems prevented the Argentine society from following the evolution of the world economy . . . I am very suspicious of any theory that puts the blame abroad for our domestic problems.

*Interview in Buenos Aires, December 7, 1988.
†Interview in Buenos Aires, December 9, 1988.

> We must think first what is wrong with us. Something in our constitution, in our culture, has to be modified.*

Or to quote Di Tella:

> We have to reincorporate ourselves into the modern world. Argentina has veered unfortunately to become some sort of Albania of the West, isolated from the world currents, feeling persecuted, while actually it is our isolationist attitude which is at the root of the problem. How to change that is not easy. The only advantage our situation has today is that we are at the end of the road and everybody is aware that we cannot continue as we have in the past.†

To foreign bankers the problem of Argentina's isolation was much more evident. As John Reed saw it from Citicorp:

> It's a society whose economy has simply never gotten itself appropriately tied to the rest of the world . . . And it's not a society that has traditionally invested its money at home. There's a tremendous tendency to invest the savings of Argentina outside of Argentina, often in Europe. It has a cumulative effect in an unforgiving world. The pace at which the global economy has marched on, and the pace at which each society has had to cope with the changes imposed from outside, have made the insular isolated economy immensely difficult.‡

After its boom years were over Argentina still seemed to retain a charmed life. During the thirties, when most Latin American countries could not avoid default, Argentina remained solvent. But it was soon suffering dangerous political changes, as the populism of President Peron encouraged the workers to think they could have jam today, as well as tomorrow. In 1956, in the midst of the global prosperity, Argentina had to renegotiate its heavy debts. Roberto Aleman, a former Minister of Finance, now looks back with near-despair at the changes which made discipline so difficult:

> We changed rules, we changed governments, we changed policies, we changed ministers, all the time. During these last forty-five years we have had inflation: for the last thirteen years high inflation. Four or five times there were attempts to bring inflation down. I was part of at least three of them. We brought inflation down

*Interview in Buenos Aires, December 7, 1988.
†Interview, December 7, 1988.
‡Interview, May 9, 1989.

> and it seemed that we were successful and then it was all turned around and inflation was back.*

It was the oil crisis of 1974, which hit all the developing countries, which began Argentina's current debt predicament. The military government welcomed the offers of huge loans to tide it over and used much of the money to build up the armed forces. Carlos Menem, now President of Argentina, liked to quote the economist J. K. Galbraith: 'When foolish bankers give foolish loans to foolish countries or governments, the external debt never gets paid back.' 'Argentina got into debt,' Menem said before his election, 'thanks to the foolishness of the actual creditors and to the foolishness of the government that contracted this debt.'† But it had been hard for any government to resist such apparently easy loans. In the words of Roberto Aleman, who became Minister for Economy in 1981:

> It was so easy, you know, from '73 to '81. The large banks collected the money from the Arabs and other petrol countries and recycled it into borrowing countries which were prepared to take it and invest it. Argentina was just one. It was easy money, it was cheap money. In those years the interest rates were below world inflation. So it was really a negative interest rate.‡

And it was not difficult to blame the bankers. As Dr Terragno put it:

> The international banks had too much money, and high interest to pay, and they were anxious to find some countries to lend that money. And they relied upon countries that were in extreme necessity and countries like Argentina with a military government, without responsibility enough to understand the consequences of that overburden represented by that mass of money coming into the country.§

By the early eighties Argentina faced its full reckoning, with high interest rates, low commodity prices, rising debts and no new lenders. The Falklands War toppled the military regime but left still heavier debts and appalling problems for its successors. President Alfonsin took over to head the democratically elected government with a fanfare of hope. But he faced the full rigours of the debt, and all the

*Interview in Buenos Aires, December 6, 1988.
†Interview in Buenos Aires, December 8, 1988.
‡Interview, December 6, 1988.
§Interview, December 7, 1988.

perils of trying to cut back spending and induce realism in the minds of a democratic electorate. There was popular clamour to default on the debt, but the government and Central Bank resisted. As Arturo O'Connell, then on the board of the Central Bank, described it: 'We are a country of European emigration, so for us to re-establish links with the industrialised countries was an overwhelming priority . . . To stop paying debt would have meant an outright conflict with them.'* Argentina was thus saddled with a debt of 60 billion dollars whose repayment looked less and less likely. It was effectively bankrupt – but not visibly so. As Di Tella described it late in 1988:

> If we can analyse Argentina as if she were an American company, such a company many years ago would have applied to the courts for receivership . . . But the problem is that there isn't an international commercial court because we have sovereign debt – which is a very distinguished way of calling a very nasty sort of debt. We have to re-create a situation equivalent to this imaginary court and imaginary receivership. This is a very harsh statement because I am saying that we will be unable to pay in full. But this opinion is really shared by the financial community.†

There was a terrible social price to be paid for recovery. Very little of the huge loans had gone into productive construction which could benefit the country in the long term, while much was spent on military build-up and huge amounts had left the country soon after it arrived. The rich, with their mobile wealth, had benefited, while the poor, whose standard of living had already declined, would bear much of the cost of repayment. As Di Tella put it:

> Rich Argentinians found that any properties or investments in Argentina were very expensive compared to similar properties in the United States . . . The country subsidised rich Argentinians to invest elsewhere: now poorer Argentinians will have to pay the debt. This may sound a very demagogic statement but facts are facts.‡

This was the explosive prospect which faced any future government in the elections in May 1989; but it appeared still more explosive after the choice of the Peronist candidate Carlos Menem, the bewhiskered Lebanese immigrant who proclaimed himself as 'the last caudillo' and who called for a 'grace period' temporarily to suspend the repayments

*Interview, December 9, 1988.
†Interview, December 7, 1988.
‡Interview, ibid.

of debt. Menem was more realistic and pragmatic than he looked or sounded, and he appointed a former businessman, Miguel Roig, as economics minister; but he had evoked all the populist hopes of the Peronists whom he praised. And his election coincided with a full-scale economic crisis, with record inflation at about 100 per cent a month. In early June the discontent flared up into the worst rioting and looting for twenty years, in which at least fourteen were killed.

The outgoing President Alfonsin was only too relieved to hand over to Menem who quickly increased taxes and cut back expenditure, promising 'surgery without anaesthetic.' He had said six months before his election: 'We are going to set up a social pact, quite similar to those signed by countries that some time ago were able to emerge from their crisis, like Germany and Italy or Spain, which made their entry to the European Economic Community possible.'* But he faced a much more divided country than the Europeans; and many Western bankers were now saying privately, as they wrote down their debts, that Argentina was disintegrating into chaos.

Argentina remained an extreme case; but its mounting debts and its social problems were repeated elsewhere in Latin America, where the cost of repayments was hurting the poor much more than the rich. Bankers lectured governments about the need for adjustment and realism, but most of the impact fell on people who had never had any opportunity to be unrealistic. For many young democracies, the cutbacks and austerity produced an explosive predicament; and there had been a terrifying warning in March 1989 in Venezuela which was considered a relatively stable democracy. When President Perez, a relatively popular leader, began to impose his economic reforms they were met with furious riots and looting in Caracas during which hundreds were killed. It was a moment of truth for the bankers, as much as the politicians; for it gave notice that the price of harsh measures could undermine the stability on which they depended. 'If Venezuela cannot adopt sound policies without bloodshed,' complained the conservative *Economist*, 'the outlook is bleak for the jittery new democracies in Peru, Brazil and Argentina.'

All Latin Americans now faced the prospect that their nations' debts were cutting them off from the world's development, leaving them still more dependent. As Carlos Fuentes, the Mexican author and diplomat, said in 1987:

> We can certainly visualise a Latin American world, in itself, of economic crisis, political fragility and erosions both physical and

*Interview in Buenos Aires, December 8, 1988.

psychic, that will make it difficult for us to enter the twenty-first century on our feet, but rather dragged by the chariots of a few advanced nations . . .

We have become net exporters of capital, to the tune of 45 billion dollars a year. We thus contribute to two ephemeral solutions: alleviating foreign deficits and adding resources to foreign banks. We also contribute to two more permanent disasters: we sacrifice our own development while we damage the industrial nations, since without our development, they will become less developed themselves.*

All the Latin Americans were now de-developing countries, paying out huge funds to richer countries instead of receiving them. 'It's a paradox of the workings of the international financial system,' said O'Connell, 'that the less developed countries are exporting capital to the more developed countries, to the richest country in the world, to the United States . . .' It was still more paradoxical that they should be paying back the United States when it had become the world's biggest debtor, with a total debt more than all of Latin America's. The chief lender was now also the chief borrower, and both Americas were in hock together: but the United States was not subject to any of the disciplines that bore down on the Latin Americans; for the other rich countries were still prepared to lend and invest in it, and the United States was itself responsible for issuing the world currency on which foreign debts were based. While the International Monetary Fund could insist on other countries cutting back their public spending and deficits, the US could still postpone any harsh measures, and allow the dollar to devalue.

Americans themselves were beginning to compare their situation to the Latin Americans'. 'They went on consumption binges, they went on borrowing binges,' said Peter Peterson in New York. 'For a while they had overvalued currencies as we did. Our pattern, I'm sorry to say, has certain elements of commonalty.'† And John Connally, who had experienced debt from both sides, shared the same worry:

I think the future generations will feel that the 1980s was a time of easy living for the United States, that we lived beyond our means, we failed to live up to our responsibilities and we failed to be realistic in facing up to our economic problems . . . We complain about the Third World countries and the amount of debt that they

*Speech to International Press Institute, Buenos Aires, May 11, 1987.
†Interview, November 22, 1988.

have; but in one decade the United States of America went from the largest creditor nation to the largest debtor nation in the world. That's an enormous swing, and I think it forebodes ill for us, and for the stability of the international monetary system, because the dollar is the reserve currency of the world.*

Europeans as well as Americans were alarmed by the implications of America's debts. In the words of Sir Kit McMahon in September 1988:

> I think it's an enormously difficult situation. It's not yet realised how serious it is that the world's richest country should be getting itself into half a trillion dollars of debt and the consequences will be very serious. What has actually happened is that power has shifted to Japan and it is only just beginning to be realised . . .
>
> America will probably have to raise taxes and interest rates and have some degree of recession before they are out of it; and this combination in some form or other will not be very happy for the Latin American countries.†

The Latin governments, as they were continually pressed by Washington and the bankers to cut back their spending, were still more aware of their creditor's own debts: as though they were two drunks leaning against each other. Or as Dr Terragno more soberly put it:

> The United States is in a very peculiar situation with respect to Latin America. In the past it had a kind of political domination or influence. I feel that is fading away because world conditions have changed a lot. The idea of universal dominion, of proper imperialism is not related to nowadays. I feel the Latin American countries have now more freedom to manoeuvre than in the past.‡

They now began to see the United States in their own image, as a country that had lived too long in an unreal world, and must come to terms with the wheels of fortune. As Menem said six months before his election:

> The US should be humbler and not so domineering towards the rest of the world. That is what we, Argentinians, can teach not only the US but some other countries in the West. This is the world we live in, where people's possibilities increase and disappear.§

*Interview, December 1, 1988.
†Interview, September 27, 1988.
‡Interview, December 7, 1988.
§Interview, December 8, 1988.

In both the Americas the awkward fact was beginning to catch up: that the countries' debts, as much as individuals', were narrowing future choices and opportunities. And in the meantime the East Asian countries were still saving and building up national surpluses which extended their scope, both political and financial. Japan, now the world's chief creditor, was bound to play a greater role in both the Americas. The new Bush administration in 1989 began to look for new solutions to alleviate the Latin debt crisis: all the more anxiously after the riots in Venezuela and Argentina. But they were constantly looking towards Japan, which alone had the financial strength and surplus to resolve it.

The Japanese had their own interest in Latin America. They already had very large investments – particularly in Mexico, as a beachhead into the North American market. They were looking to the Latins to provide growing markets for their exports as other regions became saturated; and they were building up their political links with the major countries: Brazil even had a million citizens of Japanese origin who had earlier settled as farmers. Japan would gain obvious benefits from using part of its surplus to mitigate the Latin debt, while extending its own investment and trade in the developing world.

American bankers were loth to see the Japanese move into their traditional backyard. But the involvement of the master-lender could provide a much more stable and longer-term settlement than one debtor could offer another. And as the world's money-system became still more closely interlocked the Japanese, however reluctantly, were bound to become aware in any negotiations of the source of their power: that they had the money.

CHAPTER ELEVEN

THE GLOBAL BAZAAR

We find things beautiful, as well as serviceable, somewhat in proportion as they are costly.

THORSTEIN VEBLEN, 1899

Objet, cache-toi.

FRENCH STUDENTS' SLOGAN, 1968

Christmas reveals the full frenzy and unity of the global market-place, as Asians and Westerners, lenders and borrowers are all drawn into the festival of spending. Countries which have never seen snow or holly, never believed in Christ, send snowy Christmas cards and listen to the carols tinkling in the shopping malls, from Singapore to Sydney, from Stockholm to Cape Town. Santa Claus in his winter robes pops up in tropical climates. The hemispheres are bound together by their interest not in a common god, but in a common zeal for spending, buying the same gift-wrapped cameras, Sony Walkmen, Chivas Regal whisky or Suchard chocolate, in the annual climax of the money-religion.

The duty-free airport shops, the most placeless of all places, provide the magic circles of the cult of spending. For some of the most valued objects, like whisky bottles, they account for as much as a fifth of all world sales. The duty-free sales, worth 8 billion dollars a year by 1987, set the pace for much of the rest; and every year 3,000 delegates converge on Cannes, for the Tax Free World Exhibition where companies rent châteaux or yachts to entertain their clients.* The airport shops can defy all geographic logic: Anchorage in Alaska can import whisky from London and then sell it to passengers flying back to London; and a single jumbo may be carrying up to two tons of its passengers' alcohol and tobacco. Many passengers find the duty-free arcades in Singapore or Schiphol much more exciting than the cities outside: as if the brand-names are the real destinations. In the

*For an account of the festival, see *International Herald Tribune*, November 3, 1988.

Pacific airports, which take the place of Western railway stations, the duty-free shops at Christmas and the New Year can look like looted streets as Japanese tourists clean out the shelves in Honolulu or Hong Kong in a few hours; while the passengers display the brand-names on their clothes, carrier-bags or cartons like walking hoardings.

It was the global brand-names which were the marketing wonder of the eighties, as they exercised their power to confer magical status and glamour on to their owners in exchange for ever higher prices. A parade of honoured names – from Cartier to Burberry, from Hermes to Dunhill – stare out from every international hotel, shopping centre or airport arcade. They proclaim all the instant mobility of the new wealth: they offer jewellery, accessories, electronics and clothes which can all be carried on the person, together with luggage, the instrument of both status and escape, as if all the rich had become refugees. There is nothing new about displaying your riches on your body, or combining wealth with ornament. Arab souks weigh the intricate gold jewellery to calculate its value. In medieval Europe personal display had become so excessive that strict sumptuary laws were passed to limit the ostentation. But the late twentieth century has developed a new kind of portable wealth, carrying not gold and jewels but fantasies and magic names whose splendour has only recently been recognised across the world.*

How has this new jewellery so rapidly taken hold? They were all based on selling fantasies of different kinds, to attract the surplus wealth, and their histories throw an interesting light on the psychology of the eighties. The success of many of them depends on aristocratic associations from monarchic Europe, projected by clever salesmen into a global mass market. Cartier, the French court jewellers in the nineteenth century, had already penetrated a discreet American clientele in the 1920s; but it was not till the 1970s that they hit the global jackpot with 'Les Must de Cartier' which led into watches, leather goods, pens and spectacles. Their formula was simple: to invest ordinary objects with the romance of jewels and scent. 'We're not selling watches to tell the time,' says Cartier's young president Dominique Perrin; 'we're selling them to people who belong to a certain social class . . . who want to show off.'†

It was the Paris fashion-houses who set much of the pace: from their haughty headquarters they learnt how to mass-market their reputations for elegance and chic, spreading out from French

*For some details see: Walter J. Salmon and Karen A. Cmar: 'Private Labels are Back in Fashion', *Harvard Business Review*, May–June 1987, p.107.
†*International Management*, December 1987.

boutiques to global outlets. They were able to convert their famous labels – which buyers in the sixties had torn off – into the badges of glory in the seventies and eighties, and the key to undreamt-of profits. It was a remarkable trick of converting an exclusive trade into a mass market, which still looked exclusive. Almost a century earlier Thorstein Veblen had analysed how the rich preferred hand-made articles because they showed their expensiveness – which was the secret of haute couture. Now the most skilful marketers were able to give mass-produced objects the appeal of the hand-made through labels and clever advertising – with amazingly rapid results. In the nineteenth century Louis Vuitton sold hand-made luggage in two shops in Paris and Nice: in the 1970s Henri Racamier, who had married a Vuitton, began to sell the luggage on a bigger scale. Today the name is one of the world's status symbols.

Promoting the labels required a subtle blend of mystique and salesmanship, of boldness and restraint. Yves St Laurent, the neurotic recluse who first took over from Christian Dior at twenty-one in 1957, was later set up under his own name by an entrepreneurial art dealer Pierre Bergé (who later became director of the new Bastille opera in Paris) who brilliantly exploited the YSL name. He put the charmed initials on to clothes, belts, shoes, watches and handbags – he jibbed at YSL car-tyres – which were all sold in licensed shops round the world. The most wide-ranging was Pierre Cardin, the Italian-born designer who learnt about licensing at Dior and then extended it to the limit. After founding his own house he designed futuristic clothes in the sixties; and as they lost their appeal he lent his name to a jumble of products from penknives and alarm-clocks to underwear and frying pans – until by 1988 840 products were called Cardin round the world. In 1982 he even bought the Paris restaurant Maxim's, together with the rights for the name which he rapidly franchised in London, Mexico and Tokyo. He now boasts 'the most important name in the world' which he compares to 'a queen or a president honouring a cocktail reception'.*

A few European legends were promoted from scratch with a more classless and youthful image. The three Italian Benetton brothers began developing their sister's dazzling home-made sweaters into a new 'industrial fashion', which they eventually sold through a global network of 4,500 shops with bright decor for the under-twenty-fives, which turned the Benetton family into billionaires. In Germany Adidas rapidly exploited global sports events to sell its sports clothes, shoes and bags, on which the magic name was displayed by the customers them-

**Forbes* magazine, May 2, 1988.

selves, like a flag or a passport. But the Europeans' chief skill was in exploiting the old images of aristocracy and quality, from Cartier and Hermès to Harrods and Fortnum's, into a new global mythology, whose names could provide instant identity to the mobile newly rich. Old British firms cultivated a more masculine snobbery. Alfred Dunhill, the London pipe-maker, turned into the makers of lighters, suits, watches and even socks for the Japanese (who account for a third of their billion-dollar sales). 'Today function is taken for granted because things do work,' says the head of Dunhill holdings, Sior Pendle. 'So you have to add value in different ways.'* Thomas Burberry began selling his gabardine raincoats in 1856 and became famous for his trench-coats in the First World War. But it was not till the 1970s that Burberrys acquired global and unisex snob-appeal, stimulated by grouse-moor advertising and shops with a club-room atmosphere.

The Americans at first pioneered much more popular names emanating from movies and comic-strips. The first name-licence was granted back in 1904 when Brown Shoes bought the rights to the comic-strip character Buster Brown to sell their children's shoes at the St Louis World Fair. Walt Disney set a new pace after he first licensed Mickey Mouse for toys in 1930. Ever since, Disney's have led the field: in the 1980s they updated Mickey to bring him 'into the modern world' and on to socks, suspenders and bikinis: while they exported Disneylands to Japan, France and Korea with a success which contradicted all theories about cultural nationalism. Mickey's most serious challenger is Snoopy, created by the cartoonist Charles Schulz in 1950, and launched into Christmas cards ten years later; by 1985 he was appearing on 5,600 different products including cookies, T-shirts and ice-cream, and the Japanese were as fascinated by his personality as the Americans.† America remained the main playground for these licensed names, which were selling more than 40 billion dollars worth of goods by the mid-eighties. But some companies were so greedy and indiscriminate in renting out their names that they threatened to wreck the name-game with overkill.

Americans were also cultivating their own hierarchy, including hallowed names from Tiffany's to LL Bean, which could ride high on the boom of the eighties; and marketing and advertising became far more skilful in selling fantasy and imagined lifestyles. The most remarkable newcomer has been Ralph Lauren, who began in Brooklyn as Ralph Lipshitz, the son of an artistic house-painter,

*London *Sunday Times*, April 3, 1988.
†*Advertising Age*, Special Report, June 6, 1985.

and soon personified a new dandy style. He took over the traditional English style where Brooks Brothers had left off, and created his own label and the brand-name Polo to conjure up an imagined upper-class English life of country-houses and infinite leisure which could be sold with very high mark-ups. He first broke through in the late sixties by selling wide ties to Bloomingdales in New York and was further boosted by designing the clothes for the film *The Great Gatsby*. By 1988 Lauren was estimated to be worth 450 million dollars, living out on his ranch in Colorado the fantasies he was marketing, but he still preserved a restless insecurity and ambition (he longed to move into Hollywood) which helped him to identify with his market which depended on insecurity. Most of his customers were outside the traditional luxury market: a survey in 1985 identified a new group of 'Ultra-Consumers', many earning less than 25,000 dollars a year, who were obsessive shoppers for designer labels and prepared to go deeper into debt to acquire the identity and 'psychic armour' which they could provide.*

The Ralph Lauren style became part of the new mythology of the American eighties, with its Parnassus at the Rhinelander mansion, the ornate château in Madison Avenue built in 1894 for the heiress Gertrude Rhinelander Waldo (who never lived in it). In 1984 Lauren took a lease on it, rebuilt the inside round a staircase copied from London's Connaught Hotel, and transformed it into a kind of museum of vanished England, packed with hunting-boots, cricket-pads, silver sports-trophies, steamer-trunks, polo-sticks, faded school photographs – like the plunder from a country-house attic. Against this mystique he could sell still more expensive tweeds, crocodile shoes, tartans and sweaters as the keys to social acceptance. His advertisements were even more escapist, featuring blonde Anglo-Saxons in leisurely pursuits enjoying what Lauren called the 'whole atmosphere of the good life'. In the reality of contemporary Manhattan, insecure, workaholic and largely non-blonde, it was comically irrelevant. But any period of money-mania and social upheaval, like a century earlier, was likely to induce a longing for an earlier age of leisure and security; and social observers talked about the 'Ralph Lauren Presidency' of the patrician Anglo-Saxon George Bush.†

It was the Far East which provided the real bonanza for the purveyors of Western names and labels, who made few concessions to Oriental differences: huge hoardings of lanky American cowboys smoking Marlboro cigarettes stare out over Hong Kong harbour, to

*For details of Lauren's techniques and career see Jeffrey A. Trachtenberg: *Ralph Lauren: The Man Behind the Mystique*, Little Brown, Boston, 1988.
†See Alessandra Stanley in the *New Republic*, December 12, 1988.

small people who have never seen a cowboy or an empty space. But the limited living-spaces and growing prosperity of the East Asians provided the ideal setting for global labels. Even in China Pierre Cardin opened a Maxim's restaurant in Beijing in 1983 – followed by a Minim's selling Western fast-food – and Yves St Laurent advertised a perfume with the tactless name of Opium.* But it was the Japanese who became the most intensely name-conscious, with a special obsession with Louis Vuitton bags. As their earnings increased they urgently needed to transmute money into status without appearing ostentatious or un-middle class, and the label provided the solution. Japan seemed to be taking to a new extreme Veblen's theories that beauty was associated with cost, as some exporters found they could double the sales by doubling the cost. And the old Japanese ceremonial exchanges of gifts, with immaculate wrappings and trappings, was developed into a packagers' paradise, reaching a climax at the end of the year. The East had now reversed its older relationship with the West, when its own exports of spices, silk, lacquer or Ming were associated with excessive luxury. Now they exported the more practical objects like cars, electronics and computers, and imported luxury from the West with a special fondness for brand-names. 'People buy Reebock sneakers not knowing that they are British products made in Korea,' said Kenichi Ohmae. 'Some people like Adidas which are German products but made in Taiwan. Our people have become lovers of brands as opposed to products of certain origin . . . This is a major change.'†

Are these products the beginning of a genuinely global marketplace where national tastes and attitudes are beginning to dissolve? The global labels have been heavily analysed by sociologists, historians, and, above all, advertising agents. Daniel Boorstin, the American historian, has traced how brand-names and advertising since the American civil war have produced 'consumption communities' which reassure the customer that 'he would not find himself alone';‡ and he sees the consumption communities now crossing frontiers to create global clubs. 'A designer label is a community of consumers on whom some of the celebrity of the name rubs off,' Boorstin explained in 1988. The success of names like Cardin were due to 'the imperial power of prestige. It shows how little the consumer cares who the actual maker is.'§ Global selling has provided

*See Schell: op cit, pp.143, 177.

†Interview, September 22, 1988.

‡Daniel Boorstin: *The Americans: The Democratic Experience*, Vintage, New York, 1974, pp.90, 145.

§*Forbes* magazine, May 2, 1988.

a whole new vocabulary of slogans from advertising agencies. According to Ogilvy and Mather in London the consumer now has a 'global relationship' with advertising, while brand-names have an 'intimate relationship' with advertising. The late eighties were seeing 'a search for personal choice criteria' and perhaps 'a return to brand potency'. 'For youth in the sixties money was irrelevant; in the seventies a problem; in the eighties an opportunity.'*

The chief enthusiast for global marketing is Theodore Levitt, an athletic professor who strategically combines a marketing chair with editing the *Harvard Business Review* and advising Saatchi and Saatchi – who present themselves as the pioneers in the global market-place. Levitt provides his own vocabulary of globespeak, about the 'world-standard commonalty' and the 'new global reality – the explosive emergence of global markets for globally standardised products, gigantic world-scale markets of previously unimagined magnitudes . . .'† When I called on him at Harvard in 1988 he was talking about the 'heteroconsumer' and the 'pluralisation of consumption', and how more exotic products were spreading round the world, like pizzas, croissants or sushi: 'The more powerfully homogenising and relentlessly globalised the world's communications and commerce get, the more varied its products and more numerous its consuming segments seem to become.'‡ But he still insists on the unity of the global market-place in which identical products are spreading round the world, so that 'almost all companies will have to widen their geographic reach and offerings'.§

Is the world really being homogenised? Undoubtedly there are growing similarities in many kinds of consumption across the world, as any traveller can notice from the advertisements. Even food and drink are becoming more alike in the big cities. McDonalds is Japan's second-largest food chain, and the big food-makers – Unilever, Ajinomoto or General Foods – are invading each other's territories. The family meal, which used to be the stronghold of traditional tastes, is being undermined everywhere by TV, freezers and the pressures of time: even chopsticks have been abandoned by many young Japanese. 'By the end of the century,' says Charles Gebhard of Jacobs Suchard, 'the regular sit-down meal will have all but disappeared.'‖

*Ogilvy and Mather: presentation of PROJECT BADGE, 'Articulation of contemporary O&M London global beliefs about how advertising works', 1988.

†Theodore Levitt: *The Marketing Imagination*, Free Press (Macmillan), New York, 1983, pp.20–1.

‡Interview in Harvard, July 1988.

§Theodore Levitt: 'The Pluralization of Consumption', *Harvard Business Review*, May–June 1988.

‖*Financial Times*, February 10, 1988.

But regional differences of taste and habit remain far wider than they look from the big-city streets, hoardings and hamburger cafés. Most eating habits are much more resistant to change than clothes and gadgets: rooted in local crops and domestic traditions. Professor David Stout of Unilever mocks the idea of global foods – 'the edible Walkman' – as 'globaloney'. He points out that even foods with identical names, like McDonalds hamburgers, Kellogg's cornflakes or Coca-Cola, have distinct local tastes. The nearest thing to a global drink is bottled mineral water.*

Many marketing experts are highly sceptical of the jargon of global marketing: particularly J. Walter Thompson, the rival global agency to Saatchi and Saatchi. 'Nobody has yet successfully launched a brand exclusively for duty-free shops,' says a former British chairman of JWT. 'Global brand usually means a French or American or Japanese product that's widely sold in other countries. Brands need nationalities as much as people: that's part of their appeal to foreigners.' Many marketers look to global sales not for homogeneity, but for increasingly varied choice, as the next generation becomes more adventurous and less uniform: rather as a century ago the first Victorian department stores gave way to more discriminating boutiques.

The more important economic question is whether this hectic pursuit of luxury and status will continue without exhaustion? The luxury objects and brand-names are only the froth on the top of total world trade; but however frivolous, all these labels and objects provide an essential boost to employment and prosperity round the world – particularly the Third World. Ralph Lauren's Rhinelander mansion and the cat-walks of haute couture are linked through the intricate global industrial system to the factories and workers in developing countries who would lose their jobs if the frenzy subsided. The old equation of 'private vices, public benefits' now stretches out to factories in East Asia which depend on rich shoppers in Bloomingdales or Harrods. The discrepancy between the local wages and the eventual mark-up remains glaring: in Bangkok the low-paid workers who make designer-shirts can see them being sold with huge mark-ups in the downtown smart shops; while the same shirts are sold in the street markets at a quarter of the price, alongside YSL badges, Lacoste alligators or Adidas symbols which tourists can sew on themselves. But the Bangkok factories still depend on the fancy labels and fashions to open the doors to the Western markets.

*Professor David Stout, Unilever, *Financial Times* Centenary Conference, February 8, 1988.

For most of the post-war boom years the appetites and desires of Western consumers showed little signs of abating as television, cars, tourism and gadgets gave still more encouragement and scope for big spending. Then came the year 1968, when students all across the West began angrily denouncing the consumer society, and turning against their parents' materialism. The car, the central engine of the industrial economies, became an object of distrust and hatred, blamed for pollution, congestion and physical danger, and by factory workers for inhuman conditions: Fiat workers even set fire to cars they had built. Economists and even some bankers worried about the effects of rapid growth on the environment and wasting resources, culminating in the sensational report on 'Limits to Growth' published by the 'Club of Rome' in 1972. Industrialists worried that consumers were running out of new desires, as their houses filled up with television sets, hi-fi equipment and advanced gadgetry, and tourism began to look increasingly self-destructive: 'The tourist, in his search for something different,' warned the economist E. J. Mishan, 'inevitably erodes and destroys that difference by his very enjoyment of it.'*

The immediate crisis of 1968 soon passed; and the marketing experts dismissed it as a spasm, an intellectuals' fantasy. Students went back to business schools, consumers went on consuming, and the car – with the help of gadgetry, computers and improved engineering – soon became once again an object of glamour, status and sexiness. East Asians did their bit to promote more Western spending, by producing gadgetry, music-machines and glamorous electronics which could be replaced with still more novelties every year; while their own spending-power created new opportunities at home. Traditional bare Japanese homes filled up with expensive electronic equipment instead of furniture. 'I don't think saturation will ever happen,' Akio Morita of Sony told me; 'because our technology can create new products which give new facility, new joy, to the public.'†

There were still nagging doubts about whether the mounting consumption was providing real satisfaction. 'Why has economic advance become and remained so compelling a goal to all of us as individuals, even though it yields disappointing fruits when most, if not all of us, achieve it?' asked the economist Fred Hirsch in 1977, in his influential book *Social Limits to Growth*. Hirsch argued that people increasingly wanted 'positional' goods which were inherently scarce, like land, Old Masters or country-houses, and that the search for

*E. J. Mishan: *The Costs of Economic Growth*, Staples Press, London, 1967.
†Interview in Tokyo, September 20, 1988.

status was becoming self-defeating: 'If everyone stands on tiptoe, no one can see better.' And he warned that these social limits to growth would inevitably 'intensify the distributional struggle'.* The doubts continued. 'You have only to look around you at all the people who are dieting and jogging,' wrote the American economist Tibor Scitovsky in 1986, following up Hirsch's thesis nine years later, 'to realize that, with respect to some needs at least, a large part of the advanced countries' populations have not only reached but passed the point of satiety.' Like Hirsch, Scitovsky foresaw people looking more towards positional goods to provide status, which merely put up prices and, like hoarding money, did little to provide jobs for others. He concluded that: 'Faith in automatic market forces that push our economy towards full employment requires a hefty dose of optimism.'†

The global boom of the eighties, with all the boosts of fashion and fantasy, seemed to contradict these expectations of glutted consumers. Intellectuals, who are less excited by consumer gadgetry and may prefer the simple life, are notoriously wrong in assessing the tastes of ordinary people. The Midas Plague still spread through the West, defying the growing personal debts: and most economists expected still further consumption. 'There are still many people in London and New York – let alone the Third World – who could do with more to eat,' wrote Samuel Brittan, arguing with Scitovsky. 'There are also possibilities of substitution. The overcrowding of traditional beaches brings tourism to far-out places. As the price of Old Masters rises, some demand gets diverted to modern art . . .'‡

Yet there is a frenzy in the luxury market which makes many marketing experts sceptical. There is a limit to how long people can show off objects whose exclusiveness is visibly diminishing, and to the satisfaction of a 'consumption community' compared to more intimate communities. There is a limit to how many brand-names can be displayed on one body. How many more gadgets can a Japanese family cram into a tiny apartment? How often can they throw away TV sets or music centres to make way for new ones? How many more fast cars can they buy, to be jammed together in fume-filled streets? However much fantasy can take over from fact, in advertising vistas of empty roads, unspoilt landscapes and endless leisure, there comes a point when the illusion turns sour. As one marketing expert, Tom Jago, of United Distillers, put it:

*Fred Hirsch: *Social Limits to Growth*, Routledge, Kegan Paul, London, 1977, pp.5, 67.
†Tibor Scitovsky: 'Growth in the Affluent Society', *Lloyds Bank Review*, January 1987.
‡*Financial Times*, January 1987.

> I have very little confidence that the present fantasy world can go on, let alone go on growing, though there's no evidence yet of a slowing down. One could regard the whole phenomenon as a symptom of social conflict among newly prosperous societies – what do you do with all this money, with no evolved social or ethical conscience? – which will be resolved by radical changes hard to foresee.

The pace of consumption presents obvious problems for the future, which are described in the final chapter. It is making drastic inroads on some of the world's most valuable and irreplaceable resources; and it cannot do much to alleviate the poverty outside its charmed circle. The cultivation of fantasy provides an escape rather than a connection with the wider world.

The surge of new surplus money in the eighties, without any obvious home or purpose, led naturally to the invention of new ways of spending it to reassure rich customers. The richest of all, with several million to spend every year, were naturally looking for correspondingly greater reassurance. And they were competing in the area where the stakes had become highest of all: for the capture of art itself.

CHAPTER TWELVE

THE QUEST FOR GLORY

Money, thou bane of bliss, and source of woe,
Whence comest thou, that art so fresh and fine?
I know thy parentage is base and low:
Man found thee poor and dirty in a mine.

GEORGE HERBERT 1593–1633

At the peak of the money-world a strange ritual is periodically performed which, like the money-cathedrals themselves, seems to evoke a strange new religion. It can bring together the rich from every continent: a company raider from Western Australia, a media magnate from New York, an insurance tycoon from Tokyo. The participants assemble in evening dress – leathery old men with younger wives, smooth acolytes, theatrical socialites – and gaze at each other and at numbers in glossy books, and occasionally at paintings on walls. Then an eloquent preacher stands up on a pulpit to intone numbers, and to display a succession of paintings. Members of the congregation hold up their hands, while numbers flick on a screen displaying pounds, dollars or yen, generating rising emotion. They all listen to the numbers intently, looking anxiously at each other. At last a large number wins, a hammer is knocked, and they stand up and cheer. 'They rise to their feet as if in an old-time religious ceremony,' as the former museum director Thomas Hoving describes it, 'and howl with jubilation.' And at the end of the ceremony a new record number is celebrated, linked to the revered name of an artist, and the buyer reflects the glory.

It is in art that the rush of new money, as it circles round looking for recognition and reward, can suddenly visibly identify itself and take shape: where the competition for status reaches its peak. Art, as the painter Leon Golub says, 'is the ultimate consumer product of our society. No other product can go from relatively no value to millions of dollars, maybe in twenty years.'* And these theatrical

*Interview in New York, November 12, 1988.

auctions, where the new rich frantically compete for relatively few objects, raise once again the timeless questions: what do they want with their money? What are they really searching for, and what do they find? The questions became more pressing in the eighties as a new generation of rich emerged with less sense of guilt or social obligations, while they compete still more intensely to be recognised. The more the big fortunes were publicised and classified, the less satisfying the numbers became: money had lost much of its mystery. So the rich had to search further afield to show their uniqueness.

And art seems to provide the most complete escape from the curse of Midas, by which money is always turned back into money: for it can turn money into beauty. The traditional picture of the miser – of Scrooge, Volpone or Shylock, sitting grimly on a hoard of gold – may be hard to recognise in an age when the rich are displayed as constantly active, travelling and organising – or triumphantly spending large sums on great works of art. Few of the newly rich show the kind of conspicuous misery which reassures those without money. But the obsession with accumulating money, without pleasure in spending it, remains the problem of the rich: and the money-miser is now reinforced by the time-miser, who fills up his diary as well as his bank balance, and is meaner with minutes than with dollars.

There are still plenty of life-stories which reveal that money cannot buy happiness. Paul Getty, who was reckoned as the world's richest man until he died in 1976, became a legend for his miserly attitudes: he kept a pay-phone for his guests in his country-house Sutton Place in England, and he left behind him a legacy of bitter disputes and resentments among his children, of whom he had seen little. Charles Clore, the master-financier in Britain in the fifties and sixties, was divorced from his wife, alienated from his two children and spent his evenings dancing with young girls. With all his financial capital, wrote his biographers, Clore 'had created so little emotional capital with family, friends or lovers that he had almost nothing in that bank to draw on'.* Clore spent much of his later life living in exile in Monte Carlo and elsewhere in order to avoid taxes, and left behind bitter legal wrangles over his death duties. It was the fate of many multimillionaires to die without any real home, like the Flying Dutchman who had to travel the world until he could find the love of a faithful woman. It was hard to argue that Getty or Clore would

*David Clutterbuck and Marion Devine: *Clore, the Man and his Millions*, Weidenfeld and Nicolson, London, 1987, p.213.

have been happier if they had been less rich: their restlessness drove their greed, more than vice-versa. But their lack of human relationships was clearly linked to their ambition for money.

Psychologists face some difficulty in challenging the rational assumptions of money. 'The connection between money thinking and rational thinking is so deeply ingrained,' complained the Freudian Norman O. Brown, 'that it seems impossible to question it.'* But they and others are constantly reminded of the subconscious fears about the dark side of money. 'In the ancient civilisations, in myths, fairy-tales and superstitions,' wrote Freud, 'in unconscious thinking, in dreams and in neuroses, money is brought into the most intimate relationship with dirt.'† For centuries writers and painters had associated money with dirt and excrement, as suggested by phrases like 'filthy lucre' or 'filthy rich'. The discovery of gold and treasure underground, in holes or in mines, reinforced the images which connected money with darkness, squalor and death. The paintings of Bosch or Brueghel relate gold to human turds: the traditional German figure of the 'Dukatenscheisser' excretes gold coins. A Gillray cartoon in 1797 showed William Pitt excreting paper money through the Bank of England. The associations remain today. The American word 'tight-ass' still describes a miser; and London and New York dealing-rooms are famous for their scatological language, celebrated in Caryl Churchill's play *Serious Money* or Tom Wolfe's novel *The Bonfire of the Vanities*. "'Holy fucking shit!' shouted the Yale men and Harvard men and the Stanford men. 'Ho-lee fuc-king shit.'"‡ The memoirs of David Stockman, President Reagan's budget director, show the same compulsion to equate money with excrement: 'I had just unloaded several tons of horse manure into the Cabinet Room.'§

The anal origins of the money-instinct continue to fascinate. Freud in his now-notorious essay 'Character and Anal Erotism' in 1908 first described how constipated patients frequently showed three related characteristics: orderliness, parsimony and obstinacy.|| Psychoanalysts have continued to find the same connections, but many now see the obsession with money as part of a wider obsession with control. The 'control-freak', with a perfectionist's mind, who insists on keeping everything and everyone in their exact place, is a characteristic figure of our time, made more effective by computers linked to

*Norman O. Brown: *Life Against Death*, Routledge, London, 1959, p.234.
†Sigmund Freud: 'Character and Anal Erotism', 1908.
‡Tom Wolfe: *The Bonfire of the Vanities*, Cape, London, 1988, chapter 3.
§David A. Stockman: *The Triumph of Politics*, Avon, New York, 1987, p.385.
||Freud: op cit.

telecommunications which can fortify impersonal power without the need for human relationships. The solitary figure surrounded by screens, keyboards, telephones and faxes, using two or three gadgets at once, has become part of today's demonology. Psychoanalysts have found that computer experts often suffer from the same kind of mania as the newly rich. But money remains the yardstick for success, whether in computers or in any business, and money is the only effective instrument for control.

Among today's richest men is Michael Milken, the junk bond financier who earned over half a billion dollars in a year, who epitomises the control-freak, with a driving desire to make still more money, but little interest in spending it. He has lived modestly in a suburb of Los Angeles, with 'one house, one wife, one cat, and one car' and his colourless personality only comes to life when he is engaged in money-making, with an enthusiasm which casts a spell over his clients.*

I asked Dr Hanna Segal, a London psychoanalyst with a special interest in the motives of rich men and collectors, how valid Freud's observations now appear:

> Money is supposed to have no smell, to be neutral. But when you come to analyse people I think Freud's view is very amply confirmed. Freud's original view was based on the fact that the stools of defecation are the first product of the child with which he can control his environment. It's a first gift to mother, when the child is toilet trained and a first way of controlling her. I can think of a patient who was away on a holiday with her mother and whenever mother wanted to go out with a man she would sit on her pot and not perform, absolutely spoiling mother's going out.

Dr Segal, like other psychologists, sees the quest for money as closely linked to this childish desire to control.

> Basically it must be linked with some great insecurity and never, never having enough. But it's also linked with the characterological disposition of wishing to dominate others, and fantasies that it gives more control over their lives – which it doesn't. Because the essential things in life you can't buy. You can't buy love for money and you can't get things essential to psychological security – which is a good feeling about oneself and one's own value. Valued human relationships are if anything spoiled by the amassing of money.†

*See Edward Jay Epstein: *Manhattan Inc*, September 1987.
†Interview in London, March 30, 1989.

Whatever the infantile origins of the money-drive or the associations with dirt, the newly rich seek to connect their wealth with splendour and beauty, and with glories of the past. Generations of new rich have compared themselves to the Medici in fifteenth-century Florence, as the supreme transmuters of money into beauty; but they naturally remembered the Medici's patronage of art – which was much exaggerated – rather than their less romantic pervasive banking activities. Cosimo de Medici, who first established the power and wealth of the family, personally controlled the biggest bank in Europe which had a powerful hold on Florentine trade. Its loans extended through eight branches across Europe, including London and Geneva. The ledgers, still kept in Florence, record the bank's loans and repayments in meticulous detail. Cosimo clearly had a sense of guilt about his money-making, hardly surprisingly since the Church was constantly denouncing usury, and merchants hated the bankers for their exacting terms. One contemporary, Vespasiano, described how Cosimo had some money which, as he put it, 'he had not come by quite cleanly. Desirous of lifting this weight from his shoulders, he conferred with his Holiness Pope Eugenius IV who told him . . . to spend ten thousand florins on building.'* So Cosimo commissioned Michelozzo to rebuild the monastery of San Marco in Florence. And it was there that Cosimo himself prayed in his private cell.

The Medici knew how to use sponsorship and public relations to counter their unpopularity: they continued to commission great buildings and monuments, but like modern corporations they wanted their generosity to be recognised. Cosimo's son Piero commissioned Michelozzo in about 1450 to design the ornate tabernacle in the church of SS Annunziata in Florence. But an inscription inside made sure that people knew exactly how much Piero de Medici had spent: '*Costo' fior. 4 mila el marmo solo*': the marble alone cost 4,000 florins. 'This is worthy of remark,' writes the art historian E. H. Gombrich, 'by those who still believe that this type of announcement was invented by American tycoons.' The splendour of the Medici increased as their more mercenary activities faded into history. Piero's son Lorenzo was called Magnifico only as a courtesy title given to many other prominent Florentines: it was not until the nineteenth century that he was called 'the Magnificent'.

The Renaissance continued to provide the style by which great wealth was transformed into splendour and glory; and in eighteenth-century England aristocrats used immense classical country-houses

*Quoted by E. H. Gombrich: *Norm and Form*, Phaidon, London, 1966, p.37.

to proclaim their power and magnificence. The Palladian mansions like Wentworth Woodhouse, Stowe Park or Prior Park competed in length to dazzle their visitors; and because their wealth was fixed to the land, their relationship to their society was relatively straightforward. A great house, with its decoration, upkeep and entertainment, made jobs for hundreds of servants, artisans and farm-labourers – the equivalent of a large factory today but much more permanent. The prosperity of the owner was bound up with the life of the region, and the wealth was immobile. Thomas Coke, who inherited a fortune in Norfolk at the age of ten, later made the customary grand tour of Italy and was determined to improve his estate and build a grand mansion. He and his architect William Kent took thirty years to transform the landscape and build Holkham Hall which was 344 feet long. It gave him the immortality which he sought, commemorated above the entrance: 'This seat, on an open, barren estate, was planned, planted, built, decorated, and inhabited by Thomas Coke, Earl of Leicester'.

The aristocrats of the eighteenth century believed that they had a duty to build and extend mansions to give work to local people. Their ostentation was mocked by their contemporaries, including Alexander Pope who described one of the most pretentious mansions:

> At Timon's Villa let us pass a day,
> Where all cry out, 'What sums are thrown away!'
> So proud, so grand, of that stupendous air,
> Soft and Agreeable come never there . . .*

But Pope, like many of his contemporaries, accepted that Timon's extravagance was essential to the economic system.

> Yet hence the poor are cloth'd, the hungry fed;
> Health to himself, and to his infants bread
> The Lab'rer bears: what his hard heart denies,
> His charitable vanity supplies.†

The industrial revolution undermined the assumptions of territorial permanence, creating vast new fortunes and cities, while railroads and telegraphs made money much more mobile. The new industrial rich were detached from the land and more restless than their predecessors, while their money appeared still more disconnected from any community or responsibility. And the disciplines of large-scale

*Alexander Pope: Epistle to Lord Burlington, ll.99–103.
†Ibid, ll.169–72.

capitalism were bringing back the emphasis on thrift and parsimony. The miser was back with a vengeance, commemorated by Dickens' Scrooge, Harmon or Dombey: 'one of those close-shaved close-cut moneyed gentlemen who are glossy and crisp like new banknotes, and who seem to be artificially braced and tightened as by the stimulating action of golden shower-baths.'*

The triumph of the American multimillionaires at the end of the century brought a new side and competitiveness to wealth. In the 1840s there were fewer than twenty millionaires in the US; by 1891 there were estimated to be 120 men worth more than 10 million dollars, with speculation about the 'coming billionaire'; and the next year the *New York Tribune* published a list of over 4000 millionaires. This new plutocracy created a wave of political fears and resentments, not least from the old professional classes. 'The new plutocracy,' wrote Richard Hofstadter, 'had set standards of such extravagance and such notoriety that everyone else felt humbled by comparison.'† (It was a humiliation to be repeated in the 1980s as the professional classes in Europe and America were to contrast their constricted lifestyles with the new yuppies – who might include their own children.) Many British saw the new American plutocracy threatening the whole economic order. After hearing that Vanderbilt had left 94 million dollars to his son, William Gladstone said to Vanderbilt's friend Chauncey Depew in America: 'I understand you have a man in your country who is worth $100m, and it is all in property which he can convert at will into cash. The government ought to take it away from him, as it is too dangerous a power for any one man to have.'‡

The new industrial rich, without the territorial tradition of their predecessors and with huge surplus funds, looked much more actively for esteem and legitimacy. Many of them turned to philanthropy: John D. Rockefeller set the pattern of all subsequent foundations. Andrew Carnegie insisted that 'the man who dies rich dies disgraced.'§ But others began to look to art as the key to recognition and immortality: and they naturally looked back to the Medici. The fascination with the Medici had been revived in 1796 by William Roscoe, a banker and art collector, who wrote *The Life of Lorenzo de' Medici*. The newly rich industrialists (as Professor John Hale describes them) 'were intrigued to learn that commerce and manufacture could

*Charles Dickens: *Dombey and Son*, chapter 2.
†Richard Hofstadter: *The Age of Reform*, Vintage, New York, 1955, pp.136, 147.
‡Henry Clews: *Fifty Years in Wall Street*, Irving Publishing, New York, 1908. pp.360–61.
§*North American Review*, June 1889.

be made respectable, even glamorous, in the eyes of posterity were they to include payments for paintings and manuscripts in their balance sheets.' The legend of benign Medici patronage was soon to be countered by an equally exaggerated legend of their ruthless domination and incest: 'the dead and damned Medici,' as Mark Twain called them, 'who cruelly tyrannised over Florence.' But they remained the symbols of the immortality of riches and – in Hale's words – of the central paradox of the Renaissance: 'that an advancing culture, experimental in form and profound in its content, can co-exist with radically changing political institutions'.*

Many of the new American multimillionaires were grateful to be seen as modern Medici. Their relationship to their art was later much mocked. As Matthew Josephson described them in *The Robber Barons* in 1934:

> Sometimes they had the droll aspect of the aborigine who decorates his person with the *disjecta membra* of Western civilisation, with pieces of tin can for his earrings, or a rubber tire for a belt. Such is the suggestion given to us by the unforgettable picture of the hard little Henry Frick, 'in his palace, seated on a Renaissance throne, under a Baldachino and holding in his little hand a copy of the *Saturday Evening Post*.'†

Frick, the diminutive coal and steel industrialist from Pittsburg, was a favourite target, all the more visible because he lived in the last surviving great mansion on Fifth Avenue, with his superb original collection intact. Yet Frick, who had a minimal education and was brought up under the smoke of Pittsburgh, had a far brighter eye for good painting than his loftier rivals. Though he recorded the bills for Turners in the same books as the bills for coke, his taste was far bolder and more personal than that of Pierpont Morgan or Andrew Mellon, with a much greater influence on later collectors.

But it was Pierpont Morgan who became the most powerful public symbol of the conversion of wealth into art. He was primarily a master-banker, the ruthless rationaliser or 'morganiser' of American industry at the turn of the century; and the personification of capitalism. His famous bulbous nose, it was said, became an indispensable part of the world's financial system; and his presence was suitably intimidating, wonderfully captured in a photograph by Edward Steichen, who described how meeting his dark eyes was like confront-

*John Hale: *Florence and the Medici*, Thames and Hudson, London, 1977, pp.194–6.
†Matthew Josephson: *The Robber Barons*, 1934. Reprinted, Harcourt Brace Jovanovich, New York, 1962, p.346.

ing the headlights of an express train bearing down on you. Morgan soon used his great wealth to build up a hoard of art treasures, buying up whole collections from bankrupt European aristocrats – many of whose estates had recently been undermined by imports of cheap American grain. He could intimidate art sellers as he had financiers: when he bargained, it was said, he looked not at the object but at the eyes of the seller.

Morgan was frequently described as a modern Medici, though the comparison was doubly inept. Morgan, unlike Cosimo or Lorenzo, ignored contemporary art and was only interested in dead artists. He was also relatively aristocratic, descended from five generations of Connecticut landowners. The official historian of the Morgan Library, Francis Taylor, condemns Cosimo de Medici as 'a self-made man and despot who had consolidated his leadership of Florence through forced loans and punitive taxation, weapons he managed as deftly as others used the dagger'.*

But Morgan soon became a myth in his own right with more impact on the ownership of paintings, if not their creation, than any of the Medici: for he provided the main funnel through which the treasures of the old world were transferred to the new. To Europeans he appeared a caricature of American greed: a crude, silent figure, with his black eyes and famous nose, cruising down the Nile on his yacht to haggle with dealers, using the new-fangled telephone to clinch instant deals, buying chunks of civilisation wholesale without looking at individual beauty. To Roger Fry, Virginia Woolf's friend who briefly and unhappily advised Morgan, he was a monster of insensitivity: 'A crude historical imagination was the only flaw in his otherwise perfect insensibility toward art.'† Certainly Morgan saw it in wholesale terms. He merged art collections as systematically as corporations and railroads, sometimes at the same time: he bought Raphael's Colonna altarpiece, in the same year in which he bought out Andrew Carnegie to form US Steel. He also knew how to exploit art to achieve power: he built his great Morgan Library in the middle of the commercial hubbub of Manhattan, with an entrance hall like a temple where it seemed irreverent to argue about money; and in this building he compelled financiers to bail each other out of the crash of 1907, by locking them into his library until they agreed. Some art historians are inclined to equate his art with his power.

*See Francis Henry Taylor: *Pierpont Morgan*, the Pierpont Morgan Library, New York, 1970. See also Calvin Tomkins: *Merchants and Masterpieces, the Story of the Metropolitan Museum of Art*, E. P. Dutton, New York, 1970.
†Virginia Woolf: *Roger Fry, a Biography*, New York, 1940, p.141.

'Just as his reputation as a financier had prevented a financial panic on more than one occasion,' wrote David Alan Brown, 'so his art purchases set the standard for the Golden Age of American collecting.'* But Morgan established a tradition of art collecting in America as lasting as the Rockefeller tradition of philanthropy. He was more respectful of his treasures than were most of the decadent English or Italian aristocrats from whom he had rescued them. He enriched the Metropolitan Museum in New York which soon overtook the great European museums in its splendours.

What was Morgan really looking for, as he bought up his huge art collection between making his financial deals? Was he trying to atone or compensate for his greed and money-obsessions as a banker? In the reading-room of the Morgan Library a faded sixteenth-century Brussels tapestry called *The Triumph of Avarice* appears to offer a mysterious clue. It portrays a kind of mythical anthology of greed. The female figure of Avarice emerges from Hell with dragons' wings, clawed hands and feet, fingering a pile of gold coins, carried on a chariot full of ledgers and accounts, drawn by a griffin and crushing dead victims beneath it. In the foreground is King Midas with ass's ears, and beside him is King Tantalus, the Phrygian King who stole nectar from the gods and was doomed constantly to search for water. In the bottom left corner an elegant merchant is anxiously clutching illuminated pages. In the background is King Croesus with his hands bound. Above is an angel, warning of this deadly sin. The inscription, mixed from Horace and Ovid, proclaims: 'As Tantalus was always thirsty while surrounded by water, so is the miser always desirous of wealth'.

What induced Morgan to hang up this horrific denunciation of his own money-mania? Was it a sudden shaft of self-knowledge, a hidden sense of humour or an attraction to a work of art which at least showed such interest in his own métier?

As the first great industrial wealth was spread more widely the frontier between the rich and their art attracted many ingenious brokers who had learnt how to use both languages. The most celebrated was Joseph Duveen, later Lord Duveen, who had provided Morgan, Frick and others with European works of art and who continued his dealings through the thirties. He brilliantly understood the competitiveness and insecurities of his clients, while his discreet business partner, Bernard Berenson, provided the authentications of Old Masters which alone could ensure his high prices. Between them

*David Alan Brown: *Raphael and America*, National Gallery of Art, Washington, p.68.

they ensured that art could become a currency sufficiently stable to win the trust of the rich. By the mid-twentieth century many culture-brokers were following Duveen's footsteps to provide bridges between wealth and status. In New York two sophisticated public relations advisers competed for leadership. Edward Bernays, Sigmund Freud's nephew and American agent, extended his own interest in psychology to embrace the new rich. He worked in the twenties with Pierre Cartier the jeweller and Jacques Worth, his dress-designing brother-in-law, to provide discreet salesmanship to the new rich; and he was introduced to 'a new world of persuasion' by Germain Seligmann, the irascible art dealer who was the French equivalent of Lord Duveen. Seligmann 'despised modern art, but recognised its growing market' and approached his business with a cynicism which surprised even Bernays.

> When I started to work with Seligmann I believed that buyers acquired pictures and other objects because they liked them. When I finished I recognised that most important works of art were bought for other reasons. They were fashionable. Art served upward mobility in America. The dealer who knew how to project art symbols effectively reaped the profits.*

A more subtle broker between wealth, status and art was Benjamin Sonnenberg, the adviser to many multimillionaires in New York – above all to the banker Robert Lehman for whom he supplied many personal services. Sonnenberg brilliantly perceived the vanities and frustrations of the rich, and created a salon to satisfy them. He cultivated an elaborate Edwardian style including a brown bowler hat, a walrus moustache and two houses in Gramercy Park displaying his own collection of paintings of writers which provided an appropriate setting for upward mobility. 'Millionaires come to me when they've climbed to the top of a mountain,' he once told me, 'only to find that no one notices them. They're surrounded by other millionaires. My job is to get them on to a more visible peak. I make big pedestals for small men.' He employed press agents and journalists to massage his clients and arranged for hostesses to bring them into fashionable society. Most importantly, he introduced them to gallery curators – who he insisted were the key social arbiters – who gave them flattery and acceptance in return for their money. He left behind no memoir ('I don't mind shaming others, but I'd shame myself') and his will stipulated that his own art collection should be sold off.

*Edward I. Bernays: *Biography of an Idea*, Simon and Schuster, New York, 1965, pp.336, 339.

The huge new American fortunes after the Second World War, particularly oil fortunes, impatient for recognition, released a flood of new money into museums and galleries. Curators established gradations of honour and immortality, with their scale of charges – ranging from a single picture to a room to a wing. They could even sell the same immortal space three times over, as the Tate Gallery has done in London: commemorating one tycoon (Sir Henry Tate) with the whole museum, another (Lord Duveen) with a wing inside the museum, and another donor (Nomura) with a room inside the wing. 'It's like a Russian doll,' explained one trustee. Many of the new rich still stalked their art with the spirit of the jungle; and they became still more competitive and demanding, expecting recognition on a global stage. The hunt was often an extension of the original acquisitive drive. In the candid words of Norton Simon, the California industrialist who built up a billion dollar collection in Los Angeles: 'Acquisitiveness is a disease which you can get in money or business or politics or art.'*

The most enduring American collector was Armand Hammer, who began buying Russian icons and paintings in Moscow at rock-bottom prices in the twenties when he was trading with Lenin's government. He was interested, he wrote, in the imperial Russian treasures, because they 'might make a fluidly convertible commodity in the West'; though he was later 'moved and stirred by paintings as only music had previously affected me'.† And he later built up three separate collections, two of which he gave away. Yet he never seemed able to escape from the dollar signs. For Hammer the main excitement of collecting was the extreme competitiveness: 'one of the best games in the world'. As he wrote in his autobiography:

> The art world is a jungle echoing to the calls of vicious jealousies and ruthless combat between dealers and collectors; but I have been walking in the jungles of business all my life, and fighting tooth and nail for pictures comes as a form of relaxation to me.‡

Paul Getty, the oil billionaire, endowed the wealthiest of all museums in Malibu in California – which he never saw. He described himself in his gloomy autobiography as an 'incurable art-collecting addict'. He picked up his first bargains after the great crash of 1929, and he insisted that anyone who did not love art was a barbarian. But he described his acquisitions in terms of profits and bargains: he

**Forbes* magazine, October 24, 1988.
†Armand Hammer: *Hammer, Witness to History*, Simon and Schuster, New York, 1987, p.447.
‡Ibid, p.447.

bought a Raphael at Sotheby's for 200 dollars, worth a million dollars by 1976, and after the Getty Museum was opened he complained that each visitor cost him 3 dollars.* He added a funereal touch to his own acquisitions (he once gloomily showed me round his Dutch Masters in his English country-house Sutton Place, chilly and dimly lit). Even other billionaires are sceptical about his museum at Malibu. 'It's an ego trip of a dying man to perpetuate his name by building this mausoleum,' says Sir James Goldsmith. 'It's a sort of cemetery for him, scavenging the past. If instead he had used his money . . . for a foundation to encourage new creativity in future generations I would have admired him.'† After Getty died his son Paul Getty Junior, after some time as a drug addict, settled as a recluse in England and took special pleasure in supporting institutions competing with the Getty Museum's huge acquisitions: including the National Gallery in London. The British rewarded him in the traditional fashion: through the mediation of the National Gallery's chairman Jacob Rothschild he became an honorary Sir Paul.

It was the Metropolitan Museum of Art in New York – which owed much to Pierpont Morgan – which became the chief temple where wealth was sanctified and transmuted into status. As the rich became less interested in religion or philanthropy they devoted still more money to art and the recognition it gave them. The austere style of earlier Protestant benefactors, like the Morgans, Rockefellers or Astors, was overlaid by a new generation of donors who were more openly generous and less worried by guilt. 'I think collecting art has much more to do with the Jewish religion,' said one of the Met's senior officials. 'There's no real heaven in Jewish thought, and there's this feeling you must leave your good works on earth.' In the mid-sixties the Met entered a phase of aggressive expansion and publicity under Thomas Hoving, an ambitious curator and fund-raiser who had begun as a medieval art scholar at the Cloisters and later became New York's Commissioner of Parks. Hoving had been advised by Robert Moses, his predecessor as Commissioner who was a master fund-raiser: 'never give 'em a cheap ticket to immortality'; and he followed Moses' rule, extracting huge gifts from multimillionaires, including the biggest of all from Robert Lehman. Hoving irreverently describes how he coaxed millions from the rich:

> You would appeal to the inherent inferiority complex of the person and to their greed factor, and to their desire to become a member

*J. Paul Getty: *As I See It*, W. H. Allen, London, 1976, pp.276–89.
†Interview, October 12, 1988.

of high society, and the highest society of all was to be on the board of the Metropolitan Museum of Art . . . And you would go to the man always in office hours, never to dinner, never to a function, never at a gala. You would book an appointment and go to their office, and you would very simply lay out the most rational and important reasons why they should give their five million, ten million, whatever it was, and they would give it within, I'd say, six to ten seconds.

It's pure social climbing – I mean the real good type of social climbing right up that ladder step by step, out of some wretched place into society. Third wife, you know, the thirty-year-old beautiful, softic third wife, good tailor, fine house, or two or three or four, a plane, a yacht: and then, art. Because art is the ultimate imprimatur that you are rich, because you come into somebody's home, and if they casually surround you with Cézannes and Picassos and oh I guess Andy Warhol, you know they've got to be rich. It has always been that way. Frick, Morgan, the whole crowd of Robber Barons cleaned up their act through art.*

By the seventies and eighties the Met's trustees were equating art, status and money more closely and visibly. In two decades they had spent 200 million dollars on doubling the museum's space with six new wings, and they urgently needed more money, while the new rich were anxious for respectability and fame. In 1987 and 1988 the Met collected 10 million dollars each from Henry Kravis, Larry Tisch and Milton Petrie. They also began renting galleries for highly publicised parties – reaching a peak of ostentation with the 3 million dollar wedding reception in the Temple of Dendur for Laura Steinberg and Jonathan Tisch, with a 17,000 dollar wedding cake. As rich New York wives became too busy to organise their own entertainment in private houses, the Met became their prime site for display. 'In New York today,' wrote John Taylor in 1989, 'the sole remaining venue for conspicuous consumption on a Pharaonic scale is the Metropolitan Museum.'† The Met began to look more like a playground and cat-walk for the rich – the 'Club Met' or 'Rent-a-Palace' – than a centre for public education and art scholarship, to the growing resentment of the curators who watched their precious temples turned into society salons.

The Met's foreign rivals watched its escalations with mixed envy

*Interview in New York, November 21, 1988.
†*New York Magazine*, January 19, 1989.

and disdain: particularly its elderly London counterparts, the British Museum and the National Gallery, who faced financial crises under a less generous government. Like the Met they were trying to lure the new rich, Japan and Hong Kong as well as America. But they preferred much more discreet flattery, with an occasional very grand dinner attended by a Royal to imply that a large donation would permit membership of the most ancient establishment of all. And British fund-raising was simplified by the existence of only a few very rich patrons, led by a single family, the Sainsburys.

The American benefactions to art remained far bigger, and behind them lay more than social brokerage: for the museums were full of religious echoes. American businessmen who once gave money to churches were now buying art instead, as Tom Wolfe pointed out, and the arbiters of art fashions had become the new clergy or clerisy. 'Today, educated people look upon traditional religious ties – Catholic, Episcopal, Presbyterian, Methodist, Baptist, Jewish – as matters of social pedigree. It is only art that they look upon religiously.'* Lord Gowrie, the chairman of Sotheby's, has his own misgivings about the confusion with religion in the twentieth century: 'The spiritual impulse in religion, and those needs in human life, have got exported perhaps over into the arts – which is not always all that good for the arts.'† The vacuum left by the decline of religion had been partially filled by many other idols for worship, including money itself. But the hallowed museums brought the rich on to a higher level which invested them with more mystery and splendour. The venerated names of the painters became gradually merged with the names of the patrons which loomed over the rooms, until the visitors might assume that Lehman, Mayer or Astor were responsible for creating the masterpieces in the first place.

It was not only the very rich who were celebrating the marriage of art and money. Paintings became more widely desirable with high inflation in the seventies, followed by huge new fortunes in the eighties. Ordinary investors were persuaded that paintings were a safe hedge against inflation; while rich collectors saw them as a currency in their own right, more reliable than pounds, dollars or even yen. The key brokers were the two old London auction-rooms, Sotheby's and Christie's, which had both become public companies, and extended their networks through America and Europe. They related paintings to money much more closely through hype,

*Tom Wolfe: 'The Worship of Art: Notes on the New God', *Harpers*, October 1984.
†Interview in London, February 28, 1989.

snobbery and black-tie auctions. Fastidious and well-tailored men with fruity accents presided over the discreet transfers from old wealth to new; while the Sotheby Index established convincing statistics which helped to stimulate the idea of paintings as investments like shares, and encouraged a profitable confusion of values. Sotheby's became still more linked to international finance when it was bought by the American billionaire property-dealer Alfred Taubman, who had made his first fortune with garages and shopping malls. 'Alf' Taubman was now stealing a march on all rival collectors: for he was buying not only art but the brokers and sellers of art. Sotheby's was increasingly criticised – particularly by the dealers whom the auction-rooms by-passed – for encouraging a crude equation between art and money. Lord Gowrie, the urbane chairman in London who had been Minister of Arts under Mrs Thatcher, echoed some of the worries:

> I share some of the concerns about a lot of interest in art prices, compared with the lonely business of getting to grips with paint and canvas . . . We suffer to some degree from too much information. We know more about what is going on, in any given market or indeed any given set of studios, round the world than we ever did.*

The art market was interlocked with the financial system as foreign buyers came to London and New York. By the mid-eighties the auction-rooms were looking much more eagerly towards Japanese collectors fortified by the rising yen. American dealers mocked them for buying second-rate paintings by a few famous names – rather as Europeans mocked Americans a century earlier. But the Japanese often served as the underbidders – so much loved by the auctioneers – who pushed up the price eventually paid by the Europeans or Americans. They had their own reasons for choosing paintings – particularly Impressionists and specially Van Gogh whom they likened to the old Japanese woodblock purists. In 1987 one of Van Gogh's paintings of sunflowers was sold at Christie's in London for £24.7 million ($39.9 million) to the Yasuda Fire and Marine insurance company in Tokyo. There was a bitter irony in the record sum paid for the work of an artist who had been close to starvation. Westerners depicted the *Sunflowers* as a crude ploy of corporate publicity, a company logo; and even the Japanese Ministry of Finance publicly criticised Yasuda. It was left to Keizo Saji, the maverick president of

*Interview, February 28, 1989.

the Suntory whisky company, to come to Yasuda's defence. 'It was none of their business. Moreover it was a much more productive use of money than putting it into real-estate.'* The chairman of Yasuda, Yasuo Goto, insists that his motives were artistic. He had already bought paintings by the Japanese Seiji Togo, by Grandma Moses, and by Impressionists: 'I didn't think of investments at all.' When he first saw *Sunflowers* in Christie's gallery in Japan he was, he explains, 'amazed by the power and brightness – by what I would call its courage and passion'. Goto sees companies rather than individuals as the collectors of the future, and insists that 'the top-class companies should have power and morals. Power represents the best accomplishments and morals represent culture . . . Companies which don't put money into the cultural fields – which have nothing to do with making money – can't be regarded as top-rank companies.'† The painting now hangs in the company gallery at the top of the Yasuda skyscraper in Tokyo, in suitable splendour: when I saw it, it was surrounded by Impressionists from the Hermitage in Leningrad which Goto had arranged to borrow.

In New York in the meantime the more daring collectors were exploring the uncharted new jungle of contemporary paintings. Already in the sixties pictures by living painters were fetching prices comparable with Old Masters – for the first time since the Victorian era – and in the seventies the prices of some contemporary painters shot up faster than any others. It produced great excitement, but also anxiety.

> Never before [as the critic, Robert Hughes, reflected in 1984] have the visual arts been the subject – beneficiary or victim, depending on your view of the matter – of such extreme inflation and fetishization . . . What we are seeing, in the last years of the twentieth century, is a kind of environmental breakdown in the art world. It is caused, as breakdowns customarily are, by a combination of shrinking resources and exploding population.‡

It was pop art in the fifties and sixties which first attracted rich collectors. 'The awakening of the pop art movement was a national awakening,' said Ivan Karp, the owner of the O. K. Harris Gallery in New York who was one of the pioneer dealers in the SoHo district. 'It was basically an emblem or a symbol of America's coming to self-confidence: about its prosperity, about its world role, about its

*See profile by Ian Rodger, in *Financial Times*, October 15, 1988.
†Interview in Tokyo, September 19, 1988.
‡Robert Hughes: 'On Art and Money', *New York Review of Books*, December 6, 1984.

power. It was a very optimistic movement, pop art.' But Karp has his worries about the motives of some of his clients: 'There's a great deal of money out there, and it's uninformed money. There's a lot of ignorant buying, and it's distorting things. It makes for a current of distress just below the surface.'*

The archetypal collectors of the sixties were Bob and Ethel Sokolnikoff, later Scull, who had made a fortune out of taxicabs. Bob Scull (as he put it) fell 'head over heels in love' with pop art in 1961 and became obsessed with collecting, with the help of Leo Castelli, the Italian-born New York dealer, who introduced them to avant-garde painters including Frank Stella, Roy Lichtenstein and Andy Warhol. The Sculls were as interested in the painters as their paintings; Ethel invited them (all except Rothko who refused to let her up to his studio) to their East Hampton house: 'My children grew up knowing all these great men.' Above all they collected Jasper Johns, who set successive records for the highest prices for contemporary artists. 'I mean, this man was my whole life. There wasn't a thing that he ever painted that I didn't want to grab.' The Sculls were much mocked for their social climbing and avant-garde entertainment. Tom Wolfe described one of their parties where 200 celebrities watched a film, which ended – in keeping with anal theories – with the emergence of an enormous human turd.† But they helped to transform art collecting and Ethel could look down on the less adventurous collectors who followed: 'They're doctors and dentists and God knows what people, from out of the woodwork they're coming.' The Sculls' partnership ended in a bitter divorce in which Ethel fought hard to get her share of the paintings: eventually she won ten paintings, including five Johns, which were sold in 1986 for 4.8 million dollars.‡

New art attracted new money. One of the most prominent collectors is Asher Edelman, a fast-moving financier and arbitrageur who sees himself as avant-garde in both business and art. He buys and sells companies in an office decorated by Reinhardt, Basquiat and David Salle, and prefers the company of artists and dancers to businessmen.§ 'I think it's essential for me in life,' he insists; 'when I go anywhere or I am anywhere, or when I work or when I rest, to have my eyes rest on something that is beautiful.' Edelman sees some

*Interview in New York, November 12, 1988.
†Tom Wolfe: *New York Magazine*, October 30, 1966.
‡Doris Saatchi: 'Keeping up with the Johnses', *Vanity Fair*, May 1987.
§See *Business Week*, October 27, 1987.

connection between his collecting of art and money: 'A successful financier makes very specific, precise and accurate commitments: and looking at art requires that same type of discipline. But it isn't the eye, it's the discipline that brings you to the looking.'*

The most controversial contemporary collector has been Charles Saatchi, the co-founder of the global advertising agency based in London. Charles became interested in photo-realism in the early seventies with his then wife Doris, a more serious art scholar, and rapidly extended his collection into a succession of styles; by 1985 he had converted an old paint factory in Kilburn, North London, to create a much-publicised gallery. The high political profile of the agency made him an easy target for attack from the left: it had advertised the Conservative Party in Britain and had promoted the apartheid government in South Africa through a subsidiary. The artistic complaint against Saatchi was that he treated paintings like commodities, which could be hoarded to drive the price up. 'They're not collectors, they're accumulators,' Hoving said about the Saatchis. 'They buy whole outputs and whole studios . . . I don't think that counts. It's really rather a second-rate way of collecting.'† 'We call it the shotgun style of collecting,' said Karp. 'If you fire enough pellets in a number of directions you are going to hit some good things . . . Much of his own blitzkrieg type of purchasing is very ignorant purchasing.'‡

Collectors certainly found new excitements in the contemporary art scene, with its combination of high risk, fashion and theatre. But the paintings themselves were often secondary. As Karp puts it:

> I think a lot of people who become involved with the contemporary art scene enjoy the social fabric. They like the mystery, the intrigue, the personalities: they can meet the artist, they meet the dealer. There are wonderful occasions, there are openings at the museums to attend, splendiferous occasions sometimes, the auctions are very dramatic theatrical events . . . The larger portion of people who buy art at any time are not visually literate. People buy art because they feel they should ornament their lives to bring a kind of a sense of meaningful additions, an order to a life that's been ripened, that's become more prosperous.§

*Interview in New York, November 17, 1988.
†Interview, November 21, 1988.
‡Interview, November 12, 1988.
§Interview, ibid.

What did the painters themselves think about the surge of new money? A few became as obsessed with money as many of the collectors, if not more so. Andy Warhol, who broke so many taboos against sex, drugs or social restraint, did most to break the taboo against art being linked to money. He had begun his career in advertising and window-displays, he was well-attuned to marketing and trends and a shrewd businessman. He called his studio a factory and insisted that money-making was itself an art form. When the pop art movement was first taking off and he needed inspiration he was offered an idea for 50 dollars by a small gallery owner Muriel Latow. When he paid the money, Muriel asked him: 'What do you love more than anything else?' He did not know. 'Money,' she replied. 'Why don't you paint money?'*

Painting money had its own curious social history. Artists had traditionally avoided such a bleak subject, and Renaissance artists had usually only depicted gold and coins as warnings against greed, as in Morgan's *Triumph of Avarice*. But in America in the late nineteenth century a group of painters had begun to paint bank-notes, in a social climate with resemblances to the money-mania of the late twentieth century. The first of the school, William Harnett, produced a trompe l'oeil picture of a five-dollar bill in 1877 – when the civil war and inflation had discredited the new paper currency. Harnett was followed by a still more skilful painter of bank-notes, John Haberle, and both were watched and warned by the Federal Secret Service who suspected they were actual counterfeiters. Other money-painters had more radical motives, including Victor Dubreuil who painted *The Cross of Gold* which showed greenbacks and paper 'silver certificates' pinned down in the shape of a crucifix – echoing the great populist speech of William Jennings Bryan about the Cross of Gold at that time. The motives of these weird painters were varied. But they all appeared obsessively concerned with money as a kind of substitute for religion, while the trompe l'oeil provided its own commentary on money: that it is not as real as it looks.†

The early money-painters acquired a new vogue in 1988 when the Berry-Hill Galleries in New York put on an exhibition. 'Our own passion for and about money,' wrote Bruce Chambers in the catalogue, 'is a major reason for our growing intrigue with the money-painters.' Among the guests at the opening two contemporary painters shared a similar fascination: Barton Benes, an American

*Quoted by Calvin Tomkins in John Coplans, *Andy Warhol*, Graphic Society, New York.
†For an analysis see Bruce W. Chambers: *Old Money: American Trompe L'Oeil Images of Currency*, Berry-Hill Galleries, New York, 1988.

sculptor who creates images out of dollar-bills, and Stephen Boggs, an American living in London who draws pictures of money which he then sells to shopkeepers in exchange for goods. Like his predecessors Boggs has been arrested and acquitted on charges of counterfeiting; and he insists there is a connection between money-painting and social upheaval: 'In societies that get overheated to a dangerous point, the art community starts to get a little overheated – which it has done.'*

Andy Warhol back in the sixties had already become the most famous painter of money. He had taken Muriel Latow's advice and turned out paintings of dollar-bills which became his first pop art success, followed by Campbell's soup tins and mass-produced famous faces. Opinions remain fiercely divided as to whether he was an ephemeral freak or an historic influence who changed everyone's perceptions. But certainly he changed perceptions about money including those of other painters. 'I think Andy was honest about the personal, social, political relationship one-for-one with the public,' said Robert Rauschenberg. 'He shook everything up. There was never any way that you could measure what is a good Warhol, and I always admired that.'† 'Warhol was the most relaxed of the artists about his participation in the economics of art,' said Ivan Karp. 'He never decried the pleasure that he felt from selling something. He said this is an object that I make, and I am offering it to the world and if they give me something that they have for what I have made, this is a wonderful thing.'‡ Warhol was not the first painter to turn art into a business, and the boom in contemporary art would have continued without him; but he helped to break down the barriers. His Midas Touch lived on after him: his money-paintings changed hands for more and more money. It was a tribute to his flair, but it provided a bleak commentary on the age, as though money were unable to escape from money: the final nightmare of Midas.

And by the late eighties the relationship between money and art appeared to be crazier, as the rich were competing still more frenziedly for a few contemporary painters. One week in New York in November 1988 broke all records, when Christie's and Sotheby's sold 1,404 works of art for 443 million dollars, including 17 million dollars paid for Jasper Johns' painting *False Start* by Sy Newhouse, the publishing billionaire. Art collecting was becoming like a freakish extension of world finance. 'The art market, following the financial markets,

**New York Times*, December 4, 1988.
†Interview in New York, November 18, 1988.
‡Interview, November 12, 1988.

has become globally integrated,' commented the economist Henry Kaufman. 'The limited supply of art creates an enormous distortion of price behaviour. When lots of people want one painting and they have the resources, what's the market?'* The economic distortion was mixed with psychological distortion, as the ritual of the big auctions generated a mounting hysteria.

Living painters were very ambivalent, and only very few had become part of this global market. 'We're all happy when our works sell for 400 times what they went for originally,' said Roy Lichtenstein, after one of his paintings was sold for 2 million dollars. 'But it also worries me. The higher prices go, the fewer people can have your work.'† Successful painters who are still active can wryly observe their own earlier rebellious works become part of the new currency of status and investment. (Lord Gowrie observes that collectors like to buy the works of painters who were rebels when they were young.) But ageing artists who are no longer creative can watch with some bitterness as pictures they once sold very cheaply are sold and resold by the rich who pay nothing to them.

The artist who despises money, though favoured by novels, has always been rare. Art has always needed money, and money has wanted art: most great painters have enjoyed spending money and have been glad to accept it from rich people, even if they hate them. Van Gogh, the most tragically penniless, had no illusions about the value of money: 'If one has more ambition and love of money than love,' he wrote to his brother Theo, 'in my opinion there is something wrong with that man.' But he added: 'If a man has only love and does not know how to earn money, there is something wrong in him also.' And he admitted to Theo: '"Greed" is a very ugly word. But that demon does not let anybody alone, and I should be greatly astonished if it had not sometimes tempted you and me, even so that for the moment we were inclined to say: "Money is the ruler".'‡ William Blake was scornful of money: 'He feared nothing so much as being rich,' wrote his friend John Linnell after his death, 'lest he should lose his spiritual riches.'§ But even Blake, who died in penury, accepted that he could have achieved more with more money – as he movingly explained in one of his notes:

> Some people and not a few artists have asserted that the painter of this picture would not have done so well if he had been properly

*New York Times, November 26, 1988.

†New York Times, ibid.

‡Irving Stone (ed): *Dear Theo*, Signet, New York, 1969, pp.67, 73, 105.

§Frederick Tatham: *Life of William Blake*, Methuen, London, 1906, p.xiv.

> encouraged. Let those who think so, reflect on the state of nations under poverty and their incapability of art; tho' art is above either, the argument is better for affluence than poverty; and tho' he would not have been a greater artist, yet he would have produced greater works of art in proportion to his means.*

Today's artists, even the Bohemian and unconventional, are unlikely to share Blake's dread of being rich. As Rauschenberg put it: 'An artist doesn't have to be poor. It doesn't mean he's any less great because he is poor. But [being poor] is not an essential quality, and I do think that that kind of myth still somehow exists in people; like keep 'em barefoot and pregnant.'† Rauschenberg was one of the pioneers of pop art with his friends Warhol and Johns. He noticed with special interest his painting *Rebus* being sold for 6.3 million dollars in 1988, for he had vainly campaigned for legislation to allow painters to keep a proportion of the subsequent profits from selling their own work. 'For the most part it's not the collector who encourages the value of particular artworks,' he complained, 'it's the continued labour and struggles of the artist.' He is disgusted by the art buyer's sense of superiority over the artist, and he feels very ambivalent about the record price for his own earlier works, which he thinks actually frustrates the market for his current paintings which are quite different. 'It seems to me to be so exaggerated now that I don't know how I can follow as a live artist, because I certainly can't raise my prices the way Sotheby's can.' He is disgusted by the impersonality and detachment of the art market:

> I would rather have people who had some idea about art and some sensibility: a little more intimate than investment. In the very early days, when I was surrounded by contemporaries who didn't want this person to have a painting because they didn't understand it, I said: maybe their maid will . . .
>
> I still feel that art is basically communication, and if some grocery boy walks through this place here and has some kind of revelation, it's worth it. But when it gets so exaggerated, you would rather have just maybe a few friends sharing your own sensibility.‡

More radical painters, who explicitly attack the capitalist system, face ironies as they encounter the new flood of money. Leon Golub – who teaches at an American state university – has painted menacing

*Blake, Rossetti MS: 'A Vision of the Last Judgment', c.1810.
†*New York Times*, November 26, 1988.
‡Interview, November 18, 1988.

pictures of mercenaries, as symbols of unscrupulous governments' power, which have been bought by prominent capitalists including Charles Saatchi. Golub suspects that some of his collectors may see themselves as mercenaries or buccaneers who can manoeuvre their power, but he insists that paintings, wherever they are hung 'still have their striking power'. And he is resigned to artists being dependent on rich patrons:

> Art has this kind of history of prestige, of being controlled by the people who control the society, the world. It also maintains a certain kind of independence, we hope . . . Art serves power, and artists are aware of this, and artists try to get on to the power chain. They try to enter the system: they know just what they're doing . . . It's a false distinction to see the artist as pure and the society in which he is selling his work as impure.*

What do the rich collectors really find in their quest? Certainly a love of painting does not necessarily imply other qualities. 'I have to say that I've met some real horrors with wonderful eyes,' says Lord Gowrie. 'I don't think that having a good eye for painting necessarily makes you a nicer person.'† Most of the richest collectors still appear driven by commercial competitiveness, and a desire for posthumous glory, rather than a deep interest in paintings, or encouraging painters themselves as the Medici did. As Hanna Segal puts it: 'If they contend that they transform the money into beauty the way the patrons used to they are quite wrong. Because the objects they buy are already made; they don't help a young artist actually to produce.'‡

Even the immortality is somewhat unpredictable: your name on a museum will perpetuate your family's name, but it attracts attention to its misdeeds. The name of Whitney is associated with contemporary art, but also with the man who was jailed for fraud after the great crash of 1929. The name of Paul Getty has been reviled as much as revered through his vast endowment to the Malibu museum.

In their own lifetimes few of the new rich appear to achieve the kind of peace and serenity that emanates from their paintings. Having spent so much time concentrating their minds like searchlights on the details of money and prices, they find it hard to look at their paintings without thinking of their money-values. They remain driven by the kind of demonic energy and restlessness which is never easily satisfied. While they compete for beautiful paintings they show less

*Interview, November 12, 1988.
†Interview, February 28, 1989.
‡Interview, March 30, 1989.

interest in beauty in the wider sense, or in townscapes and the surrounding environment. And the art market ignores altogether the pleasures of life that carry no price-tag, like the beauties of nature, which are free.

The contest for famous masterpieces was part of the frenzy of the eighties when so much money had been made so quickly, and was looking for some kind of recognition. But it was also part of a broader escapism: for the new money was more detached from the social realities of the rest of the world – where the need for new money was increasingly desperate.

CHAPTER THIRTEEN

THE END OF THE LINE

To the hungry man do not give your fish. Give a fishing-rod.

CHINESE PROVERB

The mission of a manufacturer is to overcome poverty.

KONOSUKE MATSUSHITA

As Western spenders extend their motivations and desires round the rich countries, so the gap widens with the rest of the world. Supermarkets overflowing with designer brands, scented bathsalts or flavoured pet-foods contrast still more sharply with shack-shops with bare shelves or tiny markets in the sand selling single cigarettes. While Western factories turn out more and more temporary luxuries, the poor countries still lack the basic needs for health and survival – clean water, sanitation, cheap tractors or hospitals. The high-speed global system of synchronised factories, sophisticated marketing and competitive consumption peters out into stagnation on the edge of the world.

The two faces of Christmas – the season of frenzied acquisitiveness and the season of compassion – become still more at odds, while the consumer fantasies look still more unreal against the realities of poverty. As the Pope said in his New Year message of January 1988:

> Side by side with the miseries of underdevelopment, themselves unacceptable, we find ourselves up against a form of *superdevelopment*, equally inadmissible, because like the former it is contrary to what is good and to true happiness. This superdevelopment, which consists in an *excessive* availability of every kind of material goods for the benefit of certain social groups, easily makes people slaves of 'possession' and of immediate gratification, with no other horizon than the multiplication or continual replacement of the things already owned with others still better. This is the so-called civilisation of 'consumption' or 'consumerism' which involves so much 'throwing-away' and 'waste'.

> An object already owned but now superseded by something better is discarded, with no thought of its possible lasting value in itself, nor of some other human being who is poorer.*

The consumer society shows its ironies in the enclaves of luxury tourism within the Third World. Rich Western tourists long to 'get away from it all', away from the pressures and disciplines of money and time, back to a simple life still symbolised by thatched huts, grass skirts and empty beaches: while the tourist industry conspires to provide appropriate settings and staff. Yet the resorts are themselves managed by the most intricate industrial system, linked into computer-booking, airline discounts and packaged tours, supplied with imported food. And beyond the palisades the real life of the country is far from idyllic, as locals rummage in the hotel dustbins for their food. The frontier is fraught with cross-purposes. While tourists are trying to cut down their eating and drinking, and to escape from industrial society, the locals desperately want to become part of it. While the tourists want to forget about money, the locals are desperate to find it. But in reality, the Westerners are part of an elaborate system of bank accounts, salaries, credits and loans, from which the rest of the world is excluded. In the words of John Reed of Citicorp:

> There are 5 billion people living on earth. Probably 800 million of them live within societies that are 'bankable' and probably 4.2 billion are living within societies that in some very fundamental way are not bankable. I think it's a great danger as we look out between now and the turn of the century that this distinction between the bankable and the unbankable parts of the world could become more aggravated. We're forming this global economy which is very much a phenomenon of the northern hemisphere – Europe, North America, Japan – with some small additions . . . Many of the problems we have on the globe, be it the global environment or health, are problems of the 4.2 billion, not the 800 million.†

Across the frontiers of the bankers' world, money becomes so scarce that it goes back to its original purpose, as the basic medium of minimal exchange. In Africa, which has been left out of so much of the transformation of the eighties, most of the population still deals with no money at all: they survive on a subsistence economy,

*Pope John Paul II: *Sollicitudo Rei Socialis*, Holy See, 1988.
†Interview, May 9, 1989.

with no savings, no stockpiles, no credit or banks. When they use coins they are for necessities. Most of the money is purely local, with a medley of national currencies which date back only to the nations' independence, whose exchange with each other is complex and expensive. When contract workers come home after their stint in another country, they often arrive with notes and coins concealed all over their person, like walking banks.

The fundamental contrast is between surplus and waste, and shortages and starvation; and it has become much more visible to the rich countries through the rapid expansion of their communications, including TV, jet planes and satellites, which can reveal the full extent of famine and starvation. The new technologies can move information instantly: satellites in space can detect potential crop failures and famines before they have happened; and television can project the images of famine into thousands of millions of homes. For the first time in history, people know what is happening at the other end of the world, *while* it is happening.

> Several times in the 1980s a world-wide public has shown that it is not prepared to accept the sight of children suffering and dying on its television screens in the 'loud emergencies' of drought or famine. That reaction itself represents a fundamental change in ethos from times when famine or natural disaster were accepted as inevitable . . .*

The effect can be powerful but often simplistic – and too late. 'There is no better spur to tangible action,' said a recent report on famine in 1985, 'than beaming starving people in the South via television into the living rooms of the North. But it is a sad and belated way of making the point.'†

The inability of the rich countries to reduce world poverty through the years of their boom marked the most fundamental failure in the economic management of the eighties. The World Bank, which regarded the reduction of poverty as their main goal, had to recognise both a moral and an economic disaster. As its president Barber Conable put it in September 1988:

> Poverty on today's scale prevents a billion people from having even minimally acceptable standards of living. To allow every fifth human being on our planet to suffer such an existence is a moral outrage.

*Peter Adamson: *State of the World's Children*, UNICEF, 1989
†*Famine: a Man-made Disaster*, A report for the Independent Commission on International Humanitarian Studies, Pan, London, 1985.

> It is more: it is bad economics, a terrible waste of precious development resources. Poverty destroys lives, human dignity, and economic potential. It must be fought with resolution and overcome with sustainable growth.*

The inability to connect up the surpluses of the richer countries with the desperate needs of the poorer ones appeared still more glaring with the improvements in transport. The fact that food could be flown out very quickly in huge cargo planes to remote corners of Africa showed up all the more exasperatingly the political problems of getting it through to the people who needed it. 'Who has ever seen a starving military officer or merchant, let alone aid worker?' asked the report on famine. 'It is a question of who has access to that food.'† There have been many famines in which sufficient food has been available close by: and the Indian economist Amartya Sen has shown the importance of democracy and free communications to provide the mechanism by which people have an entitlement to food from their government; which India has achieved but China has not.

The ease with which goods *can* travel across the continent is revealed by the one kind of product which most rich countries are always glad to sell, and poor countries to buy: weapons. Through the eighties arms sales became still more important to the national economies of not only industrialised nations but many developing countries – led by Brazil and China who have each sold billions of dollars worth of weapons to the Third World, including both Iran and Iraq. The mobility of arms marked a deadly contrast with the immobility of people, food or development projects. If the incentives to export and maintain hospitals, granaries or tractors had been half as strong as the incentives to sell arms, the developing world could have faced a much more hopeful future. 'It is a terrible irony,' as Willy Brandt wrote in his introduction to the Brandt Report on Third World problems in 1980, 'that the most dynamic and rapid transfer of highly sophisticated equipment and technology from rich to poor countries has been in the machinery of death.'‡ Or as the Pope put it in 1988:

> We are thus confronted with a strange phenomenon: while economic aid and development plans meet with the obstacle of

*Address to the Board of Governors of the World Bank: Berlin, September 27, 1988.

†*Famine*, op cit, p.63.

‡*North–South, a Programme for Survival*, Pan, London, 1980, p.14. (I served as its editorial adviser.)

> insuperable ideological barriers, and with tariff and trade barriers, *arms* of whatever origin circulate with almost total freedom all over the world.*

But to bring food to whole populations, and to build up their own food supply, required much more fundamental solutions than arms salesmen or military officers could produce. It required peace and political settlements, and effective popular pressure and monitoring which could only come from some kind of democratic representation. But it also required commercial motivations which ensured that farmers had sufficient reason to grow more food and to ensure that it was properly distributed. This basic motivation of money had been visibly lacking in the continent which had become the chief disaster-area of the eighties, Africa. And in the meantime the rich countries had lost confidence in their ability to solve the problems with money.

The disillusion with aid became much more visible through the eighties. At the beginning of the decade the Brandt Report called for urgent emergency action, including additional aid of 4 billion dollars a year, to stem the growing starvation and poverty; but it was met with scepticism in America and most of Western Europe; and in the following years many Western governments decreased their aid budgets, complaining that most aid had been wasted and insisting that Africans must now help themselves. As Paul Volcker described the problem of Africa in 1988:

> I don't think you're going to do it by giving money away. We've tried that . . . To really get these countries moving with momentum and some lasting quality, they're going to have to do it themselves, in very large part. They've got to have the institutions, the psychology, the injector, the ideology . . . they've got to have reasonably effective coherent government. It hasn't got much relationship to how much aid they have got.†

It was certainly true that huge sums of money had been diverted and misused by African governments; and that the wastage and corruption had been insufficiently revealed and confronted. But what was striking about the failures of aid to Africa, as in the build-up of debt in Latin America, was the willing connivance of the richer countries in projects and policies which were visibly unproductive at

*Pope John Paul II, op cit.
†Interview, November 19, 1988.

the time. Both receivers and givers were caught up in a process which was curiously detached from any realistic attitude to money.

The lack of realism in the new African nations went back to their origins after the Second World War. In the fifties and sixties the former imperial powers hastily granted independence to their colonies without enough forethought or preparation; and in a political mood which combined guilt, relief and short-term opportunism. Africa became a political laboratory in which idealistic European politicians and economists encouraged new black leaders to experiment with state planning and Utopias much more boldly than they could in their own continent. But they were not just socialist Utopias. Both conservatives and socialists, Europeans and Americans, were inclined to romanticise Africa, influenced by the past history of slavery and exploitation, by the idealism of the Second World War and the Atlantic Charter. Many politicians liked to see the Africans as having the kind of innocence and freedom from greed that they never expected among their own people, and to provide aid without thinking very seriously about how it would be used.

In fact Africa presented all kinds of obstacles to the easy flow of funds to its people. The new nationalism, often within too-small nations built round illogical colonial frontiers, split the continent into awkward and often unviable units. Western countries poured aid to the governments, not to the people; and the new African élite was concentrated in the towns, ambitious to build up industrial states, rather than to improve agriculture. The town-dwellers wanted cheap food above everything, so the governments set food prices too low to provide money-incentives to the farmers; and food producers – unlike those in the rest of the developing world – failed to keep pace with the rapidly rising populations. But the aid-giving countries gladly connived. They readily agreed to build ambitious industrial projects – steelworks, dams, airports, convention centres – which suited their own business interests and contractors much better than more modest and difficult plans to grow more food. The donor and receiver governments entered into a convenient relationship which excluded the interests of most of the population, and the central problems of poverty.

Even without man-made mistakes the new African nations faced intractable economic problems which they could not resolve alone. They needed to import food and bare necessities to lift themselves up from absolute poverty; yet many of the commodities which provided their basic exports were losing their value. And most of the continent was still subject to the natural disasters and erratic communications which had been a large cause of its original backwardness. In the arid regions on the edge of the desert, the multiplying population was generating a vicious circle, using up the topsoil and the trees so that the desert encroached still further – which was not only catastrophic to the local people but a danger to the whole global ecology. But these urgent problems were not helped by the grandiose aid projects.

Most of the ambitious industrial projects proved useless without markets to sell their products: they stood deserted like 'cathedrals in the desert' and monuments to false hopes. Hotels and convention centres merely helped to serve an unproductive bureaucracy and housed elaborate diplomatic jamborees led by the meetings of the Organisation of African Unity. For some countries international diplomacy became the only major industry, mostly financed by aid money, so that one group of diplomats was paying for another: in 1980 Sierra Leone spent two-thirds of its annual budget on the OAU summit.* The dream of an Africa which would rapidly join the industrialised world soon collapsed, giving way to the reality of an exploding population which was still less able to grow its own food.

The newly independent African nations had been determined to control their own national economies: but they found they were less and less able to control the serious movements of money. They desperately needed hard currencies – whether dollars, sterling or yen – to provide the precious links with the outside world, and they imposed exchange controls with great effort to stop foreign money leaving their country. But multinationals could adjust their accounts within their own company, underpricing their exports from an African country, and overpricing their imports, to avoid having too much local currency; while some companies like Lonrho, the ubiquitous African multinational, had enough political influence with black leaders to be allowed to get money out. 'If you've got muscle,' says their director Paul Spicer, 'you can talk to the government and come to an understanding . . .'† But the more serious drain on hard currencies was through the pervasive networks of the unofficial economy.

The incentives of money were still asserting themselves in an underground black market which had been estimated at half of black Africa's total economic activity – making nonsense of the official

*Martin Meredith: *The First Dance of Freedom*, Abacus, London, 1985, p.310.
†*South* magazine, October 1988.

statistics of the World Bank and the IMF. Intricate smuggling, money-dealing and money-changing have defied the formal frontiers. Togo, which mines no gold, has exported 150 million dollars worth of gold in a year – smuggled from its neighbours Ghana or Niger. Brazzaville in the Congo, which produces no diamonds, has exported millions of dollars worth of the stones, which cross the river at night from Kinshasa in Zaire. Small countries like Gambia or Djibouti depend on smuggled goods and currencies for much of their national income. Lomé, the capital of Togo, is now reported to be the centre of the West African black market, with an unofficial money-clearing house on the beach which can exchange most currencies.* The black-market routes between nations, across rivers, lakes or the sea, provide the trade-links through the continent which the national frontiers have sought to prevent. Small aircraft landing in forest airstrips or unnamed tankers docking at night, can carry long-distance illicit trade, including arms from South Africa across the continent, and oil in return. There is no lack of ingenuity among African entrepreneurs, switching between currencies and commodities: 'Such sophistication and mobility,' says one observer of the underground economy, Howard Schissel, 'should make Wall Street arbitrageurs blush.'†

In the eighties both Africans and Westerners had to recognise that they could only revive the continent's fortunes through the basic motivations of money – all down the line. The donors had often forgotten that the poorest people, as much as anyone else, need commercial incentives. They had given away food to starving regions in ways which all too easily undermined the local money-system; and they had learnt painfully that effective aid has to be very closely linked to the kind of equipment, people and education that could lead to a self-sustaining economy. Credit and rudimentary banking systems were now seen as the key to agricultural improvements: farmers needed credit to buy equipment, and the Chinese agricultural miracle of the eighties depended heavily on credit schemes which brought more peasants into the market economy. 'The main attraction of credit,' said the famine report, 'is that used intelligently it gives the borrower a power over its use which as a beneficiary of free aid, he, or she, never has.'‡ By the eighties most African states were beginning to change their priorities, to recognise the necessity of reviving agricultural production through proper incentives. They had virtually

*'Africa's Underground Economy', *Africa Report*, New York, January–February 1989.
†Ibid.
‡*Famine*, op cit, p.136.

abandoned the first faith in state enterprise and controls. 'The primacy accorded the state,' said the declaration of the Organisation of African Unity in 1985, 'has hindered rather than furthered economic development.'

But however much more realism Africans had acquired, and however much more food they could grow, many of them would continue to depend on the generosity of the industrialised world for their survival. Africans still wanted above all to become part of the world's economic system; but they seemed further away from it than ever.

In the seventies Africans could still hope that the growing prosperity of the richer countries would eventually help the poorer countries, as they became linked into the global system of trade. The more the rich consumed, the more they would need the raw materials which only the poor countries possessed. The multinational corporations would look still further afield for cheap labour, and more products would be made in Africa for export back to Europe. The 'world factories' of the future would stretch still further afield, bringing together components wherever they could be made most cheaply.

When the global boom of the eighties got under way, the rich countries *did* benefit some poorer countries – but only a few. The chief beneficiaries were the countries in South East Asia which were close to the Japanese market, which were favoured by multinationals, and whose people had the education and skills to become part of the manufacturing system. The 'Tigers' – Korea, Hong Kong, Singapore and Taiwan – had already (as Lee Kuan Yew put it) 'plugged into the international grid'. Now Thailand, Malaysia, Indonesia and even the Philippines were joining the escalator, providing cheap labour to make shirts, radios or air-conditioners for the richer countries.

But the boom was far less global than the developing countries had hoped. The rich countries never generated the surging demand for raw materials which the poorer ones had counted on. The most valuable commodity in the developing world, oil, was back in glut. The old mainstays of heavy industry, like copper, bauxite or iron ore, lost much of their demand in the new computerised industrial revolution. Still more seriously, the multinational corporations became much more automated, robotised and capital-intensive, so that the cost of labour for many of their products, including cars, became less important. The corporations were less inclined to venture further abroad, and some retreated back home where they were closer to their main market – particularly America. Industry and capital were becoming still more mobile: but people were as static as ever.

By the end of the eighties the world was looking less like a single market-place, and more like three competing markets – North America, Western Europe, and East Asia – each stretching out to their closer neighbours for both workers and customers. The world factory was giving way to the regional factory; but the factory became more demanding as it became more disciplined and interconnected, and less developed countries found it still more difficult to acquire the skills. The multinational corporations, the old bogeymen of the sixties and seventies, were now being courted and wooed as the bringers of technology and training. It brought a new poignancy to the saying: 'If there's one thing worse than being exploited by a multinational corporation, it's not being exploited.'

The new economic atlas left out huge areas and populations from its money-maps, as if they had dropped out of the world – including most of China and India and Russia. And it omitted almost the whole of one continent: Africa. Most of the old commodities which had provided Africa's trade for centuries – whether spices from Zanzibar, jute from Tanzania, cocoa from Ghana or copper from Zaire and Zambia – were now in oversupply or superseded. Africa's prospects of manufacturing exports were strictly limited by the automation of world industry, and its remoteness from rich markets. And Africa was now increasingly left off the main traffic routes. Many coastal towns had acquired their first international stimulus as ports-of-call on the way between Europe and the East. Later the airlines had extended their own networks and disciplines to stopover airports on the way to Asia or South Africa. But now jumbos could fly non-stop to Bombay or Cape Town, and most of Africa was on the way to nowhere.

How can the continent ever rejoin the economic map of the world, and become part of the producing system? The multinational corporations hold many of the keys; for they, not governments or bankers, are the masters of producers. The wastage of so much aid and lending in Africa in earlier decades had resulted from its lack of connection with actual production, so that the money left little behind. And developing countries now have to depend still more heavily on the multinationals for their training, technology and access to world markets.

Many multinational heads, particularly the Japanese, accept in theory the responsibility to extend their technology and skills to help the poorest countries: Akio Morita of Sony, who joined the Live Aid rock show in Japan to appeal for aid to Africa, said afterwards:

> People are starving not only there, but in many other places on

earth, and yet I know there is the technology available to feed everybody . . . If we can figure out how to accomplish the task of feeding the world, we may end up with a population problem and a space problem, which might yet lead to another food problem. But I am optimistic enough to believe technology will solve all these problems.*

And the Japanese multinationals now face a special test and opportunity. Not only because they have shown themselves as the masters of new technologies, with a flexibility and adventurousness which Western corporations have lacked. But also because they, not their government, hold the massive surplus which can be deployed to help the developing world. Japan's position is quite different from that of the United States forty years ago, when the federal government held the huge surplus which they used to launch Marshall Aid for the recovery of Europe. In the words of Toyoo Gyohten of the Ministry of Finance:

It is the Japanese private companies who are making the surplus. I'm sure they're quite anxious to use those moneys for the expansion of their business or their further profit. They are motivated by those private capitalistic ideas. There are many areas where financial resources are needed not simply for those capitalistic maximum profit motives. So how can we bridge this discrepancy between the holder's position and what those needy persons or countries desire? In that sense governments and various international institutions can play a very important part.†

Japanese corporations traditionally put forward idealistic aims in their public statements, mottoes or company songs. Konosuke Matsushita, the grand old man of Japanese industry until he died in 1989 founded the electrical giant which includes Panasonic. He called his own collection of essays *Not for Bread Alone*, and he first outlined his business philosophy fifty-five years ago: 'the mission of a manufacturer is to overcome poverty . . .'‡ Such a mission is unlikely to be pursued on a global scale without much greater commercial incentive. Corporations responsible to shareholders are unlikely to forgo their profits in order to help the starving people in a distant and almost unknown continent. But there is now a clear opportunity, as Gyohten suggests, for some kind of discreet subsidy. The Japanese government

*Morita: *Made in Japan* op cit, p.252.
†Interview, September 8, 1988.
‡Konosuke Matsushita: *Not for Bread Alone*, PHP Institute, Kyoto, 1984, p.22.

has recently massively increased its budget for aid, not only to its neighbours in East Asia but also to Africa – which implies more genuine altruism. The linking of generous government aid to the skills of the private corporations may yet prove to be the most effective means to eliminate poverty in Africa in the nineties.

The Agony of Ghana

The future of Africa would depend largely on the attitudes of the Africans themselves, and particularly their relationships to money, which had been so often ignored in the past. The high cost of Africa's illusions about money can be summed up by the story of Ghana, the first and most prosperous of the black states to become independent after the Second World War. Ghana at first embodied all the optimism about Africa's future; then it went through successive coups and disasters; now it is heralded by the West as a showpiece of African realism and recovery. But it is more useful to hear the story through Ghanaians themselves.

When the British colony the Gold Coast became independent in 1957 and changed its name to Ghana, it provided a kind of pageant of cheerful expectation, as if it were going back to the youth of the world: at the independence celebrations even Vice-President Nixon appeared relaxed. The Prime Minister Kwame Nkrumah, with his resounding laugh, became the prophet of the 'African way of doing things', proclaiming his slogan: 'Seek Ye First the Political Kingdom'. The heady air of freedom distracted people from the real problems of the economy, and Ghana had large foreign reserves as a legacy from its colonial masters, which helped to conceal its mistakes. As Tsatu Tsikata, now an influential official, put it later:

> I recall the euphoria that even the little children in those days had about independence. Freedom was the great cry in '56 and '57 in Ghana: and that was one of the earliest words that some of us learnt in the English language. There was a really great feeling of relief that a great historical burden had been lifted. Perhaps within that euphoria lay the seeds of subsequent problems, because some of the problems about what to do about this newly won independence, what to use it to create, perhaps were glossed over in the mood of the time.*

*Interview in Accra, March 17, 1989.

Nkrumah enjoyed a honeymoon period with the Western nations, including the British Conservative government, who dispensed aid and loans for grand projects. When Harold Macmillan visited Ghana in 1960 – I watched him being rowed in a surf-boat on to the shore – it was still in the first glow of optimism. Market-mammies chanted their greetings, cocoa crops were booming, and European companies were extending credit, bribes and loans for dams, ports or hotels. Macmillan himself talked in Ghana about the 'wind of change' sweeping through Africa – before he repeated the phrase in South Africa – and reflected that Ghana was 'not more corrupt than is absolutely necessary'.*

But Nkrumah was not much interested in economic problems, and Ghana soon became the forerunner for economic disasters elsewhere: the projects collapsed, the cocoa price fell, the reserves were run down. The economic kingdom never followed the political kingdom. Nkrumah became a paranoid dictator, surrounded by cronies and incompetents, and was toppled by a coup which brought a military government to power for three years. He was followed by an ineffective university professor, Dr Kofi Busia, who faced appalling economic problems with declining cocoa prices and huge repayments of debt; and by 1972 he was in turn overthrown by General Acheampong whose government was economically naïve and increasingly corrupt, and who was in his turn toppled by his officers and succeeded by General Akufo-Addo. A year later Akufo was supplanted by junior officers led by Flight-Lieutenant Jerry Rawlings, a much more populist leader who had simplistic views about removing corruption: he executed generals, flogged market-traders and razed the main market in Accra to the ground. He promised a return to civilian rule which lasted only two years after which a confused coup brought Rawlings back to power. But in the meantime the economic hardship was now for the first time causing near-starvation, as revealed by the 'Rawlings chain'. As Tsikata describes it:

> The economic decline started from the middle seventies when the resources were really run down. We did find that we were reduced to imports of food which were barely animal feed. But by the early eighties with the drought and the bush fires, near-famine situations were reached in Ghana for the first time in many decades. The people really got very thin, and their collar-bones were showing. They even made a joke about it: they called it the chain, which was the chain around their necks. They really joke about it to survive, you understand . . .†

*Alistair Horne: *Macmillan 1957–1986*, Macmillan, London, 1989, pp.188–9.
†Interview, March 17, 1989.

It was in the early eighties that Ghanaians experienced their real moments of truth. In the words of P. V. Obeng, now chairman of the Committee of Secretaries in Rawlings' government:

> Food was so short that we had to hide food from our neighbours and friends which we never used to do before. After enduring so many years of unattained hopes for our independence a lot of us slipped into hopelessness. People's faith in themselves also got lost and a lot of our people began to see salvation in spiritualism.*

The breakdown of the economy brought about very personal conversions. The present Minister of Finance, Kwesi Botchwey, who had earlier been a hard-line socialist, described conditions before he instituted the reform programme:

> I had a terrible personal experience. My sister died in a hospital, just from a shortage of oxygen. I remember well: the nurses were standing by us, helpless, and some of them had seen this happen so much they were not particularly moved. When I asked them how oxygen could be short in the hospital, they gave me a long lecture which I dismissed as some ex-post-rationalisation of delinquent conduct. But it had a real effect on me. Three years after the programme, I have been back at the same hospital, and I've seen the change in the attitudes, the liveliness, and the greater commitment to work: which reinforces one's view that when economic conditions deteriorate, people get cynical, they don't care, they just want to live.†

The harshness of the conditions at last gave some greater realism. The IMF insisted that Ghana must take the most drastic steps before it received any further loans; and the Rawlings government now included ministers who were much better able to understand the economic realities. Botchwey persuaded Rawlings that he must accept the IMF's recommendations which included a rapid devaluation of the currency, heavy cuts in government offices and allowing food prices to increase.

After 1983 Ghana undoubtedly achieved remarkable improvements. The World Bank and the IMF, encouraged by the new policies, wanted to make Ghana a showcase for the rest of Africa. They opened up their own loans, and encouraged other banks to follow. Inflation dropped from over 200 per cent a year to below 30 per cent;

*Interview in Accra, March 16, 1989.
†Interview in London, March 5, 1989.

private businesses revived; and there were signs of greater individual enterprise. Botchwey claims that: 'the African view of money – of how to make money and sustain it – has changed from a longing for government handouts to a certain realisation now that yes we can make money provided the environment is right.'*

Most remarkably, the use of new technology was soon causing a rapid increase in food production. The project 'Global 2,000', which had been set up by a rich Japanese entrepreneur, Ryoichi Sasakawa, decided to choose Ghana as a test-case for agricultural experiments; and in 1986 it established demonstration plots in Northern Ghana to increase yields of maize and sorghum, led by a Korean agronomist, Dr Hong. He insists that 'the productivity of the major crops in many African countries can be tripled, quadrupled, even multiplied ten times'. And he has his own firm Asian idea of the need for self-sufficiency:

> Sometimes if you give money free, it can be dangerous: you make the people lazy and make them expect more and more. In Oriental countries we have a saying: to the hungry man do not give your fish itself, but give a fishing-rod. Even though countries may be poor, instead of trying to bring something directly it will be wise to try to show the people how they can make use of their own resources. That's why we are not giving anything free . . .†

The extent of the Ghanaian recovery was much debated. The process of adjustment, as the World Bank called the cutbacks, was cruel. The government had not accompanied its economic liberalism with political liberalism: there were still executions on the beach. The process of urbanisation went into reverse, as those who had come into the towns for secure jobs now found them taken away from them. As General Olusegun Obasanjo, Nigeria's former head of state, had warned:

> Adjustment is part of the process of existence of any human being or human institution. It is part of our daily experience. But adjustment must have a human face, human heart and milk of human kindness and must not ignore what I call human survival and dignity, issues of employment, food, shelter, education and health.‡

And behind the outward miracle, Ghana had now massively increased its dependence on financial support from the World Bank,

*Interview, ibid.
†Interview in Ghana, March 17, 1989.
‡Quoted by Professor Adu Boahen, see opposite.

the IMF and others. Over five years it had received no less than 2.6 billion dollars in aid, and it was still a long way from sustaining itself: much of the new business activity was linked to the machinery of aid. Botchwey insists that the conditions in Ghana are now so improved that aid can make it self-sustaining.

> If you put an egg and a stone in the same temperature for a given period the chicken will break out of the egg, but not the stone: because the internal conditions in the egg are very different from the stone's. The over-dependence on aid really depends on how the aid is used . . . If aid goes into sensible, well-costed projects, into expanding the export sector to enable the country not only to pay off debt, but to fund its own imports, then the aid is complementing processes of national development that are based on an internal dynamic. So, I don't see any real danger of over-dependence.*

But Ghana for the foreseeable future will depend on continuing flows of aid and foreign currency. And some Ghanaians are worried that it is losing its real independence as the international agencies move in: as Professor Adu Boahen put it in 1989:

> If we do not put an end to this reckless accumulation of foreign debts, we stand a great risk of being recolonised by the industrialised countries and their agencies in the near future. It should never be forgotten that one of the reasons for the scramble for and the partition of Africa was the need felt by the imperial countries to safeguard their investments and loans . . . How many IMF and World Bank experts do we have in both advisory and managerial positions in this country at this very moment? We are warned.†

Would Africans, with all their outgoing exuberance of spirit, really be able to follow the East Asians' example, with its much more ascetic tradition behind it? I asked Dr Botchwey:

> I don't think Africans have to be like Asians to redevelop their countries. One of the challenges of economic management is to instil in the people the sort of discipline and productivity drive that development must come with. I think it's possible to do this without Africans losing what you call their outgoing national characteristics.
>
> In Ghana people are beginning to learn more and more of this

*Botchwey: interview in London, ibid.
†'The Ghanaian Sphinx': J. B. Danquah Memorial Lectures, 1989.

> self-sacrifice . . . When people see their leaders themselves sacrificing the luxuries of office and see where the investments are going, then they are less grudgingly willing to postpone the current consumption and invest in the nation's future. But when they don't see public investments that make any sense, when they see their leaders squandering their wealth, stacking it away in accounts abroad, then I'm sure even the Asians would begin to lose a bit of this asceticism that we were talking about.*

But there still remain doubts, from Ghanaians as well as foreigners, as to whether tropical Africans will ever embrace the disciplines of money with the same willingness as thoroughly urbanised Westerners. Kwasi Ntansah, a foreign exchange dealer, whose trade is now legalised, has his own scepticism about money:

> In Europe everything is money: your life is money. The time here now is about 5.30, and it looks casual: people are so relaxed in their moves. In Europe at 5.30 they'd be underground, rushing up and down for buses or trains. There's a stress in it. Stress is not a known disease so far in Africa.
>
> Will money have a great impact on the life-pattern of Africa? I would doubt it very much, because Africans are by nature extremely religious. Here, no matter the difficulty one is going through, one always calls God. It becomes a very good psychological relief.
>
> Money is a religion. It is a cause. You worship it. If you do it in a stream it becomes dangerous, murderous. But once you can use it in moderation for the proper purposes for which money is made, then a great deal of pleasure and peace comes out of it.†

But however hard they work, and become more money-conscious, the Ghanaians still face a world economy which is stacked against them. They still depend for 70 per cent of their exports on cocoa, which is at the mercy of the international market-place, which can always bid one cocoa producer against another.

As Botchwey says:

> When you encourage families to produce more cocoa, you see the price collapsing. When you want to do some local processing, acquiring the technology is difficult. Even when you've acquired it and produced the manufactured chocolate you can't sell it because the countries you are dealing with prefer to purchase raw beans. So,

*Interview, ibid.
†Interview in Accra, March, 1989.

> there's a real danger that if the international economic environment is not to permit a greater degree of local processing and manufacturing and free access to technology from restricted business practices, this marginalisation of Africa is going to happen.*

The future cocoa price is not set in Ghana, but in the Futures and Options Exchange in London, 'the Fox', where young dealers sit round a small floor dealing in cocoa, alongside other spaces dealing in sugar or oil, and sporadically spring into hectic shouting and telephoning to make new bargains which push the cocoa price up and down. And the contrast between the dealers and the cocoa growers in Ghana expresses all the helplessness of Third World countries in the face of world markets. However precious their resources, however hard they work, the African farmers are at the mercy of financial operators thousands of miles away, who can deprive their products of their cash value. The cocoa growers, like coffee, tea or copper producers, have tried to reach agreements with other producers to restrict their production to maintain the price. And they look with envy at the farmers in America, Europe or Japan, who can fix the prices of food to ensure reasonable incomes. But there are always new producers, including cocoa growers in Malaysia, who are determined to enter the market; and a new wave of dieting Americans can bring the price down still further, and puts hundreds more Ghanaians out of work.

The current tragedy of Africa lies in the fact that, even after it has put right its past mistakes and adjusted itself to world conditions, it still does not have the economic power to make its own bargains with other continents. It can only put forward the final argument, that the world cannot afford to see the continent degenerate into chaos. As Dr Botchwey puts it:

> If for no other reason than self-interest, sooner or later Europe, North America and Japan are going to find that their wealth cannot be sustained if this large part of the world remains poor, underprivileged, and unable to generate the resources that will enable them to acquire what they need to survive. If the poverty and degradation reaches a certain level, then even if we don't have the means to wage war, and to cause havoc in the world, the moral political problems that would come from continuing stagnation in such a large part of the world would make it impossible, or at least difficult, for the world to continue the way it's been doing.†

*Interview in London, March 3, 1989.
†Interview, ibid.

CHAPTER FOURTEEN

THE LIMITS OF MIDAS

For centuries mankind has worked on the assumption that we could pursue the goal of steady progress, without disturbing the fundamental equilibrium of the world's atmosphere and its living systems. In a very short time that comfortable assumption has been shattered.

MARGARET THATCHER, March 1989*

Behind all the tensions between rich and poor countries lie the contradictions between two kinds of wealth: the financial wealth represented by money, and the wealth of natural resources represented by minerals, oil, raw materials and the land and oceans. While the developing countries hold much of the natural wealth they do not control the financial power to exploit it or the markets to consume it, which belong to the industrialised world. The more global and mobile the rich countries' money becomes, and the cheaper the transport, the greater their power over static resources. The world markets offer distant communities the choice between rapidly adjusting to their own pace of change, or being left off the economic map.

The new pace of money remains hard to comprehend. Economists have always compared money to water in their metaphors – whether flowing in streams, rivers or oceans; turned on by taps; frozen or awash with liquidity. Like water, money finds its own level, leaks, seeps, floats and flows into pools. But the scale and speed of the flows have so suddenly increased – when hundreds of billions of dollars can cross the world in a day – that the water-metaphor breaks down. Much of the world's money now resides in a single pool, which has also become totally mobile. 'All of a sudden,' as John Reed described it, 'these pools of money become rather dynamic.'† Money, in fact, is no longer like water: it is much more like air.

It is the last stage in the long progression of trade. In the eighteenth century any major country had to own or control its own natural

*Address to the International Conference on the Ozone Layer, London, March 1989.
†Interview, May 9, 1989.

resources – whether food, timber, or coal for its security. To acquire them, countries went to war. But today it is through financial power that the rich nations ensure their access to the world's wealth. If they control the money, they can buy where they like. The images of national power in the 1980s are not warships or armies: they are the abilities to control financial markets, to bid down producers, to translate blips on the screen into the physical resources that the country needs to survive. The more global and instant the market-place, the more effective and pervasive this power becomes: for when everything is for sale, money can buy information, experience, influence. It can even buy the future.

This book has tried to describe how the new mobility of money has speeded up the changes in ordinary people's lives, and the shifts in the balance of power at every level. It has enabled individual entrepreneurs to borrow billions, to reach out across the continents to buy whole corporations and then sell them again, all in a few days. It has enabled agile financiers to become billionaires within a few years by making money out of money. It has accelerated the industrial triumph of Japan and other East Asian nations which have hardly any natural resources, which have competed with America with all its wheatlands and minerals. It has allowed commercial communities including the overseas Chinese to create financial networks across the globe, through which their money constantly moves in search of investment and profit. With all this mobility financial power has shifted in a few years across the hemispheres, away from America and Europe, towards the Far East. The willingness of the East Asians to save, and the eagerness of Westerners to spend, has multiplied the East's advantage over the debt-loaded corporations and nations of the West; and within a decade America has emerged as the world's biggest debtor, and Japan as the biggest creditor.

For those who have been able to channel and exploit them, the flows of money have provided breathtaking opportunities. Many young Asian countries have harnessed advanced technologies and communications to manufacture products which have provided spectacular material benefits. By latching on to the global bazaar, first as producers, then as consumers, they have lifted their own standard of living in a single lifetime from poverty and hardship into comfort and security, and turned luxuries into necessities. With money they have found greater choice and freedom, greater scope for individualism, and sometimes more genuine democracy, and easier relationships with neighbouring countries.

But the downside has been equally rapid. Countries in Latin

America with immense natural wealth have become crippled by debts too easily contracted, which have then drained their capital away to the richer nations. Other countries, particularly in Africa, which have become bogged down in disasters, whether man-made or natural, have quickly found themselves outside the magic circle of growing prosperity and bankable wealth, with a widening gap between the haves and the have-nots. And even within the rich countries many old industrial communities and cities have been rapidly undermined by unseen competition from the other end of the world, and have found themselves not only without funds, but without confidence, information, or a sense of the future – in a world they cannot understand.

The forsaken communities around the world feel a renewed fear of money, as a mysterious disembodied force. For in the eighties money has become far more abstracted from ordinary people – as its masters control them through cryptic messages on screens, and buy and sell companies which they have never seen. These communities see big money appearing once again with its old faces of greed and aggression which threaten their settled societies. Raiders and financiers have thrived on the aggressive style of hunting and war, with their language of predators, sharks or war-chests. The billions have raced round the world far ahead of other controls and understandings; and the mobility of money has weakened the forces which used to constrain it, including the nation itself.

There have been many premature epitaphs on the nation. In the sixties many economists saw multinational corporations as overwhelming the states. 'The nation-state is just about through as an economic unit,' wrote the American economist Charles Kindleberger in 1969, foreseeing the evolution of a much more international corporation which 'has no country to which it owes more loyalty than any other, nor any country where it feels completely at home'.* These earlier fears about multinationals soon appeared exaggerated as they remained firmly based on their home countries, and subject to their controls. And the emergence of the Japanese corporations, rooted in Japanese patriotism and co-ordinated by their home government, appeared to contradict the picture of homeless giants. But the mobility of funds in the eighties, which stimulated waves of cross-border takeovers in the West and which encouraged the Japanese to set up factories abroad, began to call into question the role of national governments once again. In Japan it is the

*Charles P. Kindleberger: *American Business at Home*, Yale University Press, 1969, pp.182, 207.

corporations, investing another billion dollars every day, which command the surplus and the real financial decisions, which can often be at odds with their government's policy; while the faster flows of money across frontiers undermine many national controls. Kenichi Ohmae of McKinsey's in Tokyo pictures a world in which frontiers are withering away:

> Money flows freely across the national boundaries. Some 200 billion dollars of currency is exchanged every day in London, Tokyo and New York – only those three markets. We have to accept that in today's economic activities we cannot really think about national boundaries. The problem is with the governments: they are still living in this nineteenth-century nationalism – in the narrowest sense. They measure goods that flow in from one country to another, measuring tonnage, when information, money and many intangibles flow across the national borders which could be much more valuable.*

Personally I do not think that either nations or communities will readily surrender their powers to control these economic forces. Human beings in the past have never tolerated for long the predatory and revolutionary power of money without constraining it. The eighties, it is true, have wrought many changes which appear to have no real precedent – including the global market-place, the return of conservative governments in the West, the discrediting of alternatives to capitalism. But there have always been cycles of predation and protection, of surges of individualism and returns to more communal values, children reacting against their parents' materialism. Pure money-values still have their Midas-like limitations. Families still require broader and more stable values than any financial statistics can measure. Communities still need to balance the incentives of personal ambition with the need for continuity and social fairness. Individuals still look to their national politicians and governments to defend their interests. The nation still represents their ultimate security and continuity. And many bankers as well as politicians foresee a backlash against the mobile power of money. To quote John Reed of Citicorp:

> To most of us life is not jumping from New York to Tokyo and back. The tension between mobile capital and plain vanilla day-to-day living I think is a real one. Communities worry that their own economic resources may not be available for their own

*Interview, September 22, 1988.

> use: as bankers we often hear this. A community group will say: how can we be sure that our savings are going to be available to this community when the time comes? And then we see in the United States today a foreigner buying an American company, and there's a communal sort of sense that says: hey, this is something that was part of our society, it was sort of ours, it's now going to be owned by somebody who lives in a different community. Will that somehow disrupt our life? And so these tensions between mobile money and a more day-to-day existence are modern tensions that we see increasingly around us.*

But the power of money is also coming up against a more absolute limit – not from people, but from the earth itself – which calls for a more important role for nations and governments. The consumer society reaches its end-point when it destroys the forests and oceans on which human beings depend for their health. Westerners munching hamburgers are in effect devouring whole territories in central America. Japanese throwing away chopsticks are destroying rainforests of irreplaceable timber. Africans cutting down scrubland for firewood are turning their continent into a desert. The apparently limitless financial wealth of people confronts the very finite wealth of the planet, with its own bottom line which can never be calculated in purely monetary terms, and with fixed assets which can never be replaced. Without some restraint, commercial aggression inevitably invades the wildernesses which are essential for the world's climate and continuity.

Many bankers and financiers accept the need to restrain this destructiveness – including Sir James Goldsmith, who has made part of his fortune from selling off forests for timber:

> The last hundred years have been the greatest disaster this world has ever seen because we have destroyed the environment. Today everything is secondary, tertiary, almost unimportant, compared to the protection of the planet . . . Many people have at last become aware that the planet is in danger, that we have destroyed our seas, our air, pulled down our forests, and that we will eventually destroy ourselves. Some people say the solution is to go back to the pre-industrialised age, to go back to tribal living and cultural living. I don't believe that's possible. If we have any wisdom, it is possible to move into a post-industrial age, to create a posterity and working circumstances which will allow us to try and

*Interview, May 9, 1989.

put some things right that have gone wrong in the last hundred years because of our shared responsibility.*

But the post-industrial society has no easy solution for safeguarding the environment. For it depends more completely than the earlier industrial society on the disciplines and incentives of short-term profit. It cannot protect the ecology without economic sacrifices which reach beyond any free enterprise system. The short time-scale of giant corporations, under the constant pressure of quarterly earnings, is inevitably at odds with the very long-term needs of conservation and protection. And Japanese corporations, with all their technological skills and longer-term horizons, are among the least concerned with other countries' environments. The basic problem is simple: the world's money-system is unable to take account of resources that cannot be commercially valued. As John Reed describes it:

> It's very hard to put value on some raw materials that aren't readily and commercially accessible. A country that is sitting on potentially very valuable deposits of ore finds it very difficult to convert that value into access to the global economic system, simply because the inability of the system to find a market solution makes it as if they did not exist. This is to the great detriment of all of us: because what it really says is that we are unable to correctly appreciate values in the current pricing system . . . It's very hard to imagine simply extrapolating for the next 100 years and assuming that there is going to be a continued divergence between the access to the global economy of a small versus a very large group of people. So clearly there are going to have to be mechanisms by which the global community stays more or less in sync with each other as we develop. We must give value to the importance of the Amazon rain-forest or hidden reserves and the potential important human talent that exists around the world.†

Global entrepreneurs and corporate raiders like to depict themselves as much-needed predators in the human jungle, bringing the benefits of competition and change to societies which have been over-protected. But an unrestrained predatory power can quickly extend beyond the financial battles, to begin destroying the environment. And some psychologists maintain that the money-making drive

*Interview, October 12, 1988.
†Interview, May 9, 1989.

is basically destructive, part of the death drive. As Hanna Segal sees it:

> Implicitly in avarice there is the death instinct; and you've only got to look towards the present unbridled reward for paper money, and death to our ecology, that life is being destroyed on earth . . . It seems to me that that is clearly an expression of the death drive, to poison yourself, your children, your grandchildren, for adding a few more noughts on something written on a computer. But then I have strong feelings about it – not only analytical, but also political.*

But even in a financial perspective, as John Reed makes clear, the destructiveness of short-term commercial interests has to be countered in the longer run: the world's accounting system makes no allowances for the need to pay for the preservation of the planet.

The problem is made much more politically explosive by the division between the two sides of the world. It is the rich countries which control the financial wealth; but it is the developing countries which hold most of the natural wealth – which remains commercially incalculable. As P. V. Obeng described it in Ghana:

> Those natural resources don't constitute wealth so long as they continue to be in the bowels of the earth. They're not available for our developmental processes. We need resources in cash and technology to enable us to extract this potential. But that cannot be accumulated from inside sources alone, in the face of our tremendous commitment to service debt, and to import expensively to meet our national requirements. So we need a topping up of resources from external sources.†

The cross-purposes between the two sides are made more bitter by the fact that the industrialised countries have already destroyed most of their own natural environment: while the poorer countries are still desperately seeking to become industrialised. They are industrialising at great cost to their ecology, damaging the ozone layer and the global climate which affect all countries. But they insist that if the richer countries want to preserve their environment they must pay for it.

The conflict emerged sharply at an international conference on the ozone layer in London in March 1989, at which the British Prime

*Interview, March 30, 1989.
†Interview in Accra, March 16, 1989.

Minister appeared as a surprising convert to the cause of ecology, with her own perspective:

> There is an irony about the environmental problems which now confront us. Since the beginning of civilisation, the main damage to our way of life has come from human malevolence and destructiveness, from wars, from weapons, from hostility. Now the damage to the environment comes from the actions of millions of people, conducting peaceful activities which contribute to their health, their well-being and their work in agriculture or industry – activities in other words which are perceived as beneficial.*

China provided the most dramatic example of new dangers: to industrialise she needed to exploit her huge coal reserves, but this would provide a serious new threat to the ozone layer, exacerbating the 'greenhouse effect'. The environment commissioner from China, Liu Ming Pu, complained:

> The developed countries consume 80 per cent of the world's resources and produce an equivalent amount of pollution . . . They can use their past accumulated wealth to manage the environment. The Third World countries cannot do this.†

Mrs Thatcher insisted that the developing countries were unnecessarily worried about the costs: the conference, she said, had shown ways of protecting the ozone layer which were compatible with continued economic growth. But her confidence was not shared by many experts; and large areas of the world's environment called for extensive spending and subsidies if they were to be saved.

It is Brazil which shows the most far-reaching confrontation between money and environment. It has by far the biggest rain-forests, whose natural ecology is crucial to the global climate as 'the lungs of the world'. But Brazil is also the Third World's biggest debtor; and many Brazilians insist that they can only repay their debts by destroying still more of their forests whose timber is sold to provide luxuries for the richer countries. Some Western bankers have proposed possible bargains: that Brazil could be forgiven part of its debt in return for some international controls over its forests. But Brazilians are very touchy about any infringement of their sovereignty; and such a huge financial settlement is only likely to be achieved against a background of a much broader understanding between the two sides of the world.

*Address to the Ozone Conference, op cit.
†*New York Times*, March 26, 1989.

In these last wildernesses Midas reaches his ultimate limits. The money-motives which have contributed so much to the world finally endanger the world's future; and the hectic connection between time and money comes up against the timelessness of the earth. The impasse can never be resolved through conventional financial arrangements between bankers, whose equations are absurdly inadequate in accounting for the world's ultimate wealth. Only national governments, working closely together through the international bodies which were so much reviled in the eighties, can effectively protect the environments for which they are responsible. The political process will require major realignment, for environmentalists cannot promise their supporters a higher material standard of living than can their opponents, whether conservative or socialist, who are both committed to maintain high economic growth. And at present any such challenge, from prey against predators, from herbivores against carnivores, seems unlikely to succeed. But the environmentalists have one of the most powerful and primitive instincts behind them – the defence of their territory. It is in preserving its own earth that human ingenuity faces its final challenge: for however much money can multiply material prosperity and wealth, it cannot multiply the land itself. As Mark Twain said: 'They aren't making it any more.'

INDEX